Confucianism and Women

SUNY series in
CHINESE PHILOSOPHY AND CULTURE

———————————————

Roger T. Ames, *editor*

CONFUCIANISM AND WOMEN

A Philosophical Interpretation

LI-HSIANG LISA ROSENLEE

STATE UNIVERSITY OF NEW YORK PRESS

Published by

STATE UNIVERSITY OF NEW YORK PRESS, ALBANY

© 2006 State University of New York

All rights reserved

Printed in the United States of America

No part of this book may be used or reproduced in any manner whatsoever without written permission. No part of this book may be stored in a retrieval system or transmitted in any form or by any means including electronic, electrostatic, magnetic tape, mechanical, photocopying, recording, or otherwise without the prior permission in writing of the publisher.

For information, address
State University of New York Press,
194 Washington Avenue, Suite 305, Suite 700, Albany, NY 12210-2384

Production, Laurie Searl
Marketing, Susan Petrie

Library of Congress Cataloging-in-Publication Data

Rosenlee, Li-Hsiang Lisa, 1968–
    Confucianism and women : a philosophical interpretation / Li-Hsiang Lisa Rosenlee.
      p. cm.—(SUNY series in Chinese philosophy and culture)
    Includes bibliographical references and index.
    ISBN: 0-7914-6749-X (hardcover : alk. paper)
    ISBN: 978-0-7914-6750-3 (pbk. : alk. paper)
  1. Women in Confucianism—China. 2. Confucianism. I. Title.
II. Series.

HQ1767.R67 2006
181′.112′082—dc22   2005014021

ISBN-13: 978-0-7914-6749-7 (hardcover : alk. paper)

10 9 8 7 6 5 4 3 2 1

For my mother, Mei-Hsiu Lin

—My first Feminist

CONTENTS

ACKNOWLEDGMENTS		ix
CHAPTER 1	INTRODUCTION	1
CHAPTER 2	CONFUCIANISM, CHINESE-NESS, AND *REN* VIRTUOUS PERSONHOOD	15
	Confucians before Confucius: *Ru* and Its Ambiguity	17
	Ru, State, and Chinese-ness	24
	Defining *Ru*: *Ren* as Confucian Virtue Ethics	34
CHAPTER 3	*YIN-YANG*, GENDER ATTRIBUTES, AND COMPLEMENTARITY	45
	Yin-yang and the Oppositional Binary of Femininity-Masculinity	48
	Yin-yang and Correlative Cosmology	50
	Yin-yang Complementarity and Gender Hierarchy	55
CHAPTER 4	*NEI-WAI*, GENDER DISTINCTIONS, AND RITUAL PROPRIETY	69
	Nei-wai, Ritualization, and Civilization	71
	Nei-wai, Functional Distinctions, and Gender Hierarchy	79
CHAPTER 5	DIDACTIC TEXTS FOR WOMEN AND THE WOMANLY SPHERE OF *NEI*	95
	Lienuzhuan, *Guifan*, and the Tradition of Virtuous Women's Biographies	96
	The Four Books for Women and by Women	103
	The Question of Female Literacy and the Virtue of Women's Speech (*Fuyan*)	110

CHAPTER 6	CHINESE SEXISM AND CONFUCIANISM	119
	Gender Oppression and Confucian Virtue Ethics	122
	Case Studies: Widowhood and Footbinding	129
CHAPTER 7	TOWARD A CONFUCIAN FEMINISM—FEMINIST ETHICS IN-THE-MAKING	149
	The Problems of Gender and the Politics of Feminism	150
	Outline of a Confucian Feminism: A Hybrid Identity	152
	Reflections and Conclusions	159
NOTES		161
BIBLIOGRAPHY		185
INDEX		197

ACKNOWLEDGMENTS

This project was first inspired by comments made regarding the viability of Confucianism to rectify itself to meet the problem of gender disparity without the import of Western ethical theories during the East and West Conference held at the University of Hawaii in 1998. As a graduate student then, I was eager to get to the bottom of the issue to see whether Confucianism is indeed sexist through and through. The book finally took shape in 2002 with tremendous help from numerous mentors at the University of Hawaii, in particular Mary Tiles, James Tiles, Roger Ames, Vrinda Dalmiya, and Ming-Bao Yue. This project also benefited greatly from the comments and encouragement of my friends and colleagues at the University of Mary Washington, in particular Craig Vasey, David Ambuel, Joseph Romero, Mehdi Aminrazavi and Cindy Toomey. Robin Wang at the Loyola Marymount University also provided instructive suggestions. Lastly, the detailed and constructive criticism of one anonymous reader from the State University of New York Press was especially critical in helping this project into its final shape. I am also grateful for the continuous support of my dear husband, Corey. Of course, all the mistakes and shortcomings that remain in this project are entirely my own. I also here acknowledge the reprint of chapter 4 which was originally published in *Asian Philosophy* 14:1 (March 2004): 41–58 under the title "*Neiwai*, Civility, and Gender Distinctions"—with permission.

CHAPTER ONE

INTRODUCTION

Discourse on gender oppression marks the modernity of China in the early twentieth century. In the late Qing period, literati belonging to the Reform Movement and to the May Fourth Movement in the era of the early Republic, in particular, capitalized on the inferiority and unspoken misery of Chinese women in history as part of an emerging nationalistic discourse. This was the discourse of the new generation confronted with China's countless defeats and humiliations at the hands of the new imperial power of Japan as well as the West. Victimized, illiterate, rural Chinese women systematically oppressed by the patriarchal family, which was in part supported by the feudal ideology of Confucianism, became the symbol of what was wrong with Old China. China was in desperate need of new value systems to replace the useless ones that were unable to withstand the military force of the West. Although what was needed to replace the old value systems was still uncertain at the time, what needed to be discarded was clear. In the nationalistic discourse of the early Republic, anti-Confucian sentiment ran high. In the political arena, a total purge of Confucianism was completed during the Communist Cultural Revolution in the early 1970s and this purge was viewed as the beginning of New China, the beginning of modernized China and of its entry into the international community of the New World. The May Fourth Movement and Communist China both radically rejected Confucianism, seeing it as the root of China's malaise and inferiority. Their nationalistic discourse, in turn, laid the foundation for the later Western feminists' and Asian specialists' representation of Confucianism as the root of gender oppression in the history of Chinese women.

Beginning in the early 1970s, there was a surge of interest in Chinese gender studies on the part of Western feminists as well as Asian specialists who often frame Chinese women's liberation chronologically in relation to Western intellectual traditions.[1] The surge of feminists' writings and the like on the condition of Chinese women formed part of the grand feminist movement toward constructing a global history of women designed to validate feminists' defiance of patriarchal social structures as well as the social construction of gender in the West. By going beyond the Western sphere, feminists intended to validate their insistence on the urgency of the problem of gender oppression, while expanding their sphere of concern to include their less fortunate sisters in the third world. The dream of forming a global sisterhood across cultural, geographical, religious, and ethnic boundaries underlies the well-meaning intent of Western feminists in their writings on the condition of third world women. While the concept of "gender" is well articulated and deconstructed in contemporary feminist scholarship, the concept of "culture" remains relatively marginal in cross-cultural studies of the problematic of gender. The lack of attention to the element of "culture" in feminist writings constitutes an obstacle to a genuine understanding of the gender system in an alien culture, where gender is encoded in the context of a whole different set of background assumptions. Indeed, our conceptual framework is that within which the world first becomes intelligible to us, since we only come to comprehend the meaning of the world through participating in a network of shared cultural assumptions of the nature of the world. Hence, in any attempt to understand an alien culture, we must first of all understand the "Otherness" of the other, and the imposition of our own cultural assumptions must be held in check.

In China, the background cultural assumption is by and large informed by Confucianism—the most prominent intellectual tradition in Chinese history. Although it is true that blunt, imperialistic statements degrading Confucianism are no longer discernible in this age of political correctness, the imperialistic sentiment of the superiority of Western ethical theories in regard to the issue of gender parity continues to be assumed in the theoretical background. For the fact that the viability of Confucianism as a *feminist* theory has never been affirmed or suggested by feminists or sinologists, whether they are sympathetic to Confucianism or not, is itself suggestive of the assumed superiority of Western theoretical traditions in relation to gender. Naturally, it begs the question: Why not Confucianism? In this project, I will try to take that first step to provide a conceptual space for scholars to imagine the possibility of Confucian feminism. However, by singling out Confucianism, I am not trying to reduce the richness of Chinese culture to a monolithic intellectual tradition. The intent here is to acknowledge the importance of Confucianism in Chinese self-representation of its intellectual traditions. Confucianism, despite all its ambiguity and complexity in historical reality, has consistently been perceived as the moral backbone and the grand synthesis of Chinese high culture. Without a genuine interest in understanding Confucianism—a complex intellectual tradition—as a source of the background assumptions in the Chinese world, Western feminists in their discourse on gender construction in Chinese society, in effect, essentialize the category of "woman," making the familiar Western gender paradigm the universal conceptual framework, within which the condition of Chinese women is comprehended and its possible liberation theorized.

If cross-cultural studies are to be genuinely cross-cultural instead of monocultural, with all others subsumed under the Western conceptual framework, the element of "culture"—that is, its background assumptions grounded in its own intellectual traditions—must be granted due respect. For if, as Simone de Beauvoir said, a woman is not born but made, we must first of all understand the symbolic, social meanings that a "Chinese woman" as a gendered as well as a cultural being signifies. If we begin with the premise that each culture is viable, and the social construction of gender in each culture is truly social and cultural, then superimposing a Western conceptual framework onto the alien Other, while at the same time rejecting the intellectual traditions of the Other collectively, is not just inappropriate, it in effect erases the subject matter that it intends to study. And worse yet, it affirms the superiority of Western culture under which all other cultures are supposedly to be conceptually subsumed, despite their localized, empirical differences.

A genuine cross-cultural study must begin with a genuine curiosity for another culture whose "otherness" cannot and should not be reduced to, nor be replaced by, our familiar conceptual schemes. Otherwise, what is made transparent in cross-cultural studies is merely our own reflection in disguise. To use a Kantian term, what is intelligible to us reflects merely the subjective conditions of our being rather than the objective reality of the world itself. In the same way, without a genuine understanding of Chinese culture, the image of victimized Chinese women popular in the West reflects more the assumptions that Western observers have in organizing the world and in making the world of others intelligible to themselves than the reality of the life of Chinese women. If culture is viewed as a substantive term that not only marks an irreducible otherness of the Other but also that permeates the very fabric of everyday life—the way of living, knowing, and being in the world—then every conceptual abstraction of the symbolic meanings of any social and cultural practices must situate them in their proper intellectual traditions. These traditions form the background conceptual scheme of the Other. In Chinese gender studies, a minimal due respect should be paid to Confucianism—the emblem of Chinese high culture.[2]

In brief, the objective of this project is fourfold: First and foremost, it is to clarify the intellectual tradition of Confucianism—its ambiguous and complex origins, its place in Chinese imperial histories as well as its distinctive ethical theory of *ren* as virtuous personhood. Second, it is to lay out the cultural conceptual schemes in the Chinese world informed by Confucianism; in particular, attention will focus on significant cultural terms such as *yin-yang* and *nei-wai* as well as the unique tradition of women's biographies in imperial histories and the literary tradition of instruction books written for and *by* women, which are indispensable to the construction of gender in the Chinese world. Third, it is to postulate possible interconnections between the Chinese gender system and Confucianism, where Confucian virtue ethics not only coexists with but also justifies and sustains the patrilineal family structure in Chinese society. Contrary to the conventional assumption about third world women made in feminist scholarship, in the following, women will not be perceived as mere victims, unequivocally oppressed by men; instead, they are viewed also as participants in sustaining and transmitting sexist practices that conform to certain cultural ideals in Chinese society.[3] In other words, women are perceived not just as natural beings but also as cultural beings who, despite the structural limitations imposed on them, also strive to achieve cultural ideals through the means available to them, which are limited in comparison with the cultural resources available to men. Finally, in the conclusion, this book will move beyond a one-sided critique of the sexist components of Confucianism and the deconstruction of the politics of feminism; it will provide a point from which to begin to conceive Confucianism as a viable resource to deploy in a move toward liberation for Chinese women by indicating what might be the steps necessary to construct Confucian feminism.

As a preliminary work to the understanding of Chinese gender systems, this project begins with a study of Confucianism. In chapter 2, "Confucianism, Chinese-ness, and *Ren* Virtuous Personhood," assumptions embodied in early Western feminist writings about the transparency of Confucianism as a collective, sexist ideology frozen in time are set aside. Instead, the meaning of Confucianism is problematized by examining its ambiguous and complex origins as the concept of *Ru* 儒, which denotes the inexact Chinese counterpart of the term *Confucianism* used by Jesuits in the eighteenth century. The prominent status of *Ru* learning in imperial histories contrasts greatly with its semantic ambiguity. The meaning of the character "*ru*" is further obscured when its etymological roots are understood in the tradition of paronomasia. The traditional, paronomastic association between the character "*ru*" 儒 and characters such as "*nou*" 懦, "*rou*" 柔, "*ru*" 孺, "*ru*" 濡, and "*xu*" 需 complicates the task at hand. The ambiguity of its semantic origins in ancient, pre-Confucius times obscures the connection between *Ru* as an intellectual discipline and Confucius, as its most prominent spokesperson. Unlike the term *Confucianism*—its secularized and simplified representation in the West—the complex term *Ru* is neither a unified doctrine nor the exclusive teaching of Confucius. At best, the teaching of *Ru* can only be approximated as the teaching of the sages and the worthies wherein the ethical teaching of Confucius—the Supreme sage and First teacher—forms a part, but an important part nonetheless.

After the problematization of the concept of *Ru*, we venture into *Ru*'s unique place in imperial histories. After the institutionalization of *Ru*'s teachings as the official orthodox teaching in the Former Han of the second century BCE until the end of Qing in the early twentieth century, the learning of *Ru* was, for better or worse, intertwined with the state ideology and politics. With the institutionalization of the Confucian text–based civil service examination system through which state officials were recruited, especially after the reform in the Song dynasty of the eleventh century, *Ru*'s status and the range of knowledge that a learned *Ru* was supposed to have were by and large defined by the state-controlled examination system, in which the hereditary emperor acted as the chief examiner. However, it is important to keep it in mind that despite its intimate connection with the state, *Ru* learning was not identical to nor dependent on state power, since as a closer look at the imperial history reveals, *Ru* official-literati did not possess substantial political power, which was in the hands of the hereditary ruling house. Moreover, *Ru*'s self-claimed social role as a mediator between the state and the virtuous *dao* of the sages and the worthies required them to rise above simple loyalty to the state. *Ru*, in other words, was the conscience, the moral backbone of the state, not a mere functionary vessel or clerk of the state bureaucracy. The fluidity of the meaning of *Ru* allows for a wide range of interpretations, and more importantly, the identity of *Ru* is a cultural rather than an ethnic one. The very possibility of Jesuits being able to take on the identity of *Ru* and be accepted into the community of the official-scholars in late-sixteenth-century China is an instance of the fluidity of the meaning of *Ru* and *Ru* learning.

Despite the ambiguity of *Ru* and the indeterminacy of Confucianism, the centrality of the ethical concept of *ren* 仁 in the Confucian tradition is unmistakable. The concept of a relational personhood interlocked with the ethical concept of *ren* in turn lays the foundation for a virtuous personhood achievable through the Confucian project of self-cultivation. Theoretically, the cultural ideal of virtuous personhood acquired through one's mastery of human relations and through embodying specific social virtues appropriate to specific social relations is open to both genders. Yet the openness of Confucian *ren* virtue ethics or relational personhood contrasts greatly with the historical reality of the lives of Chinese women. Such a discrepancy between theory and practice cannot be explained without examining the Chinese gender system in which both man and woman are genderized according to specific cultural assumptions of what constitutes a properly gendered being.

In chapter 3, "*Yin-yang*, Gender Attributes, and Complementarity", we begin with a critical reexamination of the Western conception of a universal "womanhood" as a kinship neutral category supported by a set of feminine qualities or defined by inborn biological functions. The concept of "woman" designated by the term *funu* 婦女 (*fu*, i.e., married women, and *nu*, i.e., young girls, maids) in the Chinese world is conceived within the bounds of familial relationality through and through. In other words, contrary to the Western representation of "woman" as a natural being existing prior to, and independent of, familial and social relations, a Chinese woman as *funu* is primarily perceived through familial, kinship roles. The concept of male/female whose distinction rests exclusively on biological, sexual differences, in the Confucian tradition, by and large applies to animals, not humans. Gender in the human world signifies strictly social roles and relations. It is through occupying different familial, kinship roles that a "woman" as a gendered being is made. That is to say, the process of ritualization within the kinship system coincides with the process of genderization. The Chinese gender system informed by Confucianism must be understood within the hierarchical structure of the kinship system, where a socially recognizable "man" or "woman" is made. Consequently, gender distinctions in Chinese society should not be assumed to rely on either a set of innate qualities assigned to the social categories of "man" and "woman," or the biological categories of "male" and "female."

In Western feminist discourse on gender, due to the apparent affinity between the *yin-yang* metaphor and the modern duality of femininity and masculinity, the concept of *yin-yang* is seen to be indexical of the Chinese gender system. The receptive quality of the *yin* and the expansive qualities of the *yang* are taken as the theoretical ground for the subordination of Chinese women to the patriarchal family structure. But by taking the *yin-yang* metaphor as conceptually equivalent to the dualistic paradigm of Western femininity and masculinity, one not only imposes a dualistic metaphysics onto the Chinese correlative *yin-yang* cosmology, but more importantly misconstrues the roots of gender oppression in the Chinese world. For unlike the dualistic paradigm of the feminine and the masculine in the West, *yin-yang*—a nonoppositional, complementary binary—cannot even function as an adequate theoretical justification for gender oppression in China. On the contrary, the irreducible complementarity of *yin-yang* both in the cosmos and the human body in fact suggests a rather fluid view of sexual difference between the male and the female body and consequently seems to imply a more tolerant view of gender roles in the Chinese world. But in reality, the fluidity of the *yin-yang* binary contrasts greatly with the rigidity of gender roles in Chinese society.

In chapter 4, "*Nei-Wai*, Gender Distinctions, and Ritual Propriety," we turn to the spatial binary of *nei-wai* as our point of entry into the Chinese gender system. Like the *yin-yang* metaphor, the term *nei-wai* is often equated with two mutually opposing and conflicting spheres—family and state, or private and public. Consequently the *nei-wai* distinction conventionally seems to signify a strictly physical segregation of man and woman into two different, conflicting spheres. However, this sort of rendering of the *nei-wai* as a static separation of man and woman in the personal, social, and political sphere is inadequate since it has been shown in recent historical studies on gender relations in China that women did, and were socially sanctioned to, traverse the assumed rigid boundary of the *nei* and the *wai*. Furthermore, in the Chinese world, family and state, or private and public, are not two separate realms; instead, the family is the foundation upon which a harmonious state can be built. The "private" virtue of filial piety is the root of all "public" virtues. Hence, just as in the case of the correlative, complementary *yin-yang* binary, the boundary between the *nei* and the *wai* is also a negotiated boundary.

In regard to gender, the *nei-wai* signifies a functional distinction that defines the propriety of two gendered spheres and the normative gender-based division of labor. Although the *nei-wai* boundary is primarily a ritual boundary, its regulative force, where women are formally confined to the familial realm of *nei*, the realm of domestic skills and household management, and men to the realm of *wai*, the realm of literary learning and public services, is not just theoretical but also reflected in social reality. In other words, due to the *nei-wai* distinction as a functional distinction, a regulative ideal, women of all classes are not allowed legitimate access to the literary realm of *wai*, officialdom, and personal fulfillment. Consequently, talented and learned women confined to the realm of *nei* must conceal their literary talent, since it is inconsequential to their gender identity and roles in the familial realm.

In chapter 5, "Didactic Texts for Women and the Womanly Sphere of *Nei*," the conflicting nature between women's gender identity in the realm of *nei* and their literary pursuit in the realm of *wai* along with the unique tradition of virtuous women's biographies and women's instruction books written for women and by women is further discussed. The question in regard to female literacy in the Chinese world, unlike in the West, is not so much about whether women should be educated or about women's innate intellectual capacity, but rather is centered on the propriety of women's gender identity. Chinese women are typically characterized as submissive, oppressed, and illiterate. The early literary representation of Chinese women found in the *lienu* 列女 tradition where the records of virtuous women's biographies form part of the dynastic history, however, shows otherwise. There is no shortage of examples in which women are portrayed as virtuous mothers instructing their grown-up sons about state politics and ritual propriety, or courageous maids demolishing their social superiors, or talented women proficient in argumentation. Chinese women in early literary representation are intellectual, virtuous agents going beyond their limited realm of *nei*, the realm of household management and domestic skills.

However, it is true that the wider range of virtues including non-gender-specific virtues such as *biantong* 辯通 (skill in argumentation), *renzhi* 仁智 (benevolent wisdom), and *xianming* 賢明 (sagely intelligence) found in Liu Xiang's *Lienuzhuan* 列女傳 (Biographies of Virtuous Women) had been transformed into a narrower range of gender-specific virtues in later dynastic biographies of women and in popular illustrated editions of *Lienuzhuan* especially during the Ming and the Qing periods. The virtues of female chastity and spousal fidelity, in particular, were popularized over nongender-specific virtues in the later literary representation of virtuous women. The shift of the motif in the literary representation of virtuous women might not be a sign of deliberate conservatism on the part of official-literati. Lisa Raphals in her study on the early literary representation of Chinese women proposed that it might simply be facilitated by the emotional appeal and the entertainment value of illustrations with tragic content of a self-sacrificial mother, filial daughter, and chaste wife, in the printing industry.[4] With the combination of the institutionalization of widowhood in the Yuan dynasty and the political turmoil in the late Ming and early Qing, where wifely fidelity is analogous to man's political loyalty, those female virtues of chastity and fidelity gradually became the defining female virtues in dynastic biographies of virtuous women as well as popular instruction books.

Despite the growing emphasis on fidelity and chastity, female literacy reached unprecedented heights during the late Ming and early Qing periods. The legitimacy of female authorship and readership in the realm of *nei* was validated not only by the actual high number of published women's writings in the Qing period but also by the compilation of the *Four Books for Women*—*Nujie* 女誡 (The Admonition for Women), *Nulunyu* 女論語 (The Analects for Women), *Neixun* 內訓 (The Regulation for the Inner Quarter), and *Nufan jielu* 女範捷錄 (The Concise Records of Model Women)—that were written for and by women in four different historical times; that is, Ban Zhao of Han, two Song sisters of Tang, Empress Wen of Ming, and the compiler Wang Xiang's widowed mother, woman Liu of Qing. The parity between female authorship in regard to the propriety of *nei* and male authorship in the realm of *wai* is implied in the title of the *Four Books for Women*, which defines the propriety of women just as the Confucian *Four Books* defines the learned status of men. The need for female literacy was first advocated by Ban Zhao—the first and foremost female court historian—despite her deliberately conservative tone in "naturalizing" women's inferiority in the *Nujie*. The incompatibility between virtue and talent in the realm of *nei* made popular by the Ming saying, "A woman without talent is virtuous," was strongly repudiated by talented and learned women in the late Ming and early Qing periods.

Most noticeably, in the *Nufan jielu*, woman Liu of Qing devoted a whole chapter to repudiating the assumed conflict between talent and virtue. For her, a woman could not be virtuous and ritually proper until she was literate about ancient wisdom preserved in literary forms. Woman Liu appealed to numerous learned and talented women and empresses in history as "historical precedents" for the compatibility between virtue and talent in the womanly realm of *nei*. Although the conservative "female texts and biographies" are a source for reenforcing orthodox values of gender propriety on women who are confined to the realm of *nei*, they are also a source of empowerment where women through the power of literacy become self-affirmative in their historical consciousness.

The question of female literacy and gender propriety occupied the center stage in the Qing literary discourse. The dramatic rise of female literacy and engagement in reading, writing, and publishing has implicitly challenged the orthodox gender propriety in the realm of *nei*, in which the true calling of a virtuous woman primarily rested on her self-sacrifice and fidelity to a patrilineage rather than on her personal fulfillment and pursuit in the literary realm of *wai*. In this debate we see the conservative reading of the canonical tradition on the one hand, and women's own progressive interpretation and justification for female literacy without overstepping the bounds of ritual propriety, on the other hand. Yet unlike their male counterparts, women with advanced literacy had no legitimate access to the realm of *wai*. For instance, women were not allowed to participate in the civil service examination system, through which their talent could be utilized by the state and hence justified. Because of a lack of justification, women's advanced literacy was often viewed as a useless social surplus irrelevant to their gender identity. Essentially, possessing literary talent in women is tragic in nature. The paradoxical feeling of learned women toward their own "insignificant" literary skills was a sign of the unspoken conflict between women's gender identity in the realm of the *nei* and their literary pursuit in the realm of *wai*. Although the boundary between the *nei* and the *wai* is ritualistic, it, as a regulative ideal, also deprives women legitimate access to the realm of literary learning and state governance, which are male privileges proper.

The disparity between the realms of *nei* and *wai* marks the beginning of gender disparity between man and woman. It is with this understanding of gender propriety defined along the line of *nei* and *wai* that we turn to concrete social practices in premodern China where severe subjugation of women was often justified and sustained under the banner of gender propriety and Han civility. In chapter 6, "Chinese Sexism and Confucianism," we intend to map out possible interconnections among prevailing social practices such as female infanticide, child-bride/servant, concubinage, widowhood, and footbinding, with Confucianism. Given the complexity and ambiguity of Confucianism or *Ru* stated in chapter 2, how is it possible to identify definitive links between sexist practices and Confucianism as the emblem of Chinese high culture? The roots of women's oppression in premodern China ran deeper than Confucianism as a state ideology. Confucianism's connection with gender oppression, I would propose, should be found in the institution of the family where the Confucian emphasis on the familial virtue of filial piety, the continuity of the family name, and ancestor worship is a way of life, a regulatory ideal that underpins the very concept of civility and hence humanity. In other words, the convergence of these three cultural imperatives—the virtue of filial piety, the continuity of the family name, and ancestor worship—which require male descendents, served as a powerful, cultural basis for gender oppression in premodern China.

Since the male is privileged as the sole bearer of a patrilineage, which in turn is intertwined with the religious practice of ancestor worship and the virtue of filial piety, the importance of the female depends on her success in giving birth to a male heir to carry on the family line. The purely functional role of women in relation to the whole cultural scheme of prioritizing male descendants is especially illuminating in the case of female infanticide and concubinage. In the practice of female infanticide, excess female babies are discarded to reserve family resources for the male heir required for the most important religious ritual of ancestor worship. In the practice of concubinage, the *failure* of the original wife to produce a male heir is compensated by the husband's "right" and obligation to take a concubine to maximize the possibility of producing a male heir. The practice of taking in a child-bride as the future daughter-in-law is one way for a mother to ensure the loyalty of the new bride to the patrilineage of which now the mother is also part. The emphasis on the virtues of filial piety, ancestor worship, and the three-year mourning ritual is prevalent in Confucian texts such as *Lunyu* (The Analects), *Liji* (Book of Rites), and *Xiaojing* (Book of Filial Piety). In the *Liji*, marriage is stated as having a dual purpose: first, it is to ensure the continuity of the sacrificial ceremony in the ancestral temple and second, the continuation of the family line. In the traditional account, the wife's failure to produce a male heir constitutes one of seven compelling grounds for expelling her from the marriage. Yet without entering into a marriage, a woman is also without a permanent social place of her own. It is not just in the husband's interest, but also in the wife's best interest to ensure that the family would have a male heir through any necessary means including participating in female infanticide, child-bride/servant, and concubinage.

Women's participation in prioritizing the production of a male heir to ensure their place in the patrilineage inevitably reflects the nameless nature of women's personhood. Women's personhood is altogether outside the realm of *wai*—the realm of ethical-political accomplishment and hence the realm of remembrance—wherein one's family name and one's good name are passed and remembered. The *nei-wai* distinction, together with the dual purpose of marriage defined in the *Liji*, renders a woman's presence in the institution of family purely functional and substitutable. She is, in a word, anonymous, bearing no distinct mark of her own person. The nameless aspect of women's personhood is not limited to illiterate, peasant women, since women of all classes are without rank (i.e., without official title in the *wai* independent of the accomplishments of the male members in her family). *Wen* 文 (literary learning) and *zheng* 政 (state governance) are located in the realm of *wai* and therefore are indeed male privileges proper. Women, by contrast, are fundamentally nameless and dependent beings confined to the realm of *nei*, regardless of their actual achievements in literature and state politics. In Rubie S. Watson's words, measured against her male counterpart, a Chinese woman, indeed, cannot be and is not fully personed.[5] Her familial roles as a wife and mother are purely functionary; she is there to give birth to a male heir in order to fulfill these three cultural imperatives—filial piety, ancestor worship, and the continuation of a patrilineage.

However, these three cultural imperatives could not account for these popular practices of widowhood and footbinding popularized especially during the Ming and the Qing periods. Observing widowhood after the death of one's husband, on the surface, expresses one's fidelity to the husband's lineage. Yet given the priority of having a male heir, it would seem unnecessary for a sonless widow to observe widowhood. In fact, oftentimes a young widow was encouraged by both her natal family as well as in-laws to remarry against her will, since her presence in her late husband's family was now inconsequential. In the same way, the practice of footbinding, which served no formal purpose in perpetuating male descendents, would seem superfluous and accidental. But with a deeper understanding of the encoded social meanings behind these practices, one comes to realize the sort of "social goods" that were presumed to accompany these practices perpetuated across ethnicities, regions, social classes, and historical times. For instance, the practice of voluntary widowhood, protected in imperial statute since the Tang, signified more than spousal fidelity; it signified women's own agency where women's moral intent in safeguarding their integrity as married women must take precedence over parental authority, which emphasized the power of the senior over the junior. The bestowal of imperial honors on the households of chaste widows institutionalized in the Yuan further elevated widowhood from a private virtue to a social virtue with practical consequences. Comparable to the civil service examination for men, widowhood became a means of social mobility for women; that is, a means through which women were able to acquire the highest honor—imperial recognition—because of their own actions instead of the deeds of their father, husband, or son.

In the same way, the practice of footbinding expressed more than the imposition of male sexual desires projected onto the passive female body or the victimization of women by the patriarchal system. It expressed, among other things, women's gender identity, the Han civility, and ethnic identity. It was a proper cultural marking of the female body for the people of Han, especially during the political transition in the late Ming and the early Qing periods, when Han culture was threatened by the invading barbarian, the Manchurian. A pair of bound feet with all its socially sanctioned aesthetic values and class status symbolized the ethnicity of the Han people and their political resistance to the ruling barbaric tribe of the Manchu, which repeatedly issued prohibitions on the practice of footbinding among the Han people. What is more, footbinding was also women's culture proper where women bound their own feet, and the feet of their daughters who in turn transmitted "this cultural of ours" in the inner quarters through wraps and needles instead of words and brushes. The aim of this chapter is not to somehow explain away the "sexist" components of these social practices. After all, most of these practices mentioned no longer exist as social ideals. Rather, the purpose here is to decode cultural meanings embodied in social practices so that we are able to come to see women as subjects, and to understand women's own agency in not only embracing but also actively participating in those practices in order to achieve some sort of shared cultural ideals given the structural limitations imposed on them. For without such an understanding, women in third world countries remain frozen in time as mere passive victims of their "sexist" traditions whose liberation can only be justified by Western ethical theories that supposedly rise above parochial, "cultural" moralities.

In order to go beyond the false dichotomy between the West as a moral agent and the rest of the world as a moral problem waiting to be solved, in the conclusion, we will contemplate the viability of Confucianism as a feminist ethical theory. In chapter 7, "Toward a Confucian Feminism—Feminist Ethics In-the-Making," we will seek the resources available within the Confucian tradition that could be used as the building block of a distinct Confucian feminist ethic that is practical in the sense that it takes concrete human relations as its starting point and yet is comprehensive in scope without a metaphysical grounding. It would have no need to presuppose an "original" principle underlying all other ethical principles, nor would it presuppose an absolute equality for all without qualification. First of all, our postulated Confucian feminism will affirm a relational self situated in a web of relations that are not just "add-ons" to the "core" self, but are coextensive with the substantial self. A person as a person is always a person-in-relations. The Confucian virtue of filial piety, where reciprocal care between parent and child is required, is our starting point of being human. The parent-child relationship wherein one first finds oneself in the world would be prioritized. The virtue of filial piety—one's genuine care for others—is not just limited to one's private household, since it has traditionally been extended to reach well beyond the immediate family.

Second, our Confucian feminism will affirm the centrality of the virtue of *ren* as the culmination of ideal, achieved personhood. The virtue of *ren* begins with the virtue of filial piety and is comprehensive in its scope, since a person of *ren* is also a person of *yi* 義 (appropriateness), of *li* 禮 (ritual), of *zhi* 智 (wisdom), of *shu* 恕 (reciprocity), of *xin* 信 (trustworthiness), etc. This is so because to be *ren* is also to be a person who embodies specific social excellences appropriate to specific social relations wherein the person is situated. And since there is no metaphysical ground upon which one is a person without qualification, the self will necessarily, as it were, extend itself outward beyond the familial realm, or at least maintain existing familial relationships. As the web of relationships is extended from the family to the world at large, the range of social excellences required is widened as well. Although the virtue of *ren* is comprehensive in its scope, it can only be actualized in each particular relationship governed by particular social excellence appropriate to that relationship. In sum, the virtue of *ren* is a practical ethic taking human relations as its priority without a metaphysical grounding.

Lastly, our Confucian feminism will affirm the complementarity, and the reciprocity, of *nei-wai* and *yin-yang* as the basic structure of human relations. In addition, it will also assert the basic hierarchal scheme of human relations in which inequality based on ability or moral authority, rather than an absolute equality, is the starting point among particulars. We will modify the hierarchal relationship between husband and wife and the gender-based division of labor based on the *nei-wai* distinction to meet the challenges of feminism.[6] We will discard the minister-wife and ruler-husband analogy and replace it with friendship, which is available within the Confucian five social relations. Although, like all other relationships in Confucianism, relationship between friends is also hierarchal, the hierarchy is not necessarily gender-based and the association between friends is strictly voluntary. The duration of that association also depends on an assumed common goal among its participants. Such a rectification in the context of the husband-wife relation would enable women to achieve in the realm of *wai* and be able to achieve the Confucian ideal of *junzi*—a consummated, moral subject—not only in the immediate realm of familial relations but also in the world at large.

Certainly, this book is by and large an experiment, an initial attempt to reconcile Confucianism and feminism and to go beyond a mere critique of the "sexist" nature of Confucianism and the implicit "neocolonial" assumptions in Western feminism. One way to go beyond a merely negative deconstruction of existing theories is to positively conceive the possibility of a hybrid ethical theory—Confucian feminism—where Confucian ethics with modification is also a source for women's liberation. The viability of Confucianism to rectify itself and to meet the challenges of feminism must first of all be assumed and be conceived to be a real possibility before this whole project can be even carried out. The degree of success or failure of this project is open to assessment. But what is clear is that the possibility of such a convergence between Confucianism and feminism will not only bring Confucianism forward into the twenty-first century where the issue of gender can no longer be ignored in the discourse on ethics, but also will open up the theoretical horizons of feminism where the possibility of women's liberation is no longer limited to Western theoretical paradigms.

Chapter Two

CONFUCIANISM, CHINESE-NESS, AND *REN* VIRTUOUS PERSONHOOD

It was quite evident that sexism prevailed in premodern China, given the existence of notorious social practices such as female infanticide, child-servant/child-bride, concubinage, footbinding, and widow chastity across a wide range of different historical times and regions. These practices not only reflected unbalanced gender status and power, but also called into question the state sanctioned moral teachings of Confucianism since Confucianism is understood in its historical narratives as a teaching of self-cultivation, care, and proper relations. Yet despite the state's upholding Confucian moral teachings as orthodoxy, the severe subjugation of Chinese women persisted in premodern China. In a word, there is an irreducible gap between Confucian moral teachings and the historical reality of gender oppression in Imperial China. The issue of gender oppression inevitably leads to the question of what, if anything, Confucianism as a system of ideas contributed to the social abuse of women. And, in what way could Chinese women be seen as active participants in the Confucian discourse of virtue ethics and ritual propriety?

The interconnection between Confucianism and Chinese sexism is complex. One should resist the temptation to postulate an affinity or a transparent relationship between Confucianism and Chinese gender oppression. In order not to make uncritical assumptions, scholars who engage in the field of Chinese gender studies should immediately confront the following questions: "What is Confucianism?" and "In what way could dominant social practices such as footbinding, concubinage, and the cult of widowhood be attributed to Confucian teachings?" In other words, how does one identify the "Confucian-ness" in the practice of footbinding, concubinage, etc.? Conversely, how does one identify the "sexist" components in Confucianism as a whole? Finally, is there such an inevitable causal link between "Confucianism" and "sexism"? In short, is "Confucianism" sexist through and through? In order to sort out the answers, we must first of all have a genuine interest in understanding Confucianism as a system of ideas, its unique place in Chinese civilization as well as its use and abuse by the imperial court throughout history, otherwise any attribution of women's oppression to Confucianism would seem superficial.

Since the surge of women's studies in the 1970s and even as far back as the 1930s, Confucianism in early Western scholarship on the condition of Chinese women has been commonly portrayed as a sexist, patriarchal ideology that is responsible for women's oppression in China. Most notably, early French feminist Julia Kristeva, in her book *About Chinese Women*, boldly entitled a chapter "Confucius—An Eater of Women" in 1974.[1] And as late as the mid-1990s, Confucianism was still by and large characterized by scholars as a patriarchal ideology that should be discarded as irrelevant to the modern and supposedly superior, Western way of life. For instance, Margery Wolf, in her assessment of Tu Wei-ming's popular reinterpretation of neo-Confucianism, wrote: "The Confucian principles defining the propriety of hierarchical authority structures and the orderliness of the patriarchal family system seem anachronistic in this age of multinational corporations in Fujien, and young people from Shanghai acquiring Stanford MBAs. But to my surprise, books about Confucianism still sell well, and a superb Harvard scholar named Tu Wei-ming writes cogent 'reinterpretations' of neo-Confucian thinking that are very close to being 'guides' for modern living."[2] The disparaging undertone in Wolf's perception of Confucianism is clear. For her, Confucianism—a useless ideology of Old China—is synonymous with patriarchy and misogyny. The anti-Confucian sentiment in feminist works is highly inflated. But in some sense the attribution of women's oppression in premodern China to Confucianism is not without justification, since Confucianism, as scholars generally agree, underwrote the social structure of China and dominated its intellectual traditions, especially after the establishment of Confucian teachings as the orthodox official teaching beginning in the Han dynasty of the second century BCE and lasting until 1905 with the termination of the Confucian text-based civil service examination system in the Qing, the last dynasty.

However, Confucianism should not be reduced to a set of hierarchical kinship and rigid gender roles, since in this reductionism one overlooks the dynamic aspect of Confucianism, whose ethical theory of *ren* 仁 as well as its emphasis on the lifelong project of self-cultivation and maintaining proper relations, at least at the theoretical level, are akin to the feminist ethic of care and its socially constructed self as a web of relations. Keeping in mind this theoretical feminist space within Confucianism, one might argue that a convergence or a confluence between feminism and Confucianism should be possible, along the lines of the contemporary feminist reappropriation of existentialism, liberalism, Kantian deontology, or Aristotle's virtue ethics as providing basic ethical frameworks for addressing specific feminist concerns. But, in reality the engagement between Confucianism and feminism, as Chenyang Li in his anthology on Confucianism and gender pointed out, has long been one-sided; that is, feminists criticize Confucianism for victimizing Chinese women.[3] The feminists' predominant characterization of Confucianism as a patriarchal ideology through and through not only relegates Confucianism, into an inferior position in comparison with Western moral philosophies, but more importantly it oversimplifies the roots of Chinese women's oppression.

Such a simplification, in turn, constitutes an obstacle to achieving a genuine understanding of the Chinese gender system as well as Confucian ethics.

Before we can provide any sort of satisfactory explanation for the possible connection between Confucianism and gender oppression, we will need to have a firm grasp on the meaning of Confucianism. In the following we will begin by examining the school of "Confucianism" or "*Ru*" 儒, its historical origins and representations found in pre-Qin texts, and its cultural significance to the Han people as well as to the imperial court found in the official "Biographies of *Ru*" as part of the dynastic history from the Han to the Qing dyansty. In spite of its popularity and familiarity in the West since the late eighteenth century, Confucianism or *Ru*, as will become clear later, has rather ambiguous origins in Chinese history. The meaning of *Ru* is fluid and is by and large shaped by text-based communities of official-literati whose aim often centered on the transmission of the virtuous way of ancient sages. Inevitably, the interpretation of the meaning of *Ru* differs in different historical times; there is nonetheless a shared assumption among literati in regards to the virtuousness of *Ru*. Specifically, *Ru* is deemed time and again the ultimate emblem of Chinese high culture, and hence it is indexical of Chinese-ness. In short, *Ru* not only is the fundamental Chinese cultural symbol, but more importantly it underpins the coherence as well as the civility of the identity of the Chinese people; it serves as a shared ideal in such a multiethnic state as China.

CONFUCIANS BEFORE CONFUCIUS: *RU* AND ITS AMBIGUITY

The term *Confucianism*, as noted by numerous scholars, was an "invention" of Jesuits in the late eighteenth century. It was an invention rather than a literal translation, or a representation of the culture of the literati in late imperial China, since there is no exact either literal or conceptual counterpart of "Confucianism" in the Chinese language.[4] Instead, what the Jesuits intended to represent by the term *Confucianism* is the concept of *Ru*, whose meaning, as will be argued later, is neither derivative from, nor dependent on Confucius, since its origins precede the historical figure—Confucius. Unlike the way in which Christ is centered in Christianity, Plato in Platonism, or Buddha in Buddhism, Confucianism is not a singular, unified doctrine focusing on the thought of Confucius as a historical figure. Otherwise, it would be pointless to talk about the lives of "Confucians" or *Ru* before Confucius. The complex term *Ru* conveyed by these popularized terms such as "Confucius," "Confucian," and "Confucianism" is in fact a rather opaque concept. The Jesuits' invention of Confucianism is the concept of *Ru* simplified and secularized for much easier consumption in the West. In contrast to the suggestive transparency of the Jesuits' Confucianism, the origins of *Ru* as found in pre-Qin texts tell rather ambiguous and somewhat contradictory stories of the lives of Confucians or *Ru* in ancient times.

To begin with, the term *ru* is absent in four of the *Five Classics*, except in the *Liji* (Book of Rites),[5] and *Liji* is generally agreed among scholars to have been compiled in the early Han. It is also absent in two prominent Confucian texts of the *Four Books*—that is, *Zhongyong* (Focusing the Familiar) and *Daxue* (Great Learning). The lack of reference of the term *ru* in early canonical texts seems to attest to the ambiguous as well as mysterious origins of *Ru* whose meaning and association with Confucius is anything but transparent. The earliest appearance of the term is found in the *Analects*, passage 6.13, where Confucius was reported as saying that "One wants to be a *junziru* 君子儒 not a *xiaorenru* 小人儒." In this passage, Confucius seemed to suggest that there are various kinds of *Ru*, or various ways of being a *Ru*. If *Ru*, as the Jesuits' invented term—Confucianism—seems to suggest, were a unified school of thought unequivocally centered on the teaching of Confucius, it would be rather perplexing for readers to make sense of the above quoted passage in which the term *ru* not only has no immediate identification with Confucius or his moral philosophy, but more importantly, has no inherent moral import conventionally understood as constitutive in the terms *Confucianism* or *Confucian*. What did it mean then to be a *Ru* in ancient times? How was the distinction between a *junziru* and a *xiaorenru* drawn? Finally, who were the *Ru* and what did they do?

According to the *Zhouli* (The Rites of Zhou), a ritual text of the Zhou empire compiled between the fourth and second century BCE, *Ru* originally was a designation of a Zhou official post called *Situ* 司徒, whose duty, as explained in the later Han commentary, was to teach the multitude the six arts. As said in the "*Tianguan*" chapter of the *Zhouli*, "*Ru* persuade people with *Dao*" (儒以道得民). The *Dao* here was interpreted in the Han commentary as signifying the way of the six arts. In a separate passage in the "*Diguan*" chapter of the *Zhouli*, *Ru* was mentioned in connection with *Si* 師 (i.e., master, teacher): "Combine *Si* and *Ru*" (聯師儒). The Han commentary remarked that "*Si* and *Ru* are the ones who reside in local counties teaching *Dao* and the six arts" (師儒鄉里以道藝者).[6] This traditional account of the origins of *Ru* as a designation of the Zhou official post of *Situ*—teacher of the multitude—had been consistently maintained throughout dynastic histories from the Han to the Qing in the section called "Biographies of *Ru*" or *Rulinliezhuan*, which recorded exemplary *Ru*.[7] However, if one peels away the Han commentaries, these two passages found in the *Zhouli* in fact reveal very little about the life of *Ru*, and shed little light on the connection between *Ru* as *Situ*, a humble foot-soldier residing among the people, and *Ru* as the emblem of Chinese high culture with Confucius as its most prominent spokesperson. One might ask: Why *Ru*? Why did Confucius and his followers call themselves *Ru*? And what exactly does the word *ru* stand for?

Unlike all other schools of thought such as *Daojia* (Daoism), *Yinyangjia* (the school of Yinyang), *Mojia* (the school of Mozi), or *Fajia* (Legalism) where the centrality of the study of each school is explicit, the meaning of *ru* of *Rujia* is enigmatic. The uncertainty of the meaning of the term *ru* stands starkly in contrast with its assumed transparency in the term *Confucianism* or its centrality in the Chinese culture. A venture into its etymological roots paradoxically only complicates the issue at hand. According to the *Shouwen* (Explanation of Patterns), the first comprehensive dictionary of Chinese characters compiled by Xu Shen in the early second century CE,[8] the word *ru* is defined as such: "*Ru* means soft (*rou* 柔), the title of skilled scholars" (術士 之稱).[9] The second part of the definition seems to fit into our conventional understanding of what a *Ru* is supposed to be and it is also in line with the *Zhouli*'s description of *Ru* as a humble foot-soldier residing among the people as their teacher of six arts. As for the first part of the definition, it is not entirely clear how the word *soft* is correlated with the term *ru*. The correlation between *ru* and soft, construed by Xu Shen, a Han imperial scholar of the state academy, is paronomastic in nature, and the method of paronomasia has since then become the foundation of later scholars' understanding of the meaning of *ru*. In the traditional account, the term *ru* 儒, besides the word *rou* 柔 (soft), is also paronomastically associated with the following cluster of words: *ruo* 弱 (weak), *nuo* 懦 (timid, lazy, stupid), *ru* 濡 (moist, wet), *ru* 襦 (short coat, moist), *xu* 嬬 (lesser wife, weak), and *ru* 孺 (baby, suckling).[10]

For contemporary readers who are familiar with the Western analytic tradition, these seemingly bizarre definitions of *ru* derived from paronomastic associations fall short of what a rational, literal definition is supposed to be. The semantic obscurity of *ru* was commented by Lionel Jensen in his exhaustive study *Manufacturing Confucianism*. In response to the difficulty of understanding the term *ru*, Jensen noted that: "There is also the matter of the semantic obscurity of *ru*, the oldest definitions of which are frustratingly paronomastic, puns on the sound of the word rather than definitions as *we* construe them" (emphasis original).[11] In other words, in Western eyes, the paronomastic definitions of *ru* found in the traditional account do not constitute an explanation. As Jensen went on to say, the meaning of *ru* found in Chen Jie's *Shouwen jiezi gulin* (Explanation of Patterns, Elaboration of Graphs)—a later expanded edition of *Shouwen*—formulated in the tradition of paronomasia "cannot be construed by us as explanation, for paronomasia is, as Aristotle pointed out, a form of literary entertainment."[12] It is true that in the case of *ru*, its paronomastic definitions seem to obscure more than to shed light on the meaning of *ru*. But the importance of the method of paronomasia in understanding the meaning of Chinese characters should not be so easily dismissed as a form of literary entertainment. For in the Chinese sensibility, the meaning of a given word is always derived from a cluster of words or phrases by association, instead of from a self-contained, literal definition. Judged from the Western analytic tradition, paronomasia might seem arbitrary; yet for Chinese literati, it constituted part of a "rational, explanatory account" of a given word.

The generally accepted explanation for the association between *ru* 儒 and *rou* 柔 (soft) or *ruo* 弱 (weak) centered on the nature of the work of *Ru*; that is, they were scholars, or men of letters and unlike other professions such as farmers and craftsmen, they were a class of people that did not engage in manual labor. This explanation of *Ru* conforms to the traditional account of the origin of *Ru* as the Zhou official designation of *Situ*, teacher of the multitude. More perplexing associations rest on words such as *nuo* 懦 (timid, stupid), *ru* 濡 (moist, wet), *xu* 嬬 (lesser wife), and *ru* 孺 (baby, suckling). These associations seem to suggest some fairly undesirable aspects of *Ru* and its low status. Instead of rejecting the tradition of paronomasia outright simply because it defies our understanding of a rational explanation, perhaps a more helpful way to resolve the puzzle is to take those associations as clues to the life of *Ru* in ancient times. One thing can be said for sure: *Ru*'s paronomastic associations certainly suggest a more complicated picture of the life of *Ru* than what contemporary readers might have imagined.

From a survey of pre-Qin texts of both Confucian proper and non-Confucian schools of thought, it is clear that the category of *Ru* existed prior to and was not identical with Confucius or his teachings. Moreover, the term *ru* signified for both *Ru* and non-*Ru* multiple layers of meaning, some favorable, some pejorative, and some mystical. Confucius's *junziru* and *xiaorenru* are an indication of the various ways of being a *Ru* both in and prior to Confucius's time. In the *Analects*, the term *xiaoren* (petty person) and *junzi* (authoritative person) are often paired as contrary terms, where *xiaoren* signifies moral deficiency and *junzi*, on the contrary, signifies the culmination of various moral achievements. It then can be inferred that a *xiaorenru* is a morally deficient person despite his status as a literate person.

Interestingly, the conduct of this kind of disreputable *Ru* can be found in the *Mozi*, the canonical text of *Mojia*, *Ru*'s biggest rival in the pre-Qin period.[13] In Mozi's portrait, *Ru* were a group of skilled people specialized in burial rites, a profession practiced by lazy, unproductive, yet arrogant and pretentious scholars exchanging their expertise in rituals for life necessities. *Ru* were criticized, among other things, for their excessive emphasis on the propriety of burial and three-year mourning rituals, their hypocrisy and inconsistency in maintaining kinship hierarchy, and their unproductive lifestyle. In the "Contra-*Ru*" chapter of *Mozi*: "*Ru* use elaborate ornaments and rituals to corrupt people, extend burial rites and pretend grief to deceive their parents. They set up the belief in fate and slowly cause poverty and then live in idleness. They turn away from the fundamentals and abandon works, and then are indolent and proud. They are indulgent in food and drink, are too lazy to work, often suffer from hunger and cold and are in danger of freezing and starvation without the ability to avert them.... When *junzi* laugh at them, they become angry and exclaim: 'What do undisciplined people know about the good *Ru* (良儒)?'"[14] As shown in the passage, the term *junzi* as an exemplary ideal shared is definitely not identical with *Ru* whom Mozi despised so much. Although there is no direct reference found in Confucian texts where *Ru* were said to depend on performing burial rituals as their livelihood, the importance of burial and mourning rituals in the tradition of *Ru* is evident. Proper burial and mourning rituals performed to honor one's deceased parents and one's ancestors are the most important rites of all. This is shown in the *Liji*, the ritual text of Han, wherein a disproportional amount of the writing is devoted to the discussion of burial, mourning, and ancestor worship rituals.[15] In the *Analects*, Confucius's advocacy of the practice of three-year mourning ritual as an integral part of the expression of one's filial piety also provides a well-known example (cf. *Lunyu* 17.21).

Naturally, Mozi's negative portrait of *Ru* is exaggerated. Nevertheless, from the above passage, one can tentatively infer two things: first, *Ru* in ancient times, among other things, were experts about burial and mourning rituals; second, they did not directly engage in the production of life's necessities. As Mozi went on to say about the base conduct of *Ru*, "[I]n summer they beg for grains. When the five grains are all gathered in, they resort to the funerals. All the sons and grandsons are taken along and are filled with drink and food. It is sufficient for them to manage but a few funerals," and, "When a death takes place in a rich family, they rejoice greatly, for it is their opportunity for clothes and food."[16] If Mozi's description is reliable, then ancient *Ru* could be said to function as the modern equivalents of priests in the mortuary rites. However, as Yi-Pao Mei pointed out, unlike other institutionalized religions such as Christianity and Buddhism, in Chinese native religion there is no distinct priesthood.[17] Although Mozi's remark on the base conduct of *Ru* where a *Ru* functions as the equivalent of a priest, or an ancient shaman, is commonly dismissed as a smear campaign of *Mojia* against *Rujia*,[18] the connection between *Ru* and the shaman's expertise in burial rituals nonetheless is suggestive of the religious origin of *Ru*.

The theme of *Ru* as originally ancient ritual shamans—descendants of a noble clan with specialized knowledge of astronomy and cosmology in the Shang dynasty which preceded Zhou—had been popularized by the late Qing scholar Zhang Binglin, and later expanded by the prominent scholar of the May Fourth Movement in the early Republic Hu Shi. In Zhang's essay, "*Yuan Ru*," (The Origin of *Ru*) the first systematic treatment of the meaning of *Ru* in its semantic evolution in history, the word *xu* 需 is said to be the ancient equivalent of the word *ru* 儒, and hence *xu* 需, the semantic classifier of *ru* 儒, can been seen as the graphic source for *ru*'s earliest meaning.[19] The word *xu* can be found in the hexagram of *Yijing* (Book of Changes). The fifth hexagram—*Xu* 需 (i.e., waiting)—of *Yijing*, in the received text is written as *Ru* 濡 (wet, moist). In this hexagram, the traditional juxtaposition between *ru* 儒 and its paronomastic definition—*ru* 濡 (wet, moist)—finds its "rational" explanation. In ancient writings, *xu* 需, *ru* 濡, and *ru* 儒 are all interchangeable. The meaning of the hexagram *Xu* 需 composed of *Qian* 乾 (i.e., sky) on the bottom, and *Kun* 坤 (i.e., rain) on top, according to the commentary of *Yijing*, denotes clouds above the sky; hence it is a sign of rain-in-waiting. Because of the specific ritual attire called "*rufu*" that *Ru* are associated with, as noted in the *Mozi*, *Zhuangzi*, and *Liji*,[20] Zhang came to assert that ancient *Ru* were originally descendants of a noble clan of shamans with specialized knowledge of astronomy and cosmology, and more specifically they were shamans performing ritual dances for rain for the imperial court of Shang.²¹

The mysterious origins of *Ru* are further attested in the Han text *Lunheng* (Critical Evaluation of Doctrines) whose chapters entitled "*Rushu*" or "The Books of *Ru*" are interestingly enough filled with, not philosophical essays, but mysterious accounts of the birth or legends of ancient sage-kings.²² The religious implications of *Ru* in ancient times is apparent. In addition, the legendary birth of Confucius—a son of a concubine conceived in a divine dream—as told in the tradition adds to the mystery of *Ru*. *Ru*'s semantic association with words such as *xu* 嬬 (lesser wife) and *ru* 孺 (baby, suckling) can be interpreted as alluding to the noble pedigree of *Ru* traced back to the fallen dynasty of Shang whose ritual traditions were far more sophisticated than its militarily advanced Zhou conqueror. *Ru*'s paronomastic association with *xu* 嬬 (lesser wife) and *ru* 孺 (baby, suckling), as sinologist Peter Boodberg explained, lies in this: "*ru* 孺 (with the determinative for 'child'), 'baby,' was used in ancient Chinese historical texts with the implication that it was a term reserved in the court language of the Chou period for the designation of an heir presumptive born of a concubine, rather than a first wife."²³ In other words, one might say that *Ru* were the children of lesser wives, but noble nevertheless. *Ru* as described thus far were noble descendants with ritual skills. This picture of ancient *Ru*, indeed, is anything but simple.

Zhang's juxtaposition of *Ru* with shamans, and later Hu Shi's analogy of *Ru* with Western missionaries in his "*Shou Ru*" (A Discourse on *Ru*) essay, are inventive in the sense that there is no explicit reference found in pre-Qin texts indicating that *Ru*'s ancient profession is that of ritual shamans. Nevertheless, *Ru*'s reputation as learned men with a variety of knowledge encompassing astronomy, cosmology, state affairs, and ancient canons were evident even in non-Confucian texts such as the *Zhuangzi*. As said in the "*Tianzifang*" chapter of *Zhuangzi*, "I have heard that those *Ru* who wear a round cap know the seasons of heaven; those who wear square sandals know the forms of earth, those who tie at their waist a pendant shaped like a slotted ring are able to handle affairs with decisiveness." Zhuangzi then challenged Duke Ai of Lu—a state that was full of the surviving Shang subjects and was said to be populated with *Ru*—to find true *Ru* whose ritual attire match their proclaimed knowledge. After the duke's proclamation of wearing false *Ru* attire as a capital offense, it was said, "within five days, there were no more people who dared to wear *Ru* attire (*Rufu*), except for a single old man.... The duke summoned him immediately and asked him about affairs of state. Although their conversation took a multitude of twists and turns, the duke could not exhaust his knowledge." In addition, in the "*Tianxia*" chapter of *Zhuangzi*, it was said learned men from the state of Lu (i.e., *Ru* scholars) were all capable of clarifying the meaning of canons such as *Shi*, *Shu*, *Li*, and *Yue*.²⁴ That *Ru* possessed extensive knowledge of the natural world as well as the sacred, canonical world was in turn an indication of its noble pedigree in ancient times.

As the story goes, after the fall of Shang, *Ru*, the noble clan of learned men with received ritual skills, were scattered, residing among the people and carrying with them the prophetic mission of passing on the ritual traditions of Shang in the succeeding dynasty of Zhou. Hu Shi in his "*Shou Ru*"—which builds on Zhang's "*Yuan Ru*"—suggested that the duty of the surviving *Ru*, just as its Western missionary counterpart, was not only to perform the ancient Shang burial and mourning rituals but also to transmit the sacred *Dao* of past sage-kings. Because of the various duties that *Ru* were supposed to perform as the surviving men of letters of the ritual traditions of Shang, Hu divided *Ru* into three different categories: first, *Ru* as a generic name (*daming* 達名) signified learned men with received skills in general, including burial and mourning rituals; second, *Ru*, as a class name (*leiming* 類名) signified the mastery of the six arts as designated in the Zhou official post of *Situ* as the teacher of the multitude; and lastly, *Ru*, as a proper name (*siming* 私名), took the transmission of the ancient *Dao* of past sage-kings, including Confucius, embodied in canonical texts as its private teaching profession.[25]

Given the multiplicity of meaning of being a *Ru* in ancient times, it is not surprising that Confucius remarked to his disciple Zixia, who was known for his literary skills, not to become a *xiaorenru* (petty *Ru*)—that is, a morally deficient *Ru* despite his learned status. The correlation between *ru* 儒 and humiliation stemming from the base conduct of *xiaorenru* is not limited to non-Confucian texts such as *Mozi* of *Mojia*, a competing school of thought. In the *Xunzi*, a Confucian text proper, the word *ru* 儒, curiously enough, is used interchangeably with the word *nuo* 懦 denoting "lazy, weak, timid, and ignorant."[26] *Ru* in the *Xunzi*, as in the *Analects*, is divided into *daru* 大儒 (great *Ru*) and *xiaoru* 小儒 (petty *Ru*); besides *xiaoru* there are also various kinds of degrading *Ru* such as *shuru* 俗儒 (unrefined *Ru*), *sanru* 散儒 (unaccomplished *Ru*), *loru* 陋儒 (ignorant *Ru*), and *jianru* 賤儒 (base *Ru*). In Xunzi's discussion of what constitutes a *shuru* (unrefined *Ru*), Xunzi gave a similar description of the base conduct of *Ru* as found in the *Mozi*. Xunzi's description of an unrefined *Ru* as being immodest and being dependent on others for life's necessities echoed Mozi's account of the conduct of *Ru*. However, in Xunzi's eye, the speech and talk of those detestable *shuru* were no different from Mozi![27]

The base *ru* as a common laughingstock in Confucius's time was also remarked in the *Liji*. In the chapter "*Ruxing*" (The Conduct of *Ru*) of *Liji*, Confucius remarked: "Those to whom the multitude nowadays give that name [i.e., *Ru*] have no title to it, and they constantly employ it to one another as a term of reproach." Duke Ai, after hearing Confucius's clarification of the proper conduct of *Ru* and seeing his sincerity, promised, "To the end of my days I would not dare to make a joke of *Ru*."[28] Inferring from the above passage, one might say that by the time of Confucius, *Ru*, meaning scholars identifiable by their ritual attire, certainly encompassed a broad spectrum of men of letters; some live up to the title of *Ru*, hence are respectable, and some are only *Ru* in name, hence subject to humiliation. The pretentious *xiaorenru* in turn explains the paronomastic association between *ru* 儒 and *nuo* 懦 (stupid, weak, lazy, and ignorant).

But, who were the good *Ru*? According to Confucius in the *Liji*: "*Ru* consider doing their utmost and keeping their word as their protecting coat and helmet; observing ritual propriety and appropriateness as their shield and buckler; they walk carrying the virtue of *ren* 仁 [on their head]; they dwell holding the virtue of *yi* 義 [in their arms]; the government might be oppressive, but they do not change their course, such is the way that they maintain themselves....Therefore they are called *Ru*."²⁹ *Ru* in this passage signifies a list of moral qualities, a virtuous way of being in the world, instead of a specific class of people determined by their noble lineage. Xunzi further elaborated Confucius's understanding of *Ru* as the culmination of moral accomplishments. *Daru* (i.e., great *Ru*), being the highest accomplished *Ru*, are the ones who "model after the ancient kings, unify rituals and appropriate conducts, standardize rules and measurements, use what is shallow to extend it to what is broad; use the past to extend it to the present; use one to extend to one thousand; if a matter deals with the virtue of *ren* and *yi*, even if it is among the birds and beasts, it is like distinguishing white from black for them; in dealing with strange things and bizarre transformations that have never been heard or seen before, they would be able to suddenly take up one corner [i.e., infer from what is familiar] and then be able to answer what sort of thing it is without any doubt...they would extend rule, and measure it and the thing and the explanation would coincide like two halves a tally—such are great *Ru*."³⁰

In short, the reverence toward the ancient sage-kings' legacy of virtuousness and the emphasis on the virtues of *ren*, *yi*, and *li* are unmistakably constitutive of a great *Ru*. One can tentatively conclude, echoing Hu Shi's three meanings of *Ru*, that first, *Ru* as a general term, functioned as a common name granted to all learned men with skills; second, *Ru* as a class or profession signified their expertise in burial and mourning rituals as well as their expertise in the six arts; and lastly, *Ru* as a proper name or a school of thought having Confucius as its most prominent spokesperson, denoted an unyielding reverence toward the past sage-kings and canons, but more importantly one's moral accomplishments, a virtuous way of being in the world. *Ru*, despite its ambiguous and mysterious origins, by the time of Confucius had taken on an explicitly moral dimension that anchors its existence on reverence toward the past for the sake of the present. As we will see later, *Ru*'s reverence toward traditions, including both literary and ritual traditions, in times of foreign invasion, had in turn become the ultimate guardian of Chinese high culture and thereby is synonymous with Chinese-ness.

RU, STATE, AND CHINESE-NESS

The moral dimension of *Ru* as men of letters and men of moral attributes was a unique contribution of Confucius to the ancient *Ru*. However, after the death of Confucius, the exact meaning of *Ru* still remained uncertain. The diverse meanings of *Ru* are reflected in the "*Xianxue*" chapter of *Hanfezi*, an early Qin text: "Since the death of Confucius, there have been Zizhang's *Ru*, Zisizi's *Ru*, Yen's *Ru*, Mencius's *Ru*...*Ru* is divided into eight [different branches]" (儒分為八). Nonetheless, continuing down to the Qin period, *Ru* were known and valued for their knowledge of antiquity, especially the meaning and the correctness of ancient sacrificial and worshipping rituals. The first and only emperor of Qin, despite his anti-*Ru* attitude and policy, was said to have consulted with seventy *Ru* in preparing for the sacrificial ritual to heaven on Mount Tai in 219 BCE, an imperial privilege reserved for emperor alone.[31] In 213 BCE, the infamous "book-burning" of the first emperor, where written historical records except the history of his own present state of Qin were burnt, prohibited private possession of the classics such as *Shijing* (Book of Songs) and *Shujing* (Book of Documents) as well as the texts of the hundred schools, and handed down severe punishments on those who used the past to criticize the present. In the following year, some 460 scholars were buried alive.[32] Those scholars subjected to prosecution in the Qin were said to be *Ru* scholars because of the affinity between *Ru* and their love for antiquity.

Interestingly enough, the seventy *Ru* serving the heavily legalist-oriented Qin imperial court were exempted from the prosecution and the prohibition on the possession of the classics. One can say that *Ru*, even in the Qin—the most antagonistic imperial court toward *Ru* in Chinese history—were still deemed as indispensable to the state due to their erudition in matters concerning antiquity. The strength of *Ru*, said A. C. Graham, lies in the fact that as preservers of antiquity they were seen as the guardians of Chinese civilization and hence they held the key to the full integration of the individual with his cultural identity.[33]

After the destruction of ancient literatures by the Qin court, the succeeding dynasty Han began the critical phase of recovering cultural resources and *Ru*, given their love for antiquity, naturally rose above all other schools of thought. Han, the dynasty from which Chinese native identity derived its name, marked the beginning of the complex relationship between *Ru* and the state. With the sponsorship of the Han imperial court in the second century BCE through establishing the imperial academy in which *Ru* scholars were exclusively entrusted with the duty of maintaining, compiling, and interpreting ancient canons, and through the institutionalization of the civil service examination system in which the qualification of state officials was measured based on their erudition in the classics, *Ru* consequently became the official orthodox teaching. Despite the proximity between *Ru* and the state from the early Han down to the late Qing, *Ru*, however, was not identical with, nor dependent on state power. Even in the heyday of *Ru* learning in the Song dynasty (960–1279 CE), *Ru* official-scholars held no substantial power in determining state policies, which were in the hands of the hereditary ruling house. *Ru*, at their best, functioned as moral advisors, or the conscience of the state, and, at their worst, were treated as vassals in the state bureaucracy. In fact, with a closer look at *Ru*'s actual political power within the state, one can clearly see the paradox of *Ru*'s dominant yet, at the same time, marginal place in the state politics. Nonetheless, following the institutionalization of the civil service examination system and the establishment of the imperial academy in the early Han, the status of *Ru* was intricately intertwined with the state, for better or worse.

Beginning in the early Han, with the recommendation of the *Ru* scholar-advisor Dong Zhongshu, the state adopted *Ru*'s teachings as the official teaching while excluding all other teachings in the imperial academy. The scope of *Ru* learning, at the time, was by and large undetermined, and *Ru* scholars' direct tie to actual political power limited. In the Han, the road to officialdom, besides the more conventional ones—i.e., through one's direct tie to the ruling house or to the aristocrats—by and large depended on the recommendations of high officials. Once recommended, one enrolled in the imperial academy studying the classics; the civil service examination at this time served more as a mechanism to rank and classify recommended candidates than as a recruitment device.[34] Only a very small number of scholars were selected through this method and their duty was usually "academic"; that is, they were mostly in charge of compiling and interpreting ancient canons, and writing official histories. Despite its privileged place sponsored by the Han imperial court, *Ru*'s influence on state politics remained miniscule. In fact, the Han emperor Wu, who established *Ru*'s teachings as the official teaching, was impatient with imperial *Ru* and often departed from *Ru*'s teachings of virtue-based governance. His policies were said more akin to the First Emperor of Qin who relied on legalist advisors.[35]

The first use of the civil service examination system as a large-scale recruitment device did not come until 655 CE in the Tang dynasty under the regime of the first and only female emperor Wu Zetian. In the early period of Tang before 655 CE, no more than twenty-five men were selected in any single year, and the annual average number of people who passed the examination, estimated by E. A. Kracke, was fewer than nine.[36] Under the rule of Wu Zetian, the number of candidates who passed the examination was forty-four, a significant increase of *Ru* official-literati without any imperial connections to the participation in governance. In addition, two major developments in *Ru* learning occurred in the Tang: first, the Confucian text–based civil service examination was now used as a large-scale recruitment device instead of an internal ranking device for the state bureaucracy, and second, all state officials along with the emperor had to participate in the imperial cult of Confucius where Confucius was honored as the "Supreme Sage and First Teacher" (至聖先師) in the annual sacrifice at the state-constructed temple.

Despite those significant developments, it is worthwhile to note that during the Tang dynasty from the seventh to the early tenth century, *Ru*'s influence was marginal. In the Tang dynasty (618–906 CE), just as in all the previous short-lived dynasties after the Han (202 BCE–220 CE), the imperial court was dominated by the influence of Buddhism and Daoism. In addition, numerous Tang emperors were said to be fond of the music and attire of the foreign nomadic culture.[37] The decline in *Ru* learning during the Tang was remarked in the Tang's official history, where it stated: "The recent dynasty emphasizes literature [i.e., *wen*], yet overlooks *Ru*, or it relies on the laws [to govern], the way of *Ru* has already died out, and the culture of sincerity is in decline."[38] In terms of real political power, *Ru*'s influence over state policies before the reform of the civil service examination system in the eleventh century was purely academic and marginal. In terms of historical literary representation, *Ru* despite its marginality in state politics occupied a unique place in the tradition of dynastic histories where the correlation between *Ru* learning and the civil ideal of virtue-based governance was never questioned. *Ru*, because of their expertise in antiquity, were deemed as the gatekeepers of Chinese high culture. Undoubtedly, those who compiled dynastic histories were imperial *Ru* themselves. The imperial court nevertheless sanctioned the persistent representation of *Ru* learning as a symbol of civil order throughout history despite *Ru*'s marginality in actual state politics.

During the Song dynasty (960–1279 CE), *Ru* learning had its first resurgence since the Han. Song's renaissance of *Ru* learning significantly differed from Han *Ru*, which emphasized the learning of the *Classics*. Song's *Daoxue* (the learning of the *dao*) and *Lixue* (the learning of general patterns)—or what is called "neo-Confucianism" in the West—made popular by two Cheng brothers, Cheng Yi and Cheng Hao, and by Zhu Xi, emphasized, instead, the *Four Books*. The Confucian *Four Books* composed of *Lunyu*, *Mencius*, *Daxue*, and *Zhongyong*—the latter two were originally chapters of *Liji*—in fact was compiled by Zhu Xi himself. Zhu Xi's emphasis on the *Four Books* instead of the *Five Classics* was a significant departure from the Han *Ru*, since the status of *Ru* from the Han down to the Tang, at the minimal level, was defined by their familiarity with the *Classics* shown in the section of the "Biographies of *Ru*" in dynastic histories. In the Han, scholars in the imperial academy were selected on the basis of their expertise in at least one of the *Classics*, and in the Sui—a short-lived dynasty in the late sixth and early seventh century—the official position *Rulinlang* (Officer of *Ru*) was first set up to provide an illumination of the *Classics*. This official position of *Ru* as an expert of the *Classics* later was also adopted by the subsequent dynasties Yuan (1279–1368 CE), Ming (1368–1644 CE), and Qing (1644–1911 CE) as well. In other words, *Ru* and the learning of the *Classics* were inseparable in the dynastic perception of *Ru*. Yet, in the Song, the emphasis was shifted to the learning of the Confucian *Four Books*, which can be seen as a shift of *Ru* learning from antiquity to a more narrowly defined Confucius's *Ru* where the transmission of the way of the orthodox *Ru* was clearly delineated.[39] In fact, in all dynastic histories from the Han to Qing, the biographies of exemplary *Ru* were all classified in a same section; only in the history of Song was *Ru* divided into two separate sections: *Daoxue* and *Ru*, where Song's *Daoxue* was supposedly a distinct category from the rest of *Ru* learning.[40]

Song *Ru*'s delineation of orthodox *Ru* learning reflected its preoccupation with the concern of purity, which was a reaction against the rising force of Daoism and Buddhism at the time. Interestingly enough, Song *Ru*'s *Daoxue* and *Lixue*, as scholars generally agree, is in fact a blend of Daoism, Buddhism, and Confucianism because of its overwhelming concern with cosmology, the general patterns of the inner working of things, the Great Ultimate, and a full integration of man, heaven, and earth.[41] In fact, some prominent Song *Ru* such as Zhou Dunyi (the teacher of the Cheng brothers), Zhang Cai, and Zhu Xi all had studied Buddhism in their youth.[42] But, in the Song *Ru*'s rhetoric, both Daoism and Buddhism were heterodox doctrines since the former taught deception and the latter severed one's familial ties. In Song *Ru*'s *Daoxue*, not just non-*Ru* teachings were viewed as unorthodox, early *Ru* learning such as Han *Ru* and Tang *Ru* were also omitted in Song's genealogy of the *Dao*. In the Song *Ru*'s construction, the orthodox *Ru* learning that embodied the way of the ancient sage-kings was supposedly transmitted from Confucius and his prominent disciples (excluding Xunzi since two of his disciples were later classified as legalist) directly to the *Daoxue* of Song *Ru*.

Song *Ru*'s narrowly defined *Daoxue* dominated *Ru* learning from the fourteenth to the early twentieth century. But its dominance in history had a rather controversial inception. In the 1180s, two of Zhu Xi's contemporaries attacked the *Daoxue* of Zhu Xi as hypocrisy. In 1196, *Daoxue* was further labeled as "false learning," and Zhu Xi was impeached for ten crimes. In 1199, Zhu Xi's official title and privileges were removed and his status reduced to a commoner. Not until 1209, nine years after his death, was Zhu Xi honored with the posthumous title of *Wen* 文 (i.e., literary culture), and in 1313 during the succeeding dynasty Yuan, Zhu Xi's commentaries on the *Four Books* and *Five Classics* were by an imperial decree made the official interpretations of *Ru* learning and made the basis of civil service examination.[43] However, not every *Ru* literatus was comfortable with Song *Daoxue*'s narrowly defined *Ru* learning. As late as 1255, Song's *Daoxue* was still criticized by its *Ru* contemporaries for claiming exclusive knowledge of the *Dao* of the sages and for altering *Ru* learning by incorporating Buddhism and Daoism.[44] In short, Zhu Xi's orthodox *Ru* learning of *Daoxue*, or, what is called "neo-Confucianism," was once viewed as a heterodox learning as well.

After centuries of neglect, the interest in *Ru* learning rose during the Song. After the reform of the examination system in the early eleventh century, the state allowed a relatively free and impartial competition among literati for official degrees. Consequently, there were more than two hundred degrees granted annually during the Song, a dramatic jump from the annual average of twenty-five in previous dynasties.[45] The dramatic increase in the number of *Ru* official-scholars also created an unprecedented number of literati. As estimated, by the mid-thirteenth century as many as four hundred thousand literati had participated in the state-sponsored schools or examination.[46] The increased opportunity for state examination also opened up a teaching profession for *Ru* scholars in private academies, the proliferation of which in local communities, in turn, laid the foundation for the emergence of the gentry class and the diffusion of *Ru*'s elite discourse of virtue ethics into the semiliterate commoners' everyday life as a sign of social status.

The impact of the institutionalization of *Ru* learning went beyond the number of official degrees awarded to the learned elites. The impact of *Ru* learning as proposed by Benjamin Elman can be seen in three different arenas—the political, the social, and the cultural. In the political arena, the examination had a dual function: first, through participating in an impartial examination, the privileged status of cultural elites was objectively validated; second, through validating the status of cultural elites, the state was, in turn, granted moral authority and political legitimacy to govern. What is more, after the late tenth century of Song the emperor customarily served as the chief examiner in the final examination that took place in the imperial palace, and hence symbolically all successful candidates owed political loyalty to the hereditary emperor.[47] In the social arena, the privileged gentry status as a byproduct of the examination helped consolidate the distinct gentry class whose status depended on its continuous investment of its male household members in the classical training of *wen* 文, which was intertwined with political participation (*zheng*) through the examination system.[48] *Wen* (literary learning) and *zheng* (governance) then became integral parts of the gender identity of elite males. Lastly, in the cultural arena, the examination that elevated the Mandarin dialect, through which ancient texts were interpreted, generated the unequal status not only between *Ru* and non-*Ru* but also between the Han people and the non-Han.[49] The cultural inequality, however, was offset by the fact that the state examination was also a means through which the state was able to unify its subjects based on the culture of *Ru* as the civil ideal despite the diversity of local vernaculars and customs. All in all, the civil service examination was the primary means through which *Ru* learning was able to reproduce itself politically, socially, and culturally, and it eventually became the binding thread of Chinese culture and identity in history.

After the fall of the Southern Song in 1279, the free competition of the civil service examination was suspended under the Mongol rule in the Yuan dynasty until 1315. The Mongol ruling house, which relied largely on their military strength to maintain a decentralized political system, considered *Ru* literati a useless social surplus that were synonymous with the defeated Han people who could not be entrusted with political power. Learning from the fall of two short-lived dynasties ruled by foreign invaders Liao (916–1125) and Jin (1115–1234) in the north, the Mongol leaders profoundly distrusted *Ru* literati. As Qubilai reflected on the fall of these two foreign-ruled dynasties, "While Liao perished through [excessive patronage of] Buddhism, Chin [i.e., Jin] perished through *Ju* [i.e., *Ru*]."[50] In Yuan's early period of consolidation from the late 1230s to the early 1310s, *Ru*'s self-proclaimed social role as moral advisors of the state was cast aside. Instead, *Ru* under the early Mongol rule was designated as a special privileged household called *Ruhu*

儒戶 that was exempted from minor litigations, labor services, and most taxes. To qualify, one must, first, be a direct descendent from higher degree holders, state academy students, or ranking officials of the previous fallen dynasty Song; second, one must demonstrate one's literary competence by passing the state examination.[51] *Ru* during the Yuan dynasty was reduced to a sign of a private honor for hereditary households.

The Mongols, furthermore, considered the state institution of *Ru* learning and the traditional, dynastic model of civil order as defined by *Ru* literati as "Han methods" instead of "civil methods."[52] The association of *Ru* with the cultural identity of Han began to emerge. Under the Mongol rule, the word *Han* became increasingly an ethnic identification. In 1315 when the Mongol imperial court reinstated the examination system as a recruiting device for the state, a quota system was superimposed on four hierarchically ranked ethnic and regional groups: Mongols, foreign collaborators, *Hanren* (the people of Han, i.e., Northern Chinese), and *Nanren* (Southerners, i.e., the surviving subjects of Song in the south).[53] The annual average of twenty-one degrees awarded was equally divided among all four ethnic and regional groups.[54] Obviously, this quota system was in favor of the Mongols and the foreign collaborators, given their relatively small population. Furthermore, Han *Ru* were barred from occupying higher official posts, which were reserved for the Mongols only.[55]

Despite the limitation imposed on Han *Ru* during the Yuan dynasty, *Ru* learning, in the historical narratives, signified more than the ethnic identity of Han. *Ru*, among other things, signified the cultural ideal of civil order of the sages. *Ru* as a culture-based category was clearly shown in the Jurchen of Jin dynasty's adoption of *Ru* learning as a civil ideal while at the same time preserving their distinct ethnic identity. According to Peter K. Bol in his study on the relationship between Han literati and Jurchen rule in the Jin (1115–1234), the Jurchen ruler's adopting and patronizing literati culture should be seen as part of the civilizing project that promotes civil order (i.e., *wen* 文) rather than a process of sinicization or becoming ethnically Han.[56] Under the Jurchen rule in the Jin, Han *Ru* in the north were immediately faced with not only the issue of political loyalty, but also the issue of the preservation of the tradition of *wen*—that is, *Ru* learning. It was through promoting *wen*, the culture of civility, that both Han literati and the Jurchen ruling house eventually found their common ground.[57] The term *wen* as summarized by Peter Bol has four layers of meaning: first, it signifies the civil (*wen*) as opposed to the military (*wu*) approach to the use of political power; second, it means the things used to exercise power in a civil manner—that is to say, for instance, one brings about civil order by using rites and music, the techniques of *Ru*, in humane governance; third, it refers to the literary tradition of the ancients, the canons of Chinese civilization; and lastly, it denotes one's literary accomplishment, one's literary skill in poetry composition and essay writing.[58]

Through promoting the culture of *wen* under the Jurchen rule, *Ru* learning was able to reproduce itself politically, socially, and culturally, and the rise of *Ru*'s status in these three arenas in turn gave moral legitimacy to the Jurchen ruling house. *Ru*, in other words, were the guardians of civil ideals, or, what is the same, the guardians of culture (i.e., *wen*), which was indispensable to the moral legitimacy of the state. Through adopting *Ru* learning, the Jurchens became "civilized." The Jurchen's self-conscious desire for *Ru*'s model of civility was further demonstrated in the decree of 1191 in which the Jin emperor prohibited "terming our people and our language as being barbaric (*fan* 蕃)."[59] In contrast, the Mongols who explicitly rejected *Ru* learning as a "Han method" also rejected the culture of *wen*, the civil ideal of the ancients.

How then did the Han *Ru* define themselves under the Mongol rule in which the status of *Ru* was reduced to a sign of a special, privileged household in the new taxation system without any ethical, public functions? According to Wang Wei, in his "*Yuan Ru*" essay—a critical reflection on the origin of *Ru* written in the end of the Yuan dynasty—*Ru* signified various kinds of learning, the only true one being the learning of "the sages and the worthies."[60] A good *Ru* should be like Duke Zhou or Confucius who not only was able to command a body of learning but also was able to put classical learning into effect in state affairs. In other words, a good *Ru* was not just an academic classicist or a functionary clerk in the state bureaucracy; instead a true *Ru* must also be an applied ethicist, a moral consoler of the state. According to Wang, in his time there were many "useless" *Ru* who were *Ru* in name but not in reality. Echoing Xunzi's early critique of various kinds of base *Ru*, in Wang's eyes those useless *Ru* were pretentious scholars who wore *Ru* attire, were able to master the classics, wrote commentaries as well as composed elegant poems and essays, yet were detached from state affairs and had no practical solutions to problems. "If you ask such a one [i.e., a useless *Ru*] about the affairs of the state and the world, he answers: 'I am a *Ru* and I am not familiar with that.' Or, if he has some contact with affairs but trouble arises, then he says: 'I am a *Ru* and cannot handle it.'"[61] Inferring from Wang's critical comments on his contemporary *Ru*, it is clear that the meaning and the social role of *Ru* must go beyond its functionary role as an academic classicist without being entrusted with state affairs. *Ru*, one can say, signifies the higher order of things; that is, the moral conscience of the state, and the civil ideal of the sages and the worthies.

Wang's understanding of true *Ru* as a moral category was also echoed in Song Lian's essay "*Qirujie*" (Seven *Ru* Explained). According to Song Lian, another prominent fourteenth-century *Ru* who eventually occupied a series of high advisory positions in the formative stage of the Ming dynasty from 1360 till his death in 1377, *Ru* did not mean just one thing. Song Lian divided *Ru* into seven different types: there were *youxiazhiru* (*Ru* of wandering knight), *wenshizhiru* (*Ru* of literature and history, i.e., historians), *kuangdazhiru* (unconstrained *Ru*, i.e., the style of Zhuangzi and Liezi), *zhishuzhiru* (intelligent and calculative *Ru*), *zhangzhuzhiru* (*Ru* of essay and sentence, i.e., literary critics), *shigongzhiru* (*Ru* of meritorious service, i.e., accomplished official-scholars), and lastly *daodezhiru* (*Ru* of *dao* and *de*, i.e., virtuous *Ru*).[62] In Song's eye, virtuous *daodezhiru* was the highest expression of *Ru* exemplified by the way of Confucius that emphasizes the five virtues (*ren* 仁, *yi* 義, *li* 禮, *zhi* 智, and *xin* 信) and the five relations (father-son, ruler-minister, husband-wife, old-young, and friends).[63] *Ru*, as understood by this fourteenth-century literatus, was fundamentally an applied ethic focusing on the cultivation of virtuous human relations encompassing both the familial and the political realm.

The founding emperor of the succeeding Ming dynasty, Ming Taizu (1368–98)—a former peasant and outlaw—was highly suspicious of the examination system, despite having Song Lian as one of his top advisors. During his reign, he held the examination once in 1371, abolished it in 1373, and then revived it in 1384.[64] Under his rule, there were an average of thirty degrees issued annually[65]—a slight increase from the annual average of twenty-one degrees in the previous Yuan dynasty. Only in the mid-seventeenth century, the last century of the Ming dynasty, did the annual average of degrees granted rise to nearly 110.[66] However, this increase in the number of degrees awarded in the seventeenth century is minuscule, if one takes into account the drastic increase in population from sixty-five million in the 1400s to 150 million in the 1600s.[67] The decline in the state sponsorship of *Ru* learning during the Ming becomes clear if one compares the Ming's 110 annual average in the seventeenth century with the Song's 220 annual average in the thirteenth century.

The state sponsorship of *Ru* learning continued to decline in the last dynasty Qing, a dynasty ruled by the Manchu whose rulers once attributed the fall of its preceding dynasty Ming to the high number of licentiates who were qualified to participate in the civil service examination.[68] During the Qing (1644–1911), the annual average rose only slightly to 120.[69] The increased population that reached three hundred million by the end of the eighteenth century had further intensified the competition in state examinations.[70] As a result of the narrow gateway to officialdom in the Qing, there was an increasing frustration on the part of literati toward the foreign ruling house. During the Qing, the format of the examination also became increasingly rigid and the scope of competence was narrowed in order to cope with the large number of candidates. The standardized essay format called eight-legged essay first implemented in the late fifteenth century of Ming substantially limited the scope of creativity of literati.[71] The examination questions were shifted from stressing one's ability to write social policy to the ability to explicate the meaning of the *Four Books* based on Zhu Xi's commentaries.[72] Keeping all these changes in mind, one can say that *Ru* during the Ming-Qing period had declined into what Xunzi and Wang Wei called "useless" *Ru*, who aimed at nothing beyond reciting the classics and composing elegant essays without actually engaging in state affairs.

The kind of *Ru* that the Qing court produced through the standardized examination format and the narrow scope of the orthodox *Ru* learning was more a specialized vessel or bureaucratic clerk than a high level advisor fully participating in governance. The growing frustration on the part of literati in private academies beginning in the late Ming had eventually led to the renewal of *Hanxue*; it was a returning to the learning of the Han, the learning of ancient classics, instead of the learning of Song's *Daoxue* which was sponsored by the Qing imperial court. This seemingly academic movement in the shift of the direction of *Ru* learning was more than an intellectual curiosity; it was, rather, a political movement that challenged the state's authority in the transmission of the classical texts, which in turn were perceived as the source of political legitimacy for both the state and *Ru* literati.[73] Learning and writing in imperial China were essentially political in nature; that is to say, the learning of the classics since the Han was intertwined with the state's symbolic gesture of civil governance and hence its claim to political legitimacy. The movement of literati to return to the learning of the Han in the late Qing could be read as a sign of the rising gentry dissenting against the foreign ruling house. The word *Han* signified more than the passing dynasty that ended in the second century; it was now a sign of the Han ethnic identity. The self-reflective act of *Ru* literati in redefining *Ru* learning as *Hanxue* as opposed to the state sponsored *Daoxue* was an act of reclaiming the early tradition of Han.

The link between *Ru* learning and Han ethnic identity, or Chinese-ness, was also clearly reflected in the accommodation policies of the Jesuits in their early missionary work in sixteenth-century China. In order to nativize themselves, the Jesuits, led by Father Ricci, initially took the identity of Buddhist monks but later transformed themselves into *Ru*. At first, the early Jesuits were impressed with the popularity of Buddhism among the masses. As Father Ricci observed in the late sixteenth century, Buddhist monks totaled from two to three million, and this observation led the Jesuits to take Buddhist attire to be indexical of Chinese-ness. After adopting Buddhist attire as part of the Jesuits' accommodation policy to nativize themselves, Father Ricci proudly claimed in 1584 that "I have become a Chinaman. In our clothing, in our books, in our manners, and in everything external we have made ourselves Chinese."[74] Despite their popularity with the masses, Buddhist monks in fact occupied a marginal place in Chinese society because of their designated socioreligious role as ministers of mortuary rites and their foreign origins as an Indian faith.

In fact, Buddhist monks, called in Chinese *chujiaren* (i.e., people who walk out of family), are perceived by the Chinese as altogether without any familial ties and therefore are outsiders to the norms of social life. What is more is that, in popular fictions and plays, Buddhist as well as Daoist temples are often portrayed as a breeding ground for sexual impropriety. By adopting Buddhist identity, Jesuits were seen to be marginal and wicked as well, and hence initially they made no progress in converting literati, the socially esteemed learned elites. In 1595, Jesuits abandoned their Buddhist identity and shifted to *Ru* identity. Since *Ru* identity was the identity of the socially esteemed cultural elites, it was the normative expression of Chinese civility, the sign of Chinese-ness. Father Ricci noted in 1608 that only the tradition of the literatus "belongs to the Chinese."[75] In other words, *Ru* was a gateway for the Jesuits to cross over the ethnic and cultural boundaries, so as to overcome the "foreign-ness" of Chinese culture as well as the "foreign-ness" of their presence in China. By appropriating *Ru* learning, the sacred texts of Chinese ancient culture, Jesuits themselves became nativized, that is, they became cultured. *Ru*, in the eye of the Jesuits—the Other—in turn, was synonymous with Chinese-ness.

In sum, the very possibility for Jesuits of taking on *Ru* identity and being accepted as *Ru* by Chinese literati indicates that *Ru* indeed is, as Lionel Jensen termed it, a "polysemous symbol" that signifies neither a unified, fixed doctrine frozen in time, nor an ethnic practice limited to Han literati.[76] Instead, *Ru* signifies, at the minimal level, one's participation in the textual community of the study of the classics, which in turn symbolizes, at least, the following: first, the learning of "the sages and the worthies" (hence *Ru* signifies Chinese high culture of *wen*); second, the participation in the imperial cult of Confucius that marks the learned status of *Ru* as well as the moral legitimacy of the state (hence *Ru* signifies the complex relationship between *Ru* literati and the state); third, the civil ideal of humane governance that emphasizes a reciprocal care and obligation between the ruler and the subject informed by the hierarchical kinship relations of father-son, husband-wife, and old and young (hence *Ru* signifies a state-family ritual analogy); fourth, the shared assumption of the correlation between the divine, the human, and the natural world where ancestors are revered as gods and gods as ancestors, and where exemplary persons embody the harmonious oneness of heaven, human, and earth (hence *Ru* also signifies a correlative cosmology, an immanent religious sensibility); and lastly, the participation in the lifelong project of self-cultivation, where the virtuous self is situated in a web of human relations in a ritualized community beginning with the parent-child relation, where one's filial piety is the virtuous expression of one's humanity (hence *Ru* signifies virtue ethics).[77] All in all, *Ru*, just as the myth of Han identity, as Hall and Ames summarized it, is not an isolated doctrine or ideology, but is rather a continuous cultural narrative of the virtuous way of living and thinking of Han that is both genealogical and historical.[78]

DEFINING *RU*: *REN* AS CONFUCIAN VIRTUE ETHICS

So far, we have laid out the ambiguity as well as the complexity of the meaning of *Ru*. We have yet to identify the distinctive ethical concepts that are constitutive of Confucianism, so that we can speak intelligibly of "Confucianism" or "Confucian ethics" as a discursive, conceptual category. Keeping the complexity and the ambiguity of *Ru* in mind, what is sought here is not a simple reduction of *Ru* to a list of timeless, "core" elements. Rather, the aim here is to postulate distinctive ethical concepts identified in the traditional narratives of *Ru* as "Confucian"; that is to say, to identify the binding thread that holds together the complex tradition of *Ru* as a distinct "tradition" in Chinese intellectual history. Only by approximating "Confucian" ethical concepts can we possibly begin the journey into "Confucianism" and its interconnection with gender oppression in everyday life.

Scholars generally agree that the concept of *ren* is central in the teaching of Confucius and therefore, in the literal sense, it is "Confucianism" proper. The virtue of *ren* is the defining characteristic of Confucian personhood; the category of "person" is an achieved, ethical category, instead of an a priori ontological category. For the Confucian concept of person is interchangeable with the virtue of *ren*. The category of person in the Confucian world signifies one's virtuous achievement in the lifelong project of self-cultivation or self-refinement in which the self is irreducibly relational. And with the absence of the assumption of self or gender as an ontological category, that is, without the supposition of the given-ness of "human" nature from which the modern concept of equality is derived and without the supposition of the given-ness of gender traits based on which gender hierarchy is justified, in Confucianism a person is rather a particularized achievement in a complex web of human relations beginning with the most fundamental human institution, the family. In other words, given the interchangeability of the virtue of *ren* and the concept of a relational self, one's humanity and civility are an acquired virtue. The possession of the virtue of filial piety actualized in the most fundamental human relation, the parent-child relation, is the minimal qualification of personhood. The category of person in Confucian virtue ethics signifies one's existential, moral achievements; or, to adapt Simon de Beauvoir's famous phrase—"One is not born, but rather becomes, a woman"—one might say, in the Confucian context, one indeed is not born a human but rather becomes one. Yet, if one can become human, one can also fail to meet the minimal qualification. The fragility of one's "humanity" as an acquired virtue requires a constant cultivation of one's own person as a fully cultured being, in particular, through the learning of the literary culture of *wen* and the ritual tradition of *li*.

At the theoretical level, Confucian virtue-based personhood is seemingly open to both genders. But in historical and social reality, given the structural limitation derived from the concept of *nei-wai* as a gender-based division of labor, women indeed cannot be and are not fully "personed." However, before we can examine the problem of gender disparity in detail, we need to first of all understand the Confucian concept of personhood, that is, the virtue of *ren* as the defining characteristic of Confucian virtue ethics. In the following, we will first lay out the concept of *ren* found in the *Classics* as well as pre-Qin texts, and then trace its transformation in the Confucian *Four Books* where the virtue of *ren* underlies the very concept of Confucian achieved personhood in a complex web of human relations.

Ren 仁, as scholars agree, is unmistakably a central concept that underlies the teachings of Confucius.[79] The word *ren* actually appears quite late in the Chinese language. According to Lin Yu-sheng, the word *ren* did not appear in any available oracle-bone or bronze inscription dated from or prior to the

Western Zhou period (1122–771 BCE)[80] *Ren* only appears five times in the *Shujing* (Book of Documents), twice in the *Shijing* (Book of Songs), and eight times in the *Yijing* (Book of Changes).[81] The marginality of the concept of *ren* in these classics contrasts greatly with its centrality in the sacred text of Confucius, the *Analects*, where *ren* is mentioned more than one hundred times![82] The concept of *ren*, although it was not an invention of Confucius per se, was made central in the Chinese intellectual traditions by Confucius and his prominent disciples. As Chinese scholar Fang Ying-hsien in "On the Origins of *Ren*" wrote, "The teaching of Confucius is commonly called 'The teaching of *ren*.'"[83] Hence, any attempt to understand Confucianism with Confucius as its most prominent spokesperson must begin with the distinctive "Confucian," ethical concept of *ren*, which by the time of Mencius (371–289 BCE) had become synonymous with the concept of person.

To begin with, in the Confucian concept of person or *ren*★ 人 there is no assumed coincidence of the concept of humanity with the male self with which things that are ideal are associated. The dichotomy of male rational intellect and female unconstrained emotion is a common assumption in contemporary feminist critiques of the Western canons. Simone de Beauvoir wrote in her pioneer feminist writing *The Second Sex*: "[T]he relation of the two sexes is not quite like that of two electrical poles, for man represents both the positive and the neutral, as is indicated by the common use of *man* to designate human beings in general; whereas woman represents only the negative, defined by limiting criteria, without reciprocity," and, "Thus humanity is male and man defines woman not in herself but as relative to him."[84] The male self represents both humanity in general and the ideal, while the female self can only be defined in terms of a lack in relation to the ideal. More bluntly, as Aristotle put it, "[T]he female is as it were a male deformed."[85]

The privileged status of qualities associated with the male such as "reason," "transcendence," "public," and "autonomy" over characteristics associated with the female such as "emotion," "immanence," "private," and "nature" is often construed by modern feminists as a theoretical ground for gender oppression. Genevieve Lloyd in *The Man of Reason: "Male" & "Female" in Western Philosophy* wrote:"[T]he hierarchical relations between reason and its opposites . . . have undoubtedly contributed to the devaluing of things associated with the feminine."[86] In other words, in the West, the concept of "gender" and the concept of "person" are construed as ontological categories defined by a priori masculine and feminine gender traits, and qualities associated with the masculine represent the ideal while the feminine represents a lack.

Unlike its Western counterpart, the Confucian concept of person or *ren*★ 人 is an ethical category defined by one's practical achievements, instead of being defined by male gender traits. For firstly, in the most rudimentary, linguistic level, the Chinese character *ren*★ 人 used to designate person or people in general is gender neutral. That is to say, there is no such identification between "man" and "human beings" in general either literarily or symbolically. The generic male in the Chinese language is designated by an entirely different character—*nan* 男 or *fu* 夫—that forms no connection with the character of person *ren** 人, either graphically or phonetically. Furthermore, "gender" in the Chinese world correlates with social roles instead of with "masculine" or "feminine" traits, which will be argued more fully in chapter 4. Secondly, the Confucian concept of person is intimately linked with the virtue of *ren*. Etymologically, sinologist Peter Boodberg noted, *ren* 仁 is not only a derivative of, but is in fact the same word as person or *ren** 人 in classical Chinese literature.[87] In the *Mencius* and *Zhongyong*, it was stated that "*ren* means person" (仁者人也) and "to realize oneself is *ren*" (成己仁也).[88] *Ren* is a virtuous state achievable in the complex network of human relations as the word *ren* 仁—where the radical 人 (i.e., person) is coupled with numerical two 二 (i.e., the complex of human relations)—denotes.[89] Thirdly, the homonym of *ren* 仁 as virtue and *ren** 人 as person further accentuates the ethical dimension of the Confucian concept of person as well as the relationality of the Confucian concept of self. In other words, unlike its Western counterpart exemplified by the Cartesian ahistorical self or the Platonic divine soul, the Confucian person is first and foremost an ethical achievement through interpersonal exchange in a ritualized community.

Although the interpretation of the meaning of *ren* in the *Classics* has been varied, one characteristic of the word *ren* remaining constant is the desirable, pleasing interpersonal quality or talent.[90] The word *ren* made its earliest appearance in the "*Qinteng*" chapter of the authentic "modern text" of the "Books of Zhou" in the *Shujing* (Book of Documents) where the legendary tale of Duke Zhou who intended to offer himself to the ancestors in order to take the place of the seriously ill King Wu was recorded. "I [Duke Zhou] am *ren* and capable, have many different abilities and talents, and am able to serve the spirits well."[91] *Ren* in this context seems to refer to the pleasing disposition and various talents that Duke Zhou had over the seriously ill King Wu in serving the ancestors. *Ren* as a quality of disposition or talent exhibited through interpersonal exchange is also shown in the song "*Shuyutian*" of *Shijing* (Book of Songs), which is a song on praise of the legendary hunter Shu. "Shu is away in the hunting-field, there is no one living in the street. Is there really no one living in the street? It is that there is no one living in the street like Shu, he is so good, so *ren*."[92] *Ren* in this context seems to refer to a desirable interpersonal quality that makes the community lively because when Shu was away the community seemed empty. In sum, he who possesses *ren* distinguishes himself from all others.

Ren as a qualitative distinction of one's own person can also be extrapolated from the "*Taishi*" chapter—a later forged "ancient text" of the "Books of Zhou"—in the *Shujing* (Book of Songs) where the determination of the Zhou tribe in overturning the corrupted Shang kingdom was recorded. "Although the King of Shang has thousands of thousands of common people under his rule, they are not in one mind with him, I [King Wu] only have ten ministers with me, but they are all in one mind with me. Although the King of Shang has his immediate relatives around him, he cannot compare with me having those *ren* people around me" (不如仁人).⁹³ *Ren* here clearly is made in contrast with the commoners who have no distinctive talents or abilities. This passage was repeated in the *Analects* written as a quoted statement (cf. 20.1).⁹⁴ The recurrence of the same passage in the *Analects* at least indicates the awareness, if not the continuity, of the distinguishing, interpersonal dimension of *ren* among Confucius's prominent disciples who composed the *Analects*.

After Confucius, the concept of *ren* acquired a distinct moral connotation. *Ren* found in post-Confucius, pre-Qin texts, such as *Zuozhuan* (Zuo Annual) and *Guoyu* (Discourse of the States)—both are fifth-fourth century BCE texts⁹⁵—can no longer be interpreted as a purely descriptive term of one's desirable disposition or talent; instead, *ren* is a moral category closely linked with one's empathetic ability to feel with and to love others. The moral aspect of *ren* is illustrated in the *Zouzhuan*: "The famine in the state of Qin caused people to beg for food in the state of Jin, yet the people of Jin would not give. Hence Qin Zheng said: 'Turning one's back in time of need is without affection, taking pleasure in other's misfortune is without *ren* (幸災不仁), indulging oneself in desires is not favorable, angering one's neighbors is without *yi* 義; if these four virtues are all lost, how one can safeguard the state!"⁹⁶ *Ren* here is treated as a particular virtue that is in contrast with other particular virtues such as *yi* and is associated with one's capability to empathize with the misfortune of the other. In the *Guoyu*, the empathetic dimension of *ren* is tied to one's ability to love others. "[When Zhou speaks] he doesn't speak of something far away [i.e., he always hits the mark]. Hence when speaking of reverence, he definitely speaks of heaven, when speaking of being of one mind, he definitely speaks of genuine meanings, when speaking of keeping one's word, he definitely speaks of one's own person, when speaking of *ren* 仁, he definitely speaks of *ren*★ 人 ..." since, "[m]odeling after heaven enables one to revere, following genuine meanings enables one to be of one mind, thinking reflectively about one's own person enables one to keep one's promises, loving others enables one to be *ren* ..."⁹⁷

Besides being a tender aspect of human feeling, that is, to love, and to empathize with others, *ren* in the late Spring and Autumn and early Warring States period was also understood as an altruistic concern for others, a genuine marker of one's maturity as a complete person (*chengren* 成人).⁹⁸ In the "Discourse of Qi" of *Guoyu*, the action of Duke Huan of Qi in helping other states to resist the invasion of a barbarian tribe was characterized as being *ren*: "Aristocracies everywhere all praise [Duke Huan] as being *ren*. It is because they all know Duke Huan did not do this for his own self-interest, and for this reason, all aristocracies submit themselves [to Duke Huan]."⁹⁹ Acting on the behalf of *ren* is certainly acting for the good of others, not for the good of one's narrow, selfish interest; and once that maturity is reached, one is endowed with a moral capacity to induce voluntary submission from others. To recapitulate, *ren*, after Confucius, was transformed from a purely descriptive term of a desirable interpersonal quality or talent in the early *Classics* to a distinctive moral virtue and capacity to empathize with and to love others for the good of the whole.

The loving, altruistic, aspect of one's moral personality is the defining characteristic of the concept of *ren* in the tradition of Confucian teachings. When Confucius was asked what *ren* was in the *Analects*, he responded: "It is to love others" (12.22).[100] Mencius reiterated, "The person of *ren* loves others 仁者愛人" (*Mencius* 4B/28).[101] And Xunzi put it precisely, "*Ren* means love, therefore affection" (仁愛也故親).[102] However, what distinguishes the teaching of Confucius as the "teaching of *ren*" from all others is that the concept of *ren* is elevated from a particular virtue of empathy or a qualitative distinction of one's own person to an all-embracing virtue that signifies the culmination of one's moral achievements. The virtue of *ren* becomes synonymous with the concept of humanity as an ethical achievement.[103] It is true that there are numerous passages in the *Analects* that treat *ren* as a particular virtue contrasted with wisdom (*zhi*), rightness (*yi*), or courage (*yong*); the virtue of empathy (*ren*) is only one among many. For instance, "The wise person enjoys water, the *ren* person enjoys mountains" (6.23). Or, "The *ren* person is not anxious; the wise person is not in a quandary; the courageous person is not timid" (14.28). Also in the *Mencius*, "*Ren* is the heart of a person, *yi* is the path" (*Mencius* 6A/11).[104] These passages all suggest that *ren* is treated as a particular virtue. However, when *ren* is used to signify the quality of being an exemplary person, that is, *junzi*, it encompasses all other virtues, and therefore the virtue of *ren* in Confucian teachings signifies mature, ideal humanity.

But unlike the transcendent concept of God in the Western intellectual and religious traditions, *ren* does not transcend all particular human relationships. In the West, one's relationship with God must take precedence over all human relationships, and all human relationships are primarily means to achieving one's transcendental end to unite with God. In contrast, *Ren* as the highest attainment of one's moral cultivation can only be achieved and developed in human relationships.[105] To borrow from Fei Xiaotong, the Confucian ethical concept of *ren* can be understood as "the morality of personal relationships."[106] Although the virtue of *ren* symbolizes the synthesis of all particular virtues, it must be actualized in personal relationships governed by specific virtues appropriate to each particular relationship. For instance, the virtue of affection (*qin* 親) must be actualized in the parent-child relation, the virtue of appropriateness (*yi* 義) in the ruler-minister relation, the virtue of differentiation (*bie* 別) in the husband-wife relation, and the virtue of promise-keeping (*xin* 信) in friendship, etc. Confucian ethics of *ren*, in a word, is an immanent morality of personal relationships where a person of *ren* is able to master all these relationships with appropriateness.

Furthermore, in Confucianism, the self is never seen as an isolated, autonomous individual whose essential qualities and intellectual capacities are bestowed from without and possessed solely within. Instead, a person is always a person situated in a social context; a person qua person is a self-in-relation. For a person without social relations is also a person without humanity. As

Mencius wrote, "Without a father, and without a ruler is what is called a beast" (3B/9).¹⁰⁷ The role father and ruler here signify is not so much the biological, natural relation of parent-child or the hierarchal power relation between the leader and the follower, which in fact are also shared by the kingdom of beasts, but rather they signify the reciprocal obligations embodied in these social relations. One's humanity begins with one's actualization of these human relationships; that is to say, one only comes to be in and through relations. There can be no self without the other, or, rather, there can be no self without being situated in relation with others. Hu Shi put it precisely: "In the Confucians' human-centered philosophy, a person cannot exist alone; all actions must be in a form of interaction among people."¹⁰⁸ This understanding was also echoed by Herbert Fingarette: "For Confucius, unless there are at least two human beings, there can be no human beings."¹⁰⁹ Since the concept of a relational self is interchangeable with the grand virtue of *ren*, interpersonal relationality is then not just an inevitable, existential fact of human existence, but rather it is the necessary condition for the cultivation of one's virtuous personhood.

Among all social relations, the most important ones are the *wulun* 五倫 (five relations),¹¹⁰ which begin with and are conceived of in terms of family. Three of the five—that is, the father-son, husband-wife, and older-younger sibling—are familial. The other two—the ruler-minister relation and friendship—though not familial, are often modeled after the father-son and sibling relations. As Ambrose King put it: "The relationship between the ruler and the ruled is conceived of in terms of father (*chun-fu* 君父) and son (*tzu-min* 子民), and the relationship between friend and friend is stated in terms of elder brother (*wu-hsiung* 吾兄) and younger brother (*wu-ti* 吾弟)."¹¹¹ Family, in a word, is the center of one's ever-enlarging network of social relations. To use Roger T. Ames's model of the "focus-field" self,¹¹² the self that is first situated in familial relations is the vertical, focused center while the outward extended network of social relations conceived in terms of family is the horizontal, extended field from which one's substantial personhood gradually emerges.

In the Confucian world that takes familial relations as the core of all social relations, the starting point of being human inevitably begins with the virtue of filial piety (*xiao* 孝). *Ren*, in its most rudimentary level as the loving aspect of humanity, must begin with the love and care for one's parents. Filial piety is the beginning point, the root of the virtuous character of the exemplary person, *junzi*. As taught in the *Analects*, "It is a rare thing for someone who has a sense of filial and fraternal responsibility to have a taste for defying authority; it is unheard of for those who have no taste for defying authority to be keen on initiating rebellion. *Junzi* concentrate their efforts on the root, for the root having taken hold, the way will grow therefrom. As for filial (*xiao* 孝) and fraternal (*ti* 悌) responsibility, it is, I suspect, the root of a person's character" (1.2). The familial virtue of *xiao* in the parent-child relation and the virtue of *ti* in the sibling relation in the familial realm are the basis upon which the sense of civic responsibility in the political realm is formed. The cultivation of one's filial piety is the beginning of one's humanity. The same sentiment can also found in the *Mencius*: "Filial affection for one's parents is called *ren* (親親仁也)" (7A/15), and, "He who could not get the hearts of his parents cannot be considered human (不得乎親不可以為人)" (4A/28).[113]

To prioritize the virtue of filial piety in the parent-child relation as the beginning of one's humanity however does not amount to the duality or the incompatibility between the private, internal, personal relations and the public, external, social relations. Rather, the fundamental presupposition here is that since a person is always situated in a complex network of human relations, the familial relations where one first finds oneself must be substantiated prior to all other extended social relations. The family, instead of standing in opposition to the public, is perceived as the key to a well-ordered state and consequently the world at large. "The root of the world at large is in the state, the root of the state is in the family and the root of the family is in one's own person" (*Mencius* 4A/5).[114] This order of priority as well as the interconnection between the family and the world at large is also echoed in the *Daxue*. "The ancients who wish to illustrate illustrious virtue in the world at large first order well their own states. Wishing to order well their states, they first regulate their families. Wishing to regulate their families, they first cultivate their own persons (*xiushen* 修身)" (*Daxue* the "text").[115] The starting point of one's self-cultivation (*xiushen*) must begin with one's filial devotion of serving one's parents well. "Therefore, *junzi* may not neglect the cultivation of their own person and in wishing to cultivate their own person, they may not neglect to serve their parents" (*Zhongyong* 20).[116] Learning to be human is to learn to be true to one's familial roles by building a reciprocal bond with one's parents and by caring for them and serving them well.

Yet, an uninformed love for others would only be counterproductive. Confucius was aware of the danger of an unstructured love as he commented on the six flaws that accompany the six desirable qualities of character including *ren*: "The flaw in being fond of being *ren* without equal regard for learning is that you will result in foolishness" (*Lunyu* 17.8). One's altruistic concern for others must be structured by *li* (禮), that is, informed by one's knowledge of what is appropriate and proper in a social context expressed through a shared form of ritual, a shared social grammar. This is the case since social relations must be built upon shared social meanings that are expressed through concrete means such as rituals. The importance of *li* as a shared social expression of one's roles is an indispensable part of the Confucian project of self-cultivation or the project of becoming *ren*, becoming human. As Confucius said to his favorite disciple, Yen Hui, in response to his question about *ren*: "Through self-discipline and observing *li* one becomes *ren*" (*Lunyu* 12.1). *Ren* is not a simplistic expression of one's instinctual feeling for others. It is, instead, an informed act that must be accompanied by one's knowledge of the world in which one is situated. To be *ren*, even at the most elementary level of serving and caring for one's parents, is also to be keen on acquiring knowledge of one's neighboring fellows in the community and eventually the world at large. As the *Zhongyong* goes on to say regarding *junzi*'s lifelong project of self-cultivation: "In order to serve the parents, *junzi* may not neglect to acquire a knowledge of their fellowmen; and in order to know their fellowmen, they may not dispense with a knowledge of heaven" (*Zhongyong*, 20).[117] In short, *ren* as a general virtue that marks one's humanity must be substantiated in personal relationships based on a shared knowledge as well as shared assumption of the world.

The Other, whether it is another person or the world at large, is not a limitation or an external constraint imposed on the existing self. Rather, the Other is an integral part of a relational self since the degree of one's achieved humanity is measured in terms of the success that the self has in building a balanced, harmonious network of human relations as well as in terms of the extent to which it builds these. For *ren* or humanity can only be achieved by taking in and making others part of the relational self; and in finding a place, taking a stand, or acquiring a persona for oneself, one is also at the same time helping others to establish their own. In this often quoted passage from the *Analects*, the symbiotic nature of the self and other is especially illuminating: "*Ren* persons in seeking to establish themselves establish others, in seeking to promote themselves promote others" (6.30). In other words, a virtuous person possessing *ren* is a person-in-relation-with-others where the achievement of the self intertwines with the achievement of others in what Hall and Ames called a "field of selves."[118] And since, in Confucian ethics, an absolute Other as opposed to a private ego is not presupposed, reciprocity and communicability underlies the very structure of human relations. The virtue of *ren* ultimately is a genuine, reciprocal concern for others informed and structured by *li*, a shared social expression of meanings.

The concept of *ren* and the concept of reciprocity (*shu* 恕), which is the binding thread of Confucius's teaching (cf. *Lunyu* 4.15), are synonymous in effect. For instance, when a disciple asked about *ren* Confucius responded: "Do not impose upon others what you yourself do not want" (*Lunyu* 12.2), and when another disciple asked for a practical guiding thread that one could cling to until the end of one's days, Confucius gave an identical answer, except the guiding thread now is *shu* instead of *ren*. "Zi Gong asks 'Is there one expression that can be acted upon until the end of one's days?' The Master replies 'There is *shu*: do not impose on others what you yourself do not want'" (15.24).

To recapitulate, the Confucian concept of *ren* or person interpreted so far is threefold: Firstly, unlike its Western counterpart, the concept of person is an ethical category rather than an ontological category. That is to say, the category of person that is interchangeable with the virtue of *ren*, which can only be actualized in personal relationships, is a virtuous achievement rather than a given. Secondly, the virtue-based personhood is relational. That is to say, an isolated, autonomous, private ego is not presupposed as the starting point of the existing self; instead, the existing self is conceived of always in relation with others in a social context, and it is only through such a relatedness and codependence in a participatory, ritual community that the substantial self comes to exist. In Confucian ethics, the other, instead of being a limitation of the autonomous self, is an integral part of the ever-enlarging relational self. Lastly, since an absolute other as opposed to a private ego is not presupposed, reciprocity and communicability underlie the very basic structure of human relations. The key to self-cultivation or self-actualization in the Confucian world does not lie in the exercise of one's divine, rational faculty or one's private consciousness, but lies in one's qualitative achievement in building, sustaining, and enlarging a harmonious network of human relations. By keeping the relational, ethical aspect of personhood in mind, Confucian *ren* or personhood is gender-neutral, void of any a priori determination, and in principle the ideal personhood acquired through one's mastery of human relations is open to both sexes.

However, the openness of Confucian *ren* virtue ethics or personhood at the theoretical level is in stark contrast with the social and historical reality of the subordinate status of Chinese women, who whether learned or not, are all formally limited to the realm of *nei*—the realm of concealment—and hence women are conceptually incomplete, dependent beings through and through. In order to understand such a discrepancy between Confucian virtue ethics of *ren* and the cruelty of female servitude in Chinese society, we must first of all understand how gender distinction is construed in the Chinese world on its own terms. For if we are to reject the universality of the dualistic gender paradigm in the West exemplified by the Cartesian duality of the rational mind and the unconscious body, or the Aristotelian active form and passive matter in cross-cultural studies, then we must substantiate the element of culture in our understanding of gender in the Chinese world. In other words, we will have to understand how Chinese women are marked with cultural meanings as gendered beings. Furthermore, we will have to understand what sort of means are available for women in their project of self-cultivation, that is, in their project of becoming human in comparison with the normative, Confucian project of self-cultivation culminating in the civility of *wen* available for men in social reality. In the following chapter, we will begin by examining the concept of *yin-yang*, which is often viewed as synonymous with the concept of femininity and masculinity in the feminist discourse of gender in Chinese society.

CHAPTER THREE

YIN-YANG, GENDER ATTRIBUTES, AND
COMPLEMENTARITY

The discourse on gender where the category of "woman" is seen as both a biological and a social category is a very recent phenomenon in modern China, since in traditional writings, the discourse concerning women primarily is a discourse concerning the propriety of social relations embodied in familial roles such as father/mother, husband/wife, son/daughter, etc. The term "*nuxing*" 女性 (the female sex) now used to signify both the biological female sex and to convey a sense of universal womanhood, did not appear in the Chinese language until the early twentieth century during the May Fourth Movement.[1] Before the "modernization" of literary writing in the May Fourth Movement, the concept of "*nuxing*" was traditionally designated by the term *funu* 婦女 (wives and daughters). As Tani Barlow in her "Theorizing Woman: *Funu, Guojia, Jiating*" pointed out, the term *nuxing* was originally an invention of the rising new intellectuals around the 1920s. The symbolic meaning of the invented term *nuxing* is twofold: first, it represents an end to the representation of woman as *funu* conceived within the bound of *jia* 家, or familial relationality; second, it symbolizes the beginning of "modernization" in Chinese literary writing where the kinship-neutral term *nuxing* is used as a conceptual equivalent of the Western concept of "woman" as a discursive category. This is evident in the May Fourth Movement where the term *nuxing* was perceived as a sign of "Westernization" and "modernization," and subsequently during the Communist early liberation period of the 1930s and '40s, it became a sign of Western "bourgeois" woman.[2]

The representation of "woman" as a kinship-neutral category supported by a set of feminine qualities or defined by inborn biological functions is in fact quite foreign to premodern China. For woman as *funu* is always concurrent with the discussion about different social roles, especially familial, kinship roles and along with them the observation of proper rituals and the cultivation of corresponding virtues. This is already evident in ancient writings where the word *nu* was used originally to designate young, unmarried girls, and the word *fu* for married women. In one of the earliest canons—*Shijing* (Book of Songs), the word *nu* found in the well-known first poem, "*Guansui*," refers to a virtuous young girl who is a perfect mate for the man of noble birth. "The modest, virtuous *nu* is a good mate for the king."[3] Traditionally, the young lady, the *nu*, here is understood as referring to the new bride of the legendary King Wu.[4] In the *Liji* (Book of Rites), unmarried women is designated by the term *nuzi* 女子 and unmarried men by the term *nanzi* 男子.[5] When a *nu* 女 is married, she then is conventionally called a *fu* 婦, as defined in the *Shouwen* (Explanation of Patterns), one of the earliest Chinese dictionaries. Furthermore, the word *fu* 婦 (married woman) is often used in a pair with *fu*★ 夫 (husband) to designate one of the social relations—the husband-wife relation—in the Confucian *wulun* (five relations). The representation of "woman" as *funu* in the tradition points to the prioritization of familial relations in the process of gendering. A woman belongs primarily to two different social categories: one is *nu* (unmarried girls or daughters/maids), and the other is *fu* (married women or wives/mothers).

The concept of male and female based on sexual differences alone, in the Chinese literary tradition, is not used to denote man-woman gender relations. The terms *mu-pin* 牡牝 and *xiong-ci* 雄雌, which literally mean the male and the female sex, by and large, are used to refer to animals.[6] In the *Mozi*, the terms *mu-pin* and *xiong-ci* (the male-female sex), differing from the term *nan-nu* (man-woman), explicitly correlates with the kingdom of birds and beasts. "When the sages transmitted [their knowledge], with regard to heaven and earth, they spoke of above and below; with regard to four seasons, they spoke of *yin* and *yang*; with regard to human propensity, they spoke of *nan* and *nu*; with regard to birds and beasts, they spoke of *mu* and *pin*, *xiong* and *ci*."[7] The terms *mu-pin* and *xiong-ci* belong to the realm of birds and beasts where the reproductive bodies are the primary indication of the male and the female, while the term *nan-nu*, denoting distinct gender roles and relations, belongs to the human world. The ability to draw distinctions between man and woman based on reciprocal social roles and obligations, according to Xunzi, is indexical of humanity: "[T]he reason why humans are human is not particularly because they have two feet and no hair; it is because they have the ability to make distinctions. Whereas beasts have father and son, they don't have the affection between father and son; and whereas beasts have *mu-pin* (male and female), they don't have the distinction between man and woman (無男女之別). Hence the way of humanity cannot be without distinctions."[8]

So far, two implications can be drawn here: first, the distinction between man and woman for humans differs from the distinction between male and female for animals because the latter is an instinctual distinction between the inborn reproductive bodies, while the former is a self-conscious distinction between social roles and obligations; and second, since the reproductive bodies themselves are not taken as the original basis for the distinction between man and woman, subsequently a discrete conceptual separation between the concepts of "sex" and "gender" popular in modern Western feminist writings was absent in the discussion of gender in Chinese literary traditions.[9] That is to say, sex as referring to one's bare physicality is not conceptualized as the "basic stuff" from which the effect of acculturation and socialization engenders man and woman with a set of distinct psychological traits and social roles. Gender in premodern China was not postulated as a set of inborn biological differences between the male and female sex, nor a set of feminine or masculine qualities associated with the social categories of man and woman. The attempt to define woman as a sexed being independently of social relations, in Chinese literary traditions, is rather marginal, given the cultural supposition of the Confucian concept of person as a practical achievement through one's mastery of human relations.

Familial, kinship roles are the focus point in the discussion of gender. The early representation of women found in the *Five Classics* is strictly familial; the category of "woman" is understood in terms of the roles that she occupies, not in terms of her innate "nature" either as a biological being or as a transcendent agent outside the context of familial relations. The lack of reference to woman as a category distinct from familial roles was observed by sinologist Richard Guisso. In his systematic and often critical interpretation of the traditional perception of Chinese women in the *Five Classics*, Guisso nevertheless came to the conclusion that "the *Classics* have little to say of women as persons, but deal almost entirely in idealized life-cycle roles of daughter, wife and mother."[10] This was the case in ancient writings precisely because "woman" is primarily a kinship term denoting familial relations and social roles, instead of an individuated being existing prior to or independently of social relations.

The coextensiveness of the category of woman and her familial roles as daughter, wife, and mother can also be extrapolated from Margery Wolf's ethnographic studies of women in China in which the native informant's unwillingness to draw a conceptual distinction between woman and her familial roles defied the Western observer's essentialist assumption of the category of woman, defined by a set of qualities or attributes prior to any familial relation. As Wolf observed, "It is almost impossible to get a Chinese woman to describe for you the attributes of a proper woman. She immediately translates your subject into proper wife or mother or daughter-in-law, and if you object, she tells you about a good daughter."[11] The cultural gap between the Western conception of gender as a kinship-neutral term and the Chinese conception of gender as coextensive with familial, kinship roles is made transparent. The foreign observer's intent upon obtaining a normative description of "woman" as such beyond kinship roles is frustrated by the native informant's constant translation of the subject into concrete familial, kinship roles. Yet, in the Chinese world, a woman is a "woman" only because she is also a daughter, a wife, and a mother. There are no distinct qualities of "woman" as such. And hence the description of a "proper woman" must also be concurrent with the normative representation of familial, kinship roles assigned to woman in terms of daughter, wife, and mother.

The traditional Chinese perception of gender as familial roles is also reflected in the following passage from the eighteenth-century instruction book, *Jiaonu yigui* (Inherited Guide for Educating Women), by Chen Hongmou.

"When persons of rank are in the *jia* (family, lineage unit) they are *nu* (daughters); when they marry they are *fu* (wives), and when they bear children they are *mu* (mothers). [If you start with] a *xiannu* (virtuous, unmarried girl) then you will end up with a *xianfu* (virtuous wife); if you have virtuous wives, you will end up with *xianmu* (virtuous mothers). With virtuous mothers there will be virtuous descendants."[12] Although he was writing an instruction book defining normative ritual propriety for women, Chen Hongmou assumed no foundational status for "woman" as such; women instead were conceived in terms of the familial roles of daughter, wife, and mother. In other words, to borrow from Tani Barlow, Chinese woman was not assumed as a "transcendent agent" existing prior to or beyond familial relations.[13] It is only through occupying different familial, kinship roles that "woman" as a gendered being is made. The process of gendering is concurrent with the process of ritualization within the kinship structure where kinship relations make a person recognizably "man" or "woman." The gender system in premodern China should be understood within the hierarchical structure of the kinship system, not to be assumed to rely on either a set of innate qualities assigned to the social categories of man or woman, or the biological categories of male and female.

Because of an apparent affinity between the *yin-yang* metaphor and the modern duality of femininity and masculinity in the Western perception of gender, the concept of *yin-yang* however has been seen as indexical of the Chinese gender system. The receptive quality of *yin* and the expansive quality of *yang* are often taken to be the theoretical ground for the subordination of Chinese women to the patriarchal family structure. *Yin-yang* becomes synonymous with the Western dualistic gender paradigm of femininity and masculinity. This equation, however, is problematic, since unlike its Western counterpart, the *yin-yang* metaphor is correlative, codetermining, and complementary through and through. To demonstrate this thesis, in the following we will begin by examining the assumption that *yin-yang* mirrors the dualistic opposition between the feminine and the masculine in the West. Next, we will trace the historical roots and the uses of the *yin-yang* binary in the tradition, and its complex correlation with the concept of *wuxing* (five processes) and *qian-kun*. In the end, we will problematize the conventional assumption of the intimate connection between *yin-yang* and gender hierarchy in the Chinese world. All in all, unlike the dualistic paradigm of the feminine and the masculine in the West, *yin-yang* as a nonoppositional, complementary binary cannot function as an adequate theoretical justification for gender oppression in China.

YIN-YANG AND THE OPPOSITIONAL BINARY OF FEMININITY-MASCULINITY

When Euro-American writers first began to discuss the *yin-yang* metaphor, it was commonly treated as the conceptual equivalent of the Western conception of femininity and masculinity. The Daoist tradition, where the receptive *yin* qualities in nature are emphasized, was often characterized as being feminine, and the Confucian tradition that emphasizes the need of a well-ordered human society, in contrast, was said to be masculine in orientation. Daoism and Confucianism were set up as two contradictory, dialectical forces in the intellectual history of China. The common tendency to dichotomize Daoism and Confucianism or the *yin* and the *yang*, can be found in the work of the prominent sinologist Joseph Needham. In his *Science and Civilisation in China*, Needham wrote in regard to the two distinct attitudes toward nature in the Chinese intellectual tradition: "Confucian knowledge was masculine and managing; the Taoists condemned it and sought after a feminine and receptive knowledge which could arise only as the fruit of a passive and yielding attitude in the observation of Nature."[14]

Needham employed the modern duality of femininity and masculinity to characterize Confucianism and Daoism in which the *yin* or Daoism is equated with the passivity of the feminine and hence associated with nature, and the *yang* or Confucianism represents the active, interrogative style of the masculine and hence is associated with a patriarchal society. According to Needham, the feminine orientation in Daoism signified the probability of a matriarchal society in the early, primal stage of Chinese civilization.[15] The *yin* is resolutely female, passive, and nature-oriented as opposed to its negating counterpart, the *yang*, denoting male, active, and human society. The *yin-yang* metaphor in the Western eyes is a conceptual equivalent of the Western paradigm of femininity and masculinity.

Needham's dichotomization of the *yin* and the *yang*, or the feminine and the masculine, is in line with Western feminists' interpretation of the oppositional binary of the male and the female within the Cartesian philosophical framework. Borrowing from the Cartesian mind-body duality in which the rational mind stands higher than the mechanical body, feminists such as Genevieve Lloyd commonly reinterpret gender representations in canonical texts in terms of the duality between the male rational mind that directs and the female mechanical body that receives, while the former represents the subject, or agency, and the latter the object, or passivity.[16] By situating femininity and masculinity within the Cartesian framework of the mind-body duality, genders in the West are conceived first and foremost as metaphysical, ontological categories. Secondly, the male or the masculine—such as Reason, Rational Mind, and Transcendence—is the divine, and represents the ideal feature of human existence, while the female or the feminine—such as Passion, Unconscious Body, and Immanence—is the physical, the peculiar, and represents the passive aspect of human existence. The male and female within the Cartesian framework are not just different and hierarchical, they are, more importantly, contradictory concepts negating rather than completing one another. Therefore, to equate the correlative *yin-yang* metaphor with the concept of the feminine and the masculine is to assume not only the ontological status of gender, but more importantly its dualistic, mutually negating nature.

The *yin* and the *yang* are not contradictory concepts since conceptually the *yang* does not function as the ideal and the *yin* as the defective, nor is the *yang* privileged due to its transcendent, autonomous nature over the immanent, dependent *yin*. Rather, they are two inseparable elements that are correlative and complementary. The correlative binary of *yin-yang* is characterized by mutuality and reciprocity, instead of exclusivity and incompatibility. Unlike the oppositional binary of the feminine and the masculine, the correlative pair of *yin-yang* is not exclusively female or male either. Although it is true that the *yin-yang* metaphor in the Han cosmology, especially in the work conventionally attributed to early Han scholar Dong Zhongshu, *Chunqiu fanlu* (Luxuriant Dew of the Spring and Autumn), is occasionally correlated with gender, the *yin-yang* binary is a nongender-specific concept. The correlation of the *yin* and the *yang* cannot be entirely encapsulated by limited, hierarchical gender relations between man and woman, especially if gender relations are interpreted within the dualistic framework of femininity and masculinity. For oftentimes the working of the *yin-yang* binary as a complex metaphor is cross-gender and beyond gender. The complementary *yin-yang* correlation provides a basic binary scheme for organizing various fields of knowledge such as astronomy, medicine, divination, etc., and hence it functions as an explanatory account of the inner working of the natural as well as the human world.[17] In sum, the *yin-yang* correlation, as acknowledged by various scholars, although it is applicable to gender, is not based on gender.[18]

YIN-YANG AND CORRELATIVE COSMOLOGY

The concept of *yin-yang* in its early form was not intended to denote any human relations. The *yin-yang* binary first and foremost is an astronomical concept that is cyclic and complementary. Etymologically, *yin*, as defined in the *Shouwen*, means the shady side of the mountain, and *yang* the sunny side of the mountain.[19] This semantic meaning of *yin-yang* is based on the observation of the regular succession of the sunlight and shade and the corresponding climatic changes of warmth and coldness according to the position of the sun. The *yin-yang* binary in its literal meaning denotes two cyclic, complementary changes in nature. This usage of the *yin-yang* concept as the alternation of light/shade or warm/cold is present in several ancient writings. In the *Shijing* (Book of Songs) where the word *yin* and *yang* made their earliest appearance,[20] the word *yin* is used in conjunction with the word *rain* denoting cloudy, shady weather: "Gently blows the east wind, With *yin* and with rain."[21] The word *yang*, on the other hand, denotes the sun: "Heavy lies the dew, nothing but the *yang* can dry it."[22]

The *yin* and the *yang* first used as a term in the *Shijing* appeared in the poem, "*Gongliu*," which recorded the story of Duke Liu's first settlement in Pin after his careful survey of the field: "Of generous devotion to the people was Duke Liu. [His territory] is now broad and long. He determined the points of the heavens by means of the shadows; and then ascending the ridges.

He surveyed the *yin* and the *yang*, also viewed the course of the streams and springs."[23] Within the context of a new settlement in a strange land, the term *yin-yang* in this poem probably refers to either some sort of physical feature or phenomenon related to the field surveyed. In sinologist James Legge's translation, *yin-yang* is "the light and the shade" with reference to the hills; and in Xu Fuguan's view, it referred to the north and the south of hills since the south of hills receives sunlight and hence *yang*, and the north is in shade, hence *yin*.[24] In any case, the term *yin-yang* found in the early canonical text of Zhou, *Shijing*, is in line with its linguistic origin defined by the *Shouwen* as the shady and the sunny side of hills respectively.

As a metaphor for light and shade, the *yin-yang* binary is a correlative binary, not an oppositional binary in which each negates the other conceptually. For firstly, the qualitative difference between light and shade, or warmth and cold, is only relative, not absolute as with oppositional binaries such as good-bad, right-wrong, or private-public, etc. Oppositional binaries, by contrast, are conceptually contradictory to one another; for instance, the good and the bad are mutually exclusive of one another and the exclusivity is absolute. Secondly, in an oppositional binary, the ideal is defined by its own essence not by its correlation with its opposite. That is, the good is good not because it is in correlation with the bad, but because there is something intrinsic about it that is good. Lastly, the correlation between two opposites is only an external one since the ideal is conceptually autonomous from its opposite; that is, the good is still good even if the bad is absent. By contrast, correlative binaries such as light-shade and warmth-cold are not contradictory to one another. Conceptually, warmth-cold or light-shade must be situated in a continuous spectrum in which the state of being cold and the state of being warm are always relative to one another. The correlation between warmth and cold is an internal one where the existence of one depends on and is defined by the other. Hence, the *yin-yang* binary as a correlative binary of light-shade or warmth-cold is better conceptualized as a nonoppositional binary in which the coldness of the *yin* is always in relation to and is intertwined with the warmth of the *yang*, and vice versa.

The use of the pair *yin-yang* as a nonoppositional binary continued in the post-Zhou period. Up to the fourth century BCE, *yin* and *yang* were two of the six *qi* (six breaths 六氣) of *tian* that gave rise to four seasons and five differences and, when in excess, six ailments within the human body. The cosmos was said to composed of six *qi*; and *yin-yang* as two of the six natural *qi* of *tian* can be found in some fifth-fourth century BCE texts such as the *Zuozhuan* (Zuo Annals), the *Guoyu* (Discourse of the States), the older layers of the *Guanzi*, the inner chapters of the *Zhuangzi* and the *Mozi*.[25] The reference of the six *qi* appears in the inner chapter of *Zhuangzi* where an authentic person is able to "ride upon the proper course of *tian* and *di* and chariot upon the changes of the six *qi*."[26] To be able to ride upon or take charge of the six *qi* is important because *qi*, the fluid, vital breath, is understood as the basic makeup of the world wherein the cosmos and human body are conceived as one: "Human life is the togetherness of *qi*; when it coheres there is life; when it dissipates there is death.... Hence it is said, 'There is one *qi* pervades all under heaven.'"²⁷

Life depends on the coherence of *qi* within, just as the working of the world depends on the balance of *qi* without and the imbalance of *qi* within and without invite calamity. In the *Zhuangzi*, the imbalance of the *yin* and the *yang qi* is discussed in the context of a gradually deteriorating human body: "His back was all hunched up. On top were his five dorsal inductories. His chin was buried in his bellybutton. His shoulders were higher than the crown of his head. His neck bones pointed toward the sky. His *yin* and *yang qi* are all out of proper order."²⁸ The deteriorating, dying body is the manifestation of the imbalance of the *yin* and the *yang qi* within, just as a healthy body reflects the coherence of *qi* within.

The correlation between the balance of the six *qi* and bodily health is also elaborated in the *Zuozhuan* (Zuo Annals). In the story of the Marquis of Jin's illness, the physician cited the imbalance of the six *qi* within the body as an explanatory account for his incurable illness due to sexual excess. "*Tian* has six *qi*.... The six *qi* are *yin*, *yang*, wind, rain, shade, and light. They divide to make four seasons, in sequence they make five rhythms, and in excess they bring calamity." As the physician explained, "*yin* in excess brings cold diseases, *yang* in excess brings hot diseases; wind in excess brings terminal diseases, rain in excess brings diseases of the stomach; shade in excess brings delusions, light in excess brings diseases of the heart." After laying out the correlation between the imbalance of the six *qi* and its effects on human body, the physician concluded that the Marquis of Jin's terminal illness was due to an excess of sexual intercourse. "Woman is a thing of *yang* (女陽物) but shady in season; in excess they then generate diseases of internal heat and deluding poisons."²⁹

Interestingly enough, woman here is correlated with the *yang* instead of the *yin*. This correlation obviously is inconsistent within the *yin-nu* (woman) *yang-nan* (man) correlation, and therefore it presents a difficulty for scholars in constructing a coherent interpretation for this passage. However, upon a critical examination, one would realize that the correlation between woman and *yang* here is only secondary. The *yang qi* here, just as the shady *qi*, is not a gender attribute that exclusively belongs to either gender (i.e., the *yang* is not exclusively male nor *yin* female). Rather, the focus here is the effect of the excessive *yang qi* and the shady *qi* within the body. The Marquis of Jin's terminal illness caused by sexual excess is attributed to the *yang* and shady *qi* within the female body, and in excess they lead to the corresponding diseases of internal heat and delusion in the Marquis of Jin's body. This diagnosis is entirely consistent with the physician's early correlation between the imbalance of the six *qi* and the corresponding ailments within the human body; that is, excessive *yang qi* leads to hot diseases and excessive shady *qi* to delusions. The correlation between *nu* (woman) and *yang* in this passage is only contingent. In fact, as noted by numerous scholars, this passage might indicate that, at this time, the *yin* and the *yang* were not specifically linked to gender.³⁰

In the *Mozi*, the *yin-yang* correlation is also linked to the alternation of the four seasons signifying the succession of warmth and cold. "This is why the heat and cold made by *tian* are in due proportion; the four seasons are in tune; *yin*, *yang*, rain, and dew are timely."[31] Also, "When the sages transmitted [their knowledge], with regard to *tian* (heaven) and *di* (earth), they spoke of above and below; with regard to the four seasons, they spoke of *yin* and *yang*; with regard to human propensity, they spoke of *nan* (man) and *nu* (woman); with regard to birds and beasts, they spoke of *mu-pin, xiong-ci* (male-female)."[32] In both passages, *yin-yang* is correlated with four seasons. As for the latter passage, at the first sight, it seems to indicate a hierarchical analogy between *yin-yang* and man-woman. But in fact the *yin-yang nan-nu* correlation in this passage is nonhierarchical. This thesis is fully elaborated by Lisa Raphals in her study of the correlation between *yin-yang* and gender hierarchy. Supposedly, if one adopts a strictly hierarchical analogy to interpret this passage in which heaven, above, *yang*, man, and male are placed on the superior side and earth, below, *yin*, woman, and female on the inferior side, one will immediately be confronted with difficulties as to how to place these nonhierarchical components—four seasons, human propensity, and birds and beasts—in a strictly hierarchical scheme.[33] As shown in the following table:

YIN-YANG IN HIERARCHICAL ANALOGIES*

Superior terms		Inferior terms
Above		Below
Heaven		Earth
Yang	four seasons	*Yin*
Man (*nan*)	human propensity	Woman (*nu*)
Male (*xiong*)	birds and beasts	Female (*ci*)

*table adopted from Raphals 1998, 159, with some modifications

A strictly hierarchical reading of the binary terms in the passage will result in an incoherent reading. But if one adopts a complementary scheme, then the reading will be coherent and consistent with the understanding of *yin-yang* in the fifth-fourth century BCE as two of the six *qi* correlated with the four seasons. As demonstrated in the following table:

YIN-YANG IN COMPLEMENTARY ANALOGIES*

Knowledge about	Expressed in terms of
heaven and earth	above and below
four seasons	*yin* and *yang*
human propensity	man and woman
birds and beasts	male and female sex

*table adopted from Raphals 1998, 160, with some modifications

The underlying assumption here is that contrary terms such as *yin-yang*, man-woman, male-female are not contradictory binaries such as good-bad, self-other, or public-private. Rather, just as the totality of the world is expressed through the spatial concept of above and below that is relational in nature, the totality of the four seasons is expressed through the complementary binary of *yin* and *yang* that mutually constitute it.

The connection between *yin-yang* and the regular alternation of light and shade or the seasonal succession of warmth and cold can be further illustrated by the historical association of the school of *Yinyang* with astronomic and calenderic observations. In the *Shiji* (Records of History) compiled by the great historian of Han Sima Qian, the school of *Yinyang* whose work was characterized as "arranging correctly the all-important succession of the four seasons."[34] The *Hanshu* (Official History of the Former Han) offers the following explanation of the origin of the school of *Yinyang*: "The *Yinyangjia* originates from the appointments of Xi and He, whose duty it was to observe carefully the majestic heaven, to draw up the calendar, to explore the movements of the sun, the moon and the constellations, and to indicate watchfully the seasons to the people."[35] Chinese scholar Tang Junyi following this traditional account wrote: "At its origin, the Yin-yang refers to the changes in heavenly occurrences (*tien hsiang*) and the changes of weather (*tien ch'i*)."[36] To sum up, the early *yin-yang* binary is cyclic and complementary through and through since it is modeled upon the regular succession of the four seasons which are relative and corelational rather than oppositional.

By around the third and second century BCE, the *yin-yang* concept was transformed from its initial role as two of the six *qi* of *tian* to the ultimate pair of *qi* behind all differentiations; instances of which could be found in the texts such as the outer chapters of *Zhuangzi*, *Xunzi*, *Lushi chunqiu* (Springs and Autumns of Master Lu), and *Daodejing*. The complementarity of the early *yin-yang* concept was still prominent at this time. In the *Daodejing*, the complementarity of the *yin* and the *yang* and the male and the female mode of being are evident: "Way-making (*dao*) gives rise to continuity, continuity gives rise to difference, difference gives rise to plurality, and plurality gives rise to the manifold of everything that is happening (*wanwu*). Everything carries *yin* on its shoulders and *yang* in its arms, and blends these vital energies (*qi*) together to make them harmonious (*he*)."[37] Also "Know the male (*xiong*), yet safeguard the female (*ci*), and be a river gorge to the empire. As a river gorge to the world, you will not lose your real potency (*de*)."[38] The blending of both the *yin* and the *yang* and the mode of the male and the female is the key to the knowing of the grand *dao*, although they each have distinct qualities of their own.

The ceaseless generative power derivative from the blending of the *yin* and the *yang* is analogous to the union of the male and the female; and just as the *yin-yang* binary, the male-female binary in Daoist texts is also a non-oppositional binary; that is, they complete rather than contradict each other in the formation of the myriad things. The complementarity of *yin-yang* is also found in the *Zhuangzi*: "Hence, heaven and earth are the greatest forms; *yin* and *yang* are the greatest *qi*.... The *yin* and the *yang* shine upon each other, cover up each other and govern each other. The four seasons replace each other, give birth to each other and destroy each other.... The separation and the union of the male (*xiong*) and the female (*ci*), as a result, is a common occurrence."[39] Just as the four seasons succeed and intertwine with each other, the *yin* and the *yang* as found in the Daoist texts of *Daodejing* and *Zhuangzi* are also relational terms whose dynamic interaction with and interdependency on one another forms the background assumption of the *yin-yang* binary.

The dynamism of *yin-yang* is not only present in Daoist texts but also in Confucian texts as well. For instance, in the *Xunzi*: "Therefore it is said: when heaven and earth come together, then the ten thousand existants are born; when the *yin* and the *yang* act upon one another, then all changes and transformations are arisen; and when natural propensity and conscious effort join together, then the world at large is well ordered."[40] These three binaries—heaven (*tian*)-earth (*di*), *yin-yang*, and natural propensity (*xing*)-conscious effort (*wei*)—are complementary instead of contradictory. This is the case because the totality of the complementary *tian-di* binary and its effect, the ten thousand existants, is analogous with the totality of the *yin-yang* interaction and its result, dynamic transformations; it is also analogous with the totality of the natural-the conscious and its result, harmony in the world.

The emphasis on the interactive dynamism of *yin-yang* could also be found in the third-century BCE text, *Lushi chunqiu* (Springs and Autumns of Master Lu), an eclectic anthology of the thought of *Rujia*, *Mojia*, and *Daojia*.[41] Its writings in some sense were the synthesis of the major schools of thought received in the third century BCE. In the "Great Music" chapter of *Lushi chunqiu*, the *yin* and the *yang* are said to be the two ultimate exemplars in the world and together they are complete. "The origin of sound and melody is far away. It was born in due proportion, rooted in the supreme one. The supreme one emits the two exemplars (*liang yi* 兩儀), the two exemplars emit *yin* and *yang*. The *yin* and *yang* alter and transform, one above and one below together they become a complete form."[42] All in all the *yin-yang* binary is relational and constitutive of one another through and through.

YIN-YANG COMPLEMENTARITY AND GENDER HIERARCHY

However, some might argue that the *yin-yang tian-di* and *yin-yang nan-nu* analogies found in the commentaries and the appendices of *Yijing* (Book of Changes) and Han texts, such as *Chunqiu fanlu* (Luxuriant Dew of the Spring and Autumn) and *Baihutong* (White Tiger Hall),[43] are hierarchical and gender-based. It is true that, in the Han cosmology, the *yang* and the *yin* in some passages are explicitly correlated with a hierarchical scheme where *tian*(heaven)/*yang*/*nan*(man) are privileged over *di*(earth)/*yin*/*nu*(woman). For instance, in the commentaries and appendices of *Yijing*, one finds explicit references to the *qian-kun nan-nu* analogy where the *qian* conventionally interpreted as a pure *yang* is correlated with *tian*, which is venerable, and the *kun* as a pure *yin* is correlated with *di*, which is base. The commentary, the "Discussion of the Trigrams" (*Shuogua*), says: "The *qian* is *tian*, therefore it is called the father. The *kun* is *di*, therefore is called the mother."[44] In the "Great Commentary" (*Dazhuan*) of *Yijing*, one notes: "*Tian* is venerable, *di* is base, *qian* and *kun* are thereby established; when the base and high are laid out, the noble and the mean thereby take their (proper) place."[45] It seems quite evident that the correlation between the *qian-kun* and *tian-di* binaries is hierarchical, and that the hierarchical scheme matches perfectly with the later *yin-nu* (woman) and *yang-nan* (man) correlations found in Dong Zhongshu's *Chunqiu fanlu* where the hierarchical ordering of the *yin-yang*, *tian-di*, *nan-nu* are made explicitly. Chapter 43 of *Chunqiu fanlu* is simply entitled "*Yang* venerable, *Yin* base" (陽尊陰卑). Husbands are said to be *yang*, and wives *yin*: "Husbands though base all are *yang* and wives though noble all are *yin*."[46]

However the *yin-yang tian-di* and *yin-yang nan-nu* analogies found in the *Yijing* and *Chunqiu fanlu*, and their hierarchical, gender-based tendency can be challenged and problematized in their textual and historical context. There are two things that need to be taken into account: first, the crucial differences between the *Zhouyi* (the main text of *Yijing*), and the later commentaries of *Yijing*, which is traditionally attributed to Confucius; second, the ambiguous relationship between the Han cosmology and gender, and the political climate within which it was strategically necessary to emphasize *yang* as venerable.

Firstly, it is important to distinguish the *Zhouyi* from the later commentaries attached to the received text, *Yijing*, since the *yin-yang* concept along with the *wuxing* 五行 (i.e., five processes) in the Han cosmology is commonly assumed to be part of the *Yijing* tradition. The work of *Yijing* is frequently labeled as a work of the concept of *yin-yang*. In the mixed chapter of *Zhuangzi*, the *Yijing* is characterized by the teaching of the *yin-yang* concept (易以道陰陽).[47] The concept of *qian* and *kun* in the main text of *Yijing* is seen as synonymous with the *yang* and *yin* concept. The *Yijing* itself is said to set the foundation for the correlative Han cosmology, especially Dong Zhongshu's *Chunqiu fanlu*, and hence the *Yijing* is said to function as a theoretical justification for the later development of a hierarchical correlation between *yin-yang* and *nan-nu* found not only in cosmology but also in popular, normative instruction books for women after the Han.

But, with a closer look at the *Zhouyi* (the main text of *Yijing*), one might be surprised to know that not only the popular correlation between *yin-yang* and *nan-nu* is absent, but more importantly, the term *yin-yang* itself is also absent. In fact, the *yin-yang nan-nu* analogy only occurs in the later attached commentaries of *Yijing*. In the core text, *Zhouyi*, which is generally agreed to be a Western Zhou (c. 1045–722 BCE) text, the primary concept is *qian-kun*, not *yin-yang*. In the *Zhouyi*, the *qian* and the *kun*, symbolized by unbroken and broken lines, are the primary makeup of each hexagram, which, as scholars generally agree, is originally a simplified method for divination, replacing the early turtle-shell divination method in the Shang dynasty (c. 1600–1045 BCE)[48] Unlike the later *yin-yang* concept developed around the third–second century BCE as the ultimate binary of *qi*, the *qian* and the *kun* found in the *Zhouyi* is, however, not a binary concept; that is to say, they are not used as a principal binary underlying all the sixty-four hexagrams of *Zhouyi*. Each of the eight basic trigrams is formed by three lines—that is, a combination of a uneven numbers of the *qian* and the *kun*—and each of the sixty-four hexagrams is then formed by the various combinations of two of the eight basic trigrams.[49] In other words, the *qian* and the *kun*, or the unbroken and the broken line, although they are the basic makeup of each trigram, are not used in a binary fashion since the meaning of each trigram, depends, as it were, on the unevenness of the combination of the *qian* and the *kun*. One possible objection to this would be that the *qian* and the *kun*, since they are mentioned as a pair, in a sense are binary terms. But the point here is that the meaning of each trigram is derived from the combination of either two *qian* and one *kun*, two *kun* and one *qian*, three *kun*, or three *qian*; but it is never one *qian* and one *kun*, as the way that the ultimate binary of *yin-yang* is used in cosmology.

Moreover, the focus of *Zhouyi*, as a text for divination, is not on the concept of the *qian* and the *kun*, which are also the names of two hexagrams among sixty-four possible hexagrams. The use of *Zhouyi* for divination focuses rather on a coherent interpretation of the inherently vague omen-statements ascribed to each hexagram. The absence of the *qian-kun* binary in the use of the *Zhouyi* in clearly illustrated in the following rather complete description of a divination performed in the Eastern Zhou in year 535 BCE recorded in the *Zuozhuan*:

> The wife of Duke Xiang of Wei had no son, but his concubine Zhou Ge bore to him Meng Zhi. Kong Chengqi [the grand minister of Wei] dreamt that Kangshu [i.e., the first lord of Wei] told him to establish Yuan 元 [i.e., the primary one].... Zhou Ge bore him a second son and named him Yuan (元). The feet of Meng Zhi [i.e., the first son] were disabled so that he was feeble in walking. Kong Chengzi used the *Zhouyi* to determine it, saying: "Would that Yuan [i.e., the second son] enjoy the state of Wei and preside over its altars." He met the hexagram *Zhun* 屯. He next said: "I want to establish Zhi [i.e., the first son]; would that he be capable of enjoying it." He met the hexagram *Bi* 比. He showed these to Scribe Chao. Scribe Chao said:" 'Primary receipt' (元亨); what further doubt can there be?" Chengzi said: "Is it not said of the elder?" Scribe Chao replied: "Kangshu named him (i.e., Yuan 元), so that he can be said to be the elder. And Meng is not a complete person (非人) [because of his disability]; he will not be placed in the ancestral temple and cannot be said to be the elder. Moreover, its omen-statement

says: 'beneficial to establish a lord.' If the heir were auspicious, what need would there be to 'establish' one? To 'establish' is not to inherit. The two hexagrams both say it. The younger one should be established."⁵⁰

From the above passage, it is clear that in the early use of *Zhouyi* for divination, the focus is on deciphering the inherently vague omen-statements in order to sanction a given action. In the case of Duke Xiang, his second son is said to be his legitimate heir because the omen-statement of the *Zhun* hexagram says, "Prime receipt: beneficial to determine. Do not herewith have someplace to go; beneficial to establish a lord." It is interpreted as an auspicious sign for the establishment of the second son as the lord. This is so because, firstly, the word *yuan* 元 in the omen-statement of the *Zhun* hexagram is also the name of the second son, and secondly, the statement says to establish, instead of inheriting, a lord. As for the *Bi* hexagram, its Six in the Third line says, "Ally with him the non-human"(比之非人). And that is interpreted as saying that the first son, Meng Zhi, is not a complete person because of his disability, and hence he cannot be a legitimate heir. It is clear that the omen-statement ascribed to each hexagram due to its intentional vagueness admits a highly flexible interpretation of the text in a divination. It is also clear that from the above passage in regard to the *qian-kun* binary: first, the *qian-kun* binary is entirely absent in the interpretation of the hexagrams, and second, it would be reasonable to assume that the meaning of the omen-statement (due to its inherent vagueness as a divination device) must resist any type of systematization or reduction to a single binary concept, for instance, *yin-yang* or *qian-kun*.

Only in the later attached commentaries of *Yijing* are the *qian* and the *kun* treated as the ultimate binary paralleling the *yin-yang* binary. For instance, in the "*Dazhuan*" commentary of *Yijing*, one reads: "The *qian* and the *kun* are the gateway to the changes. *Qian* is *yang* and *kun* is *yin*."⁵¹ In this passage, *qian-kun* and *yin-yang* are seemingly synonymous. The later commentaries of *Yijing*, although they are traditionally attributed to Confucius (c. 551–479 BCE) were most likely compiled in the late Qin or the early Han around the third century BCE.⁵² As A. C. Graham speculated: "[T]he Confucian appendices to the *Changes* come at latest from very early in the Han."⁵³ And, "Most or all of the appendices called the 'Ten Wings'... later to be ascribed to Confucius himself, may be dated within a few decades on either side of 200 B.C."⁵⁴ If this is the case, then the systematization of the *qian-kun* binary in the later attached commentaries of *Yijing* would seem to coincide with the systematization of the *yin-yang* binary as the ultimate binary during the third–second century BCE. During this time, Zou Yan's (c. 305–240 BCE) *yinyang wuxing* theory dominated the scene of politics. It would seem reasonable to speculate that the grand synthesis of *qian-kun* and *yin-yang* binaries in the Confucian tradition had its non-Confucian root in the grand synthesis of *yinyang* and *wuxing* made popular by Zou Yan around the mid-third century BCE.

This hypothesis can be further supported by the following two textual findings. First, the concept of *yinyang wuxing* that is prominent in the received text of *Yijing* is conspicuously absent in all pre-Han Confucian texts proper, except in the *Xunzi*, a third-century BCE text. The term *wuxing* only appears in the *Xunzi* once and the *yin-yang* concept is not prominent at all. The term *wuxing* found in the *Xunzi* is usually interpreted as referring to five kinds of moral conduct (i.e., *ren* 仁, *yi* 義, *li* 禮, *zhi* 智, *xin* 信) instead of five elements (i.e., earth, wood, metal, fire, water).⁵⁵ It is still not clear whether the *wuxing* as five kinds of moral conduct found in the *Xunzi* functions as a derivative concept of the five processes or as something altogether independent. In any case, the *wuxing* theory in Xunzi's estimation is unscholarly since it mostly deals with mysterious, esoteric matters that are unworthy of any serious attention. "They have initiated a theory for which they claim great antiquity, calling it the *wuxing*. Peculiar and unreasonable in the extreme, it lacks proper categorization. Mysterious and enigmatic, it lacks satisfactory explanations ..."⁵⁶ Xunzi's rejection of the esoteric knowledge of the *wuxing* theory seems to resonate well with Confucius's exclusion of matters concerning strange phenomena, force, disorder, or spirits in his teachings (c.f. *Lunyu* 7.21). Xunzi's negative assessment of the *wuxing* theory is an indication of its non-Confucian origin in the third century BCE. And its non-Confucian origin can in part help explain its uniform absence in all of the Confucian *Four Books*—the *Analects*, *Mencius*, *Daxue*, and *Zhongyong*—where not only the term *wuxing*, but also the term *yin-yang*, are not mentioned at all.⁵⁷

In traditional commentaries, the word *yi* 易 found in the passage 7.17 of the *Analects* is interpreted as meaning the *Yijing*, which Confucius once mentioned with reverence. However, that rendition has now been contested. According to Ames and Rosemont among others, there is also a variant *yi* 亦 (i.e., also, after all) found in the received version of the text.⁵⁸ Although the *Yijing* is used several times in the *Xunzi* as an authority, Xunzi, himself, did not consider the *Yijing* a classic essential to learning. In the very first chapter of the *Xunzi*, "An Exhortation to Learning," the *Yijing* is not even included among the five classics—i.e., the *Rituals*, the *Music*, the *Annals*, the *Documents*, and the *Songs*.⁵⁹ But if it is true that the appendices of *Yijing* were compiled by Confucius around the fifth century BCE, then Xunzi's exclusion of *Yijing* as part of the ancient canon essential to learning would be perplexing. Also, if the concept of *yinyang wuxing* were assumed to be prominent among ancient *Ru*, then the uniform absence of the *yinyang wuxing* concept from all pre-Han Confucian texts would be rather suspicious. Instead, a simpler explanation would be this: the *yinyang wuxing* concept, which is found in the commentary of the *Yijing* and later became the foundation of Han cosmology, has a non-Confucian origin, and was not integrated into the Confucian school of thought before the late Qin or the early Han.

The second reason supporting the dating of the *Yijing* commentaries as concurrent with the synthesis of the concept of *yinyang wuxing* around the mid-third century to the early second century BCE is this: if it is true that the suspicious absence of the *yinyang wuxing* concept from all pre-Han Confucian texts proper is an indication of the marginality of the *qian-kun* or *yin-yang* binary prior to the third century BCE, it would be probable that the appendices of the *Yijing* were first compiled in the mid-third century BCE during the same time when Zou Yan's *wude* 五德 (five-power) theory rose to the dominant position. This time period for the compilation of the appendices of *Yijing*, where the *qian-kun* binary is an equivalent concept of the *yin-yang* binary, is entirely consistent with our earlier estimation of the evolution of the *yin-yang* concept as the ultimate binary around the third–second century BCE. The point here is that if the *yin-yang tian-di* and *yin-yang nan-nu* correlations found in the appendices of *Yijing* are to be taken as the theoretical justification for the hierarchical correlation between *yin-yang* and *nan-nu* found in the Han text, *Chunqiu fanlu*, then the historical background upon which the *yinyang wuxing* concept was first incorporated into *Ru* teachings becomes relevant to understanding the origin of the *yinyang nannu* analogy. Specifically, if we place Dong Zhongshu's *yinyang nannu* analogy in its proper historical context, it becomes plausible that the incorporation of the *yinyang wuxing* concept into *Ru* teachings, and the emphasis on the venerable *yang* over the base *yin*, was in fact a necessary response to the rise of Zou Yan's *wude* theory in the political realm around the mid-third century BCE.

Yinyang and *wuxing*, as noted by sinologists, were originally two distinct concepts.[60] The earliest appearance of the term *wuxing* is found in the "*Hongfan*" chapter of the *Shujing* (Book of Documents) where the term *wuxing* is a classificatory concept that refers to five essential materials (i.e., wood, fire, water, earth, metal) in daily life. In this early concept of the *wuxing*, unlike the later *yinyang wuxing* concept, there is no circular movement among these five materials. It is only in the later development of the *yinyang wuxing* theory that the circular movement of the *yin* and *yang qi* in the four seasons is incorporated into the conquest cycle of *wuxing*. The synthesis of the *yinyang* and the *wuxing* can be traced back to the founder of *Yinyangjia*, Zou Yan (c. 305–240 BCE),[61] who had written more than one hundred thousand characters on the *yinyang wuxing* concept in his *wude* theory.[62] Unfortunately, none of Zou Yan's works survived today; all the information regarding Zou Yan's *wude* theory is mainly from Sima Qian's *Shiji*. According to the *Shiji*, Zou Yan was the only one in the Warring States period (c. 479–222 BCE) who had a clear view of the cyclic movement of the five powers, and his theory of *wude* had won him fame among the rulers and the princes who read his theory with awe.[63] The appeal of Zou Yan's *wude* theory lies in its ability to provide a powerful theoretical basis for a legitimate, political conquest of other states in the Warring States period, the most violent era in ancient Chinese history.

Despite his fame among the rich and the powerful, Zou Yan did not belong to the scholarly circle of his time. Although Zou Yan's *Yinyangjia* was classified as one of the six major philosophical schools of thought in the *Shiji* (second-century BCE text), his *wuxing* theory was mostly ignored or viewed negatively by scholars in the third century BCE. For instance, as mentioned earlier, Xunzi regarded the *wuxing* theory to be esoteric and unworthy of learning; in the *Hanfeizi*, Zou Yan is mentioned in connection with an inaccurate divination; and in the mixed *"Tianxia"* chapter of *Zhuangzi* where all major schools of thought were assessed, *Yinyangjia* was not even mentioned. It is possible that, noted by A. C. Graham, Zou Yan belonged to a world outside scholarly circles; he was first and foremost remembered as a *fangshi* 方 士 (i.e., a man of secret arts) promising esoteric knowledge, which was one of the subjects despised by Confucius.[64] The unorthodox origin of the *yinyang wuxing* theory in conjunction with Zou Yan's *Yinyangjia* in part explains why there is a uniform absence of the *yinyang wuxing* concept in all Confucian *Four Books*. Its marginality in scholarly circles of the third century BCE contrasts sharply with the centrality of the *yinyang wuxing* cosmology in all aspects of life in the Chinese world after the consolidation and institutionalization of *Yijing* as one of the *Five Classics* and as part of the Confucian canon proper in the early Han.

Even though it was marginal in the eye of his scholarly contemporaries, Zou Yan's *wude* theory had a great importance in the political realm in the mid-third century BCE. His *wude* conquest cycle provided a powerful theoretical basis for explaining the conquest of a fallen dynasty and thereby laid a basis for legitimating dynastic changes. According to Zou Yan, the conquest cycle of the five powers (Earth, Wood, Metal, Fire, and Water), in which each power is followed by the one that it cannot conquer (that is, Earth is replaced by Wood which is replaced by Metal, Metal then is dissolved by Fire which in turn is overcome by Water), is concurrent with the yearly cycle of four seasons where the *yang* of spring and summer is inevitably replaced by the *yin* of autumn and winter. The movement of the five powers is concurrent with the movement of history in which the rise and fall of a given dynasty is explained in terms of its affinity with the prevalent power in a specific historical time. For instance, the kingdom of sage Shun, according to Zou Yan's theory, was dominated by the power of Earth, and hence it inevitably was conquered by the Xia dynasty which was ruled by the power of Wood; and the Shang dynasty, dominated by the power of Metal, was consequently overthrown by the Zhou that was ruled by the power of Fire. According to this conquering pattern, as part of the complex *yinyang wuxing* cosmology, the next victorious dynasty would have to be ruled by the power of Water—that is, the power of the high *yin* of winter—in order to take over the Zhou dynasty's place in history.

The fallen Zhou dynasty, after the long dividing period of the Warring States, was first unified by the Qin state in 221 BCE. After the unification, Zou Yan's *wude* theory took a full effect on the First Emperor of the Qin dynasty, who declared the supremacy of the power of Water in the beginning of his regime. According to the *Shiji*, the emperor, besides declaring that his reign resided in the power of Water, also changed the name of the Yellow River to "Powerful Water" to symbolize the dominance of his regime. In the complex *yinyang wuxing* correlation, water is correlated with the color black, the seasons of autumn and winter, and then with severe punishment and death. As a result, the First Emperor of Qin selected black as the royal color, decreed the first day of the tenth month (i.e., the beginning of autumn) as the commencement of a year, and used strict laws and severe punishment to deal with all state affairs.[65]

The Qin's emphasis on the supremacy of the power of Water along with the *yin* of winter contrasts greatly with the Han dynasty that succeeded it. The Han dynasty adopted *Ru*'s teachings as the state orthodoxy, and *Ru*'s teachings was figuratively represented by the *yang* of spring, which in turn symbolizes the humane governance based on Confucius's teaching of the virtue of *ren*. Such a symbolic reversal of the *yin* and *yang* power in the early Han is evident in Dong Zhongshu's *Chunqiu fanlu*—a text intermingling ethics and cosmology—in which the *yin* is correlated with winter and punishment, and the *yang* is correlated with spring and virtue. "*Yin* is the *qi* of punishment, and *yang* the *qi* of virtue; *yin* begins in autumn and *yang* begins in spring."[66] And since heaven prefers virtue to punishment, it is natural, as stressed by Dong Zhongshu in numerous chapters, that the *yang* should be exalted above the *yin*.[67] The emphasis on the venerable *yang* in the *Chunqiu fanlu* was necessitated by the correlation of *yang* with virtue and humane governance and *yin* with punishment and death. And that correlation in part was necessitated by the Qin's emphasis on law and punishment figuratively represented by the power of *yin* in the complex *yinyang wuxing* cosmology of Zou Yan.

Within the context of the Zou Yan's *wude* theory, the Qin's emphasis on the power of Water, and its preference for the legalist tradition of law and punishment, the following two hypotheses would seem plausible: First, the integration of the *yinyang wuxing* theory into the Confucian tradition in the late Qin and the early Han was an inevitable response to the political climate in the third century BCE, which was dominated by the *yinyang wuxing* cosmology. The compiling of the commentaries attached to the *Yijing* and attributed to Confucius during this time was a necessary step taken by *Ru* scholars in order to compete with the politically favored *yinyang wuxing* school of thought. By attributing the commentary of *Yijing* to Confucius, *Ru* scholars also made the popular non-Confucian concept of *yinyang wuxing* part of the Confucian tradition. Moreover, under the Qin's repressive book-burning policy, all schools of thought and ancient canons were suppressed except writings on medicine, divination, and planting and sowing. The *Yijing*, a text for divination dealing with the esoteric knowledge of heaven and earth, was among the few tolerated by the Qin court. The availability of the *Yijing* during the Qin period in some ways also contributed to the popularity of the *yinyang wuxing* theory among *Ru* scholars during the third century BCE.[68]

Second, the emphasis on the venerable *yang* over the base *yin* in the *yinyang wuxing* cosmology was strategically necessary for *Ru* scholars in the early Han, especially for Dong Zhongshu who was instrumental in establishing the *Five Classics* (i.e., the *Shu, Shi, Yi, Li,* and *Chunqiu*) as the orthodox doctrine of the state in 136 BCE.[69] His emphasis on the venerable *yang* over the base *yin*, on the one hand, accentuated the virtue-based, humane tradition of Confucian teachings in contrast with the *Fajia* tendency of laws and punishment in the Qin, and, on the other hand, provided a symbolic separation between the present legitimate dynasty of Han and the previous failed dynasty of Qin that presented itself as residing in the power of Water, or the power of *yin* and punishment.

Keeping in mind the difference between the *Zhouyi* and the later commentaries of *Yijing* dominated by the *qiankun yinyang* cosmology, and keeping in mind the pretext under which the *yinyang wuxing* theory was first integrated into the Confucian tradition, where the venerable *yang* is emphasized over the base *yin* in Han *Ru*'s ethics and cosmology, we now return to our initial question, the question of the correlation between the complementary *yin-yang* binary and gender hierarchy where the *tian/yang/nan* is privileged over the *di/yin/nu* found in both the *Yijing* and *Chunqiu fanlu*. After the Han, the hierarchical *yinyang tiandi* and *yinyang nannu* analogies permeate intellectual discourse, especially discourse concerning the normativity of virtuous women in the role of daughter, wife, and mother. The relation between husband and wife or father and mother portrayed in these two texts is definitely hierarchical. As quoted earlier, in the *Yijing* commentary, the *qian* is *tian* and is called the father and the *kun* is *di* and is called the mother, and the *tian* is venerable and the *di* is base. In the *Chunqiu fanlu*, the *yang* is venerable and the *yin* base, and all husbands are *yang* and wives are *yin*.[70] However, it will become clear in the following that the hierarchical *yin-yang* binary in the Han cosmology is also a complementary binary. In other words, despite the hierarchical scheme in the *yinyang tiandi* and *yinyang nannu* correlation, the *yin-yang* binary is neither an oppositional binary nor a gender specific concept.

First of all, the venerable *tian/qian/nan* and the base *di/kun/nu*, despite their unequal status, are complementary pairs that complete rather than contradict one another. The ambiguity of the *qiankun nannu* hierarchy can be best illustrated through the following lengthy passage in the *Yijing* commentary, which is worthwhile quoting in full:[71]

> *Tian* (heaven) is venerable, *di* (earth) is base,
> *Qian* and *kun* take their position.
> Humble and high are thereby set out,
> Venerable and base are established ...
>
> The way of *qian* completes man (*nan*),
> The way of *kun* completes woman (*nu*).
>
> *Qian* knows the great beginning,
> *Kun* performs the completion of things.
>
> *Qian* knows with ease,
> *Kun* performs with simplicity.

What is easy is easy to know,
What is simple is easy to follow.
Ease of knowing leads to closeness
Ease of following leads to accomplishment.
Closeness enables duration,
Accomplishment enables greatness.
Duration is the worthy person's virtue,
Greatness is the worthy person's field of action.

By means of the easy and the simple,
One grasps the ways of the whole world.
When the ways of the whole world are grasped,
Therein lies perfection.

In the beginning of the passage, the correlation of *tian-di, qian-kun*, and *nan-nu* in which the *tian/qian/nan* is privileged over the *di/kun/nu* is clearly hierarchical. According to the dualistic paradigm of the West, it would seem that the former of the correlation functions as the ideal while the latter is the dependent, derivative one. As one reads on, such a definitive hierarchical scheme begins to slip away, and what is left in the end is instead a complementary scheme in which the different strengths of the *qian* and the *kun* are shown to complement rather than negate one another in one's complete knowledge of the world. There is no definitive hierarchical relationship between the knowledge of the great beginning and the ability to bring things to completion, or between duration and greatness, or between virtue and action. In addition, the correlation between the *qian-kun* binary and different modes of knowing is non-gender based. As Alison Black summed it up: "[I]t is not absolutely clear that knowing is here suggested as a specifically masculine activity in contrast with a specifically feminine activity of doing or completing. It could quite conceivably have been introduced in a gender-free context."[72] The correlation between gender hierarchy and the Chinese cosmological thinking of the *qian-kun* binary in the *Yijing* is at best ambiguous. We can even go a step farther to say that the hierarchical *qiankun tiandi* and *qiankun nannu* analogies are complementary and possibly non-gender based.

The complementarity of the *yin-yang* binary is prominent in the *Chunqiu fanlu* as well despite its explicit use of the venerable *yang* and the base *yin*. Even though the *yang* is correlated with virtue and nurturing spring, and the *yin* with punishment and severe winter, the *yang* is by no means conceived of as absolute good in and of itself. The *yin* and *yang* are mutually dependent and mutually constituting. The efficacy of the whole depends on the complementary working of the two, since "the *yang* of spring and summer and the *yin* of autumn and winter are not just found in *tian*, but also within people. If a person is without the *qi* of spring, how can he extend the love and be tolerant to the masses? If a person is without the *qi* of autumn, how can he establish his dignity and accomplish anything? If a person is without the *qi* of summer, how can he bring prosperity and happiness to life? If a person is without the *qi* of winter, how can he mourn the dead and pity those passed away?"[73] Just as the four seasons with their distinct qualities complement one another in the yearly cycle, the *yin* and the *yang* each has its own irreducible worth and significance that brings completion in one's own person. The emphasis is neither on the innate superiority of the *yang* attributes as opposed to the innate inferiority of the *yin* attributes, nor on the autonomy and agency of the *yang* in contrast to the dependency and passivity of the unconscious *yin*. The focus is on the harmonious working of both the *yin* and the *yang*. As Dong Zhongshu put it precisely, "The *yin* by itself cannot produce, the *yang* by itself cannot produce, it is when the *yin* and the *yang* together participate in the *tian* and the *di* then there is life."[74]

Even though the *yin-yang* binary is correlated with gender in the Han cosmology, it is nevertheless not a gender-specific concept; by that, I mean, the *yin-yang* metaphor is not limited to, nor does it genealogically stem from the assumed gender hierarchy in the human world. Unlike the Western gender-based dualistic paradigm of femininity and masculinity, the hierarchical *yin-yang* metaphor in the Han cosmology is often cross-gender and beyond gender. For instance, the way of *yin-yang* in the *Chunqiu fanlu* is applicable to not only the husband-wife relation, but also the father-son, and the ruler-minister relation as well. "The propriety of the ruler-minister, father-son and husband-wife relations are all taken from the way of *yin-yang*."[75] Although it is true that the feminine and masculine attributes can be applied to nongendered beings as well, such as the form-matter, or mind-body binary, gender underwrites the basic polarity in the West; that is to say, the inferior is conceived of as an effect of femininization and the superior as the effect of masculinization. By contrast, in the Han cosmology, the analogy among wife, son, and minister is not an effect of femininization in the role of the socially subordinate. Instead, the hierarchical yet at the same time complementary relation between the superior and the subordinate, or the *yang* and the *yin*, functions as the basic binary upon which all social relations are based. Hence, the hierarchical scheme of the way of the venerable *yang* and the base *yin*, although it is applicable to gender, is not based on gender per se.

Since gender does not underwrite the *yin-yang* binary, the *yang* is not exclusively male, neither is the *yin* female. The hierarchical relation of the venerable *yang* and base *yin* can be applied to all hierarchical social relations without femininizing and masculinizing the inferior and the superior respectively. Regardless of one's gender, one can be *yang* and *yin* at the same time depending on one's social roles and places in relation with others. "The ruler is *yang* and the minister is *yin*; the father is *yang* and the son is *yin*; the husband is *yang* and the wife is *yin*."[76] The father who is *yang* in relation to the son is also *yin* in relation to the ruler as a subject. The son who is *yin* in the father-son relation is also *yang* in the husband-wife relation. When the wife bears a son, she then becomes socially superior to the son and to the future daughter-in-law in the hierarchical kinship system. Instead of seeing the *yin* and the *yang* as innate gender traits, the *yin-yang* binary is merely a placeholder for registering hierarchical, yet at the same time, complementary binaries such as parent-child, ruler-minister, husband-wife, virtue-punishment, and spring-autumn, etc.

The complementarity, and nongender-specific orientation of the *yin-yang* binary can also be illustrated in medical texts where the *yin-yang* binary forms the basic structure of classical Chinese medical theory. Charlotte Furth in her detailed study on the *yin-yang* metaphor in Chinese medical texts wrote: "In Chinese cosmology *yin* and *yang* were not attributes of sexed bodies, but themselves the foundation of gendered meanings diffused in bodies and in the world at large." This is the case because the *yin* and the *yang* are not innate gender attributes based on the inborn sexual differences between the male and the female body. The *yin* and the *yang* as the basic binary are the sources from which gender, among other things, derives its meanings. The *yin* and *yang* with their distinct qualities provide Chinese medical theory a uniquely androgynous model for the ideal medical body. As Furth went on to say, "[T]he normative medical body of the Yellow Emperor [i.e., *Inner Classic of the Yellow Emperor* or *Huangdi neijing*], incorporating both yin and yang relationships, was androgynous."[77] Chinese medical theory rejects what Furth called the "one-sex" masculine model of classical European medicine.[78] Instead, the balance of the *yin* and the *yang* constitutes the image of a healthy human body. Lisa Raphals, in her study on the *yin-yang* binary in Chinese medical texts, also pointed to the same conclusion that the harmony between the *yin* and the *yang* is the key to bodily health.[79] Excessive *yin* or *yang* in the human body would only lead to calamity. In the classical medical text, *Huangdi neijing*, one reads: "As for *yin* and *yang* and the four seasons, they are the origin and end of the ten thousand things; they are the root of life and death," and, "If *yin* predominates, *yang* becomes ill; if *yang* predominates, *yin* becomes sick. When *yang* prevails there is heat, when *yin* prevails there is cold."[80] A healthy body is a body with balanced *yin* and *yang* within, not the domination of one over the other.

To sum up, the evolution of the *yin-yang* metaphor as discussed so far is as follows: first, in early literatures compiled in or before the fourth century BCE, the *yin-yang* binary was two of the six *qi* of *tian* modeled upon the regular succession and alternation of the four seasons. The *yin-yang* binary, at this stage, was a cyclic pair that was nonhierarchical and nongender-based. Secondly, when the *yin-yang* binary became the ultimate pair of *qi* around the third-second century BCE, the correlation between *yin-yang* and gender was merely contingent. Thirdly, even when *yinyang tiandi* and *yinyang nannu* analogies became a common aspect of the *yin-yang* metaphor found in the appendices of *Yijing* and Dong Zhongshu's *Chunqiu fanlu*, the *yin-yang* binary, though explicitly hierarchical, was complementary as well; that is to say, the *yin* and the *yang* despite their unequal worth and distinct functions were not contradictory. And despite the applicability of the hierarchical *yin-yang* metaphor in the *yinyang wuxing* cosmology to social relations including gender, the *yin-yang* binary was not a gender-specific concept.

In contrast to the Western feminist assumption of gender as the basic metaphysical polarity underlying all aspects of human knowledge of the world, the *yin-yang* binary as the ultimate binary in Chinese cosmology is not based on gender. As Alison Black concluded in her study of the *yin-yang* binary, "It is probably safe to say that the basic polarity [of Chinese cosmology] is not one of gender. Not only do yin and yang not *mean* 'feminine' and 'masculine' etymologically or invariably or primarily. Gender in fact depends on too many other concepts in order to develop into something significant itself" (emphasis original).[81] In other words, in Chinese cosmology, *yin-yang* and femininity-masculinity are not synonymous concepts. Furthermore, the *yin-yang* binary is by and large a complementary binary whether correlated with hierarchical social relations or not. The privileged status of things associated with the male such as reason, mind, and transcendence as opposed to things associated with the female such as passion, body, and immanence is, according to the feminist interpretation, the foundation of a theoretical account for gender oppression in the West. But by contrast, the *yin-yang* binary cannot function even as a foundation of a *theoretical* account for the unequal distribution of social resources and power between man and woman. The correlation between the *yin-yang* and hierarchical gender relations by itself cannot explain why and does not represent the way in which Chinese women were devalued. For even at the theoretical level, the *yang* does not function as the ideal in and by itself apart from the putatively subordinate *yin*. This is in contrast to the way in which the Cartesian rational mind can conceptually function apart from the mechanical body. Nor does the *yang* act as a transcendental agent acting outside the immanent world of *yin*; it does not act as a Kantian autonomous, moral agent who wills beyond the mechanical laws of nature.

On the contrary, the complementarity and the dynamic interaction between the *yin* and the *yang* both in the cosmos and in the human body suggests a rather fluid view of the sexual difference between the male and the female body and consequently, if applied to gender, might even suggest a more tolerant view of gender roles. This possibility was noted by Charlotte Furth: "[I]n Chinese biological thinking, based as it was on yin-yang cosmological views, there was nothing fixed and immutable about male and female as aspects of yin and yang. These two aspects of primary ch'i are complementary and interacting.... In medicine yin and yang permeate the body and pattern its functions, and here as elsewhere they are interdependent, mutually reinforcing and capable of turning into their opposites. This natural philosophy would seem to lend itself to a broad and tolerant view of variation in sexual behavior and gender roles."[82] However, in reality, as Furth also noted, the fluidity of the *yin-yang* binary in Chinese cosmology and medical theory contrasts sharply with the rigidity of gender roles, in the Chinese gender system.[83] In sum, the complementary *yin-yang* metaphor is not a theoretical determinative of the hierarchal gender roles in social reality.

Yet, in early Western feminist writings on gender relations in China, the receptive qualities of *yin* are taken as the theoretical basis for the inferiority and the subordination of Chinese women. For instance, Marjorie Topley wrote: "The inferiority of women was supported by an ideological superstructure that equated them with the *yin* cosmic element: dark, empty, negative, and, in Confucian interpretations, inauspicious."[84] In the above passage, the *yin* is resolutely female or feminine, which is an inferior, contradictory concept to the supposedly positive, auspicious element of *yang*. This interpretation of *yin*, however, can only be supported by the background assumption of the natural inferiority of *yin* and the causal connection between the inferior *yin* with the female gender. This background assumption in turn is rooted in the dualistic gender paradigm of the West where the unequal distribution of power between genders is conceptually based on the natural superiority of the masculine attributes and the defective feminine attributes that are defined as relative to the masculine ideal without reciprocity.

However, the *yin* and the *yang* are irreducibly complementary. The imposition of the dualistic paradigm onto the *yin-yang* metaphor is inappropriate and misleading since it not only reduces the Chinese gender construction to two sets of innate gender traits that are contradictory and ontological, but more importantly overlooks the relational aspect of gender that emerges out of kinship roles in the Chinese world. Gender cannot be reduced to the innate attributes of sexed bodies in terms of a feminine *yin* and a masculine *yang*, especially in a world where the *yin-yang* binary is not contradictory, and gender itself is not even conceived as an ontological category beyond concrete familial relationality. It is with this understanding that we now turn to the concrete marking of gender in terms of social roles embodied in the concept of the *nei-wai* binary.

CHAPTER FOUR

NEI-WAI, GENDER DISTINCTIONS, AND
RITUAL PROPRIETY

In comparison with the metaphor of *yin-yang*, the spatial bipolar of *nei-wai* has been relatively neglected.[1] The term *nei-wai*, when correlated with gender, is often equated with these two mutually opposing and conflicting spheres—family and state—which in turn signify a distinct separation between private and public, or woman and man. However, as shown in the previous chapter, the imposition of the Western dualistic paradigm onto the Chinese complementary, correlative thinking is inappropriate. This being the case, the seemingly unproblematic congruity between *nei-wai* and private-public or family-state calls for a reexamination. The conventional emphasis on the nature of the separation of man and woman in a literal and physical sense in understanding Chinese gender construction overlooks the symbolic functions of the dynamic and correlative metaphor of *nei-wai* in the process of genderization. Consequently, the early analysis of the problem of gender relations in the Chinese world and its connection with Confucianism is also one-sided. With the emphasis of the static nature of the *nei-wai* in gender constructions, China along with its stable family structure, in the Western eye, appears to be frozen in time. Early sinologist Olga Lang, though sympathetic to Chinese culture, wrote in her one of the pioneering studies on Chinese family and society: "[I]mperial China was a static civilization," and Confucianism was a "great force intensifying the stagnant character of Chinese civilization,"[2] Foucault's summation of the Western imagery of China accentuates the rigidity of Chinese culture: "In our traditional imagery, the Chinese culture is the most meticulous, the most rigidly ordered, the one most deaf to temporal events, most attached to the pure delineation of space; we think of it as a civilization of dykes and dams beneath the eternal face of the sky; we see it spread and frozen, over the entire surface of a continent surrounded by walls."[3]

The shared Western image of China as a stagnant civilization frozen in time and surrounded by rigid walls and gates is, in part, supported by the perception of Chinese family and social structure in which both man and woman have their separate places defined by the line separating the *nei* from the *wai* with no transgression permitted. However, it will become clear later that the *nei-wai* binary as a marker of gender distinction and propriety is a dynamic interplay between what is central and what is peripheral, or fundamental and derivative. The boundary between the *nei* and the *wai* is constantly moving and being renegotiated, depending on the unique makeup of its social and political context. Its multilayers of meaning cannot be encapsulated by the static representation of the separation between the family and the state or the private and the public in a dualistic fashion, wherein women's oppression is conveniently summed up by the seclusion of the domestic life separated from the public life of men. In numerous studies on gender relations in Imperial China, the usual rendering of the *nei-wai* as a static separation of man and woman in the personal, social, and political sphere has been shown to be inadequate, since women did and were socially sanctioned to traverse the assumed rigid boundary of the *nei* and the *wai*.[4]

The *nei-wai* distinction signifies more than just the ritual propriety of gender relations; it functions also as a marker of civility. In other words, the *nei* and the *wai* embody not only the process of genderization and ritualization but also the process of civilization within and without. The spatial binary of *nei-wai* along with the idea of the differentiation between man and woman (*nannuzhibie* 男女之別), as Lisa Raphals suggested, is better understood as functional "'distinctions between men and women', rather than the strict and inflexible physical, social, and intellectual separation that has so often been assumed."[5]

In the following, we will begin by examining the historical roots of the spatial binary of *nei-wai* along with the concept of the differentiation between man and woman (*nannuzhibie*) and the concept of *li* 禮 in the *Five Classics*, the Confucian *Four Books* as well as pre-Han texts such as the *Guanzi*, *Mozi*, and *Xunzi*, and Han texts such as the *Yantie lun* (Discourse on Salt and Iron), *Huainanzi*, and *Hanshu* (Book of Han). Such a historical, textual study will enable us to locate the philosophical roots of the term *nei-wai* whose symbolic functions in the process of genderization through boundary marking are extended beyond gender and is intrinsically intertwined with the very defining feature of a civilized society. Once the dynamic, multifaceted layers of meaning of the term are clear, we will then focus on the symbolic functions of *nei-wai* in the process of genderization through assuming a definitive gender role in the household economy and its correlation with gender hierarchy through the concept of the "Threefold Following or Dependence" (*sancong* 三從). The complexity of gender cannot be fully understood without grasping the shifting nature of the *nei* and the *wai* and their symbolic functions in defining civility and gender propriety. The seemingly unproblematic gender hierarchy supported by the separation between genders marked along the line of the *nei* and the *wai* is further complicated by the authority of the mother in the Chinese kinship structure and by a socially sanctioned occasional boundary crossing and redrawing in historical reality. Instead of assuming an immediate congruity between *nei-wai* and gender hierarchy, private-public, or family-state, we begin with a textual study of the term to uncover its historical roots and to reveal the hidden yet assumed equivocation between *nei-wai*, ritualization, and civilization.

NEI-WAI, RITUALIZATION, AND CIVILIZATION

It is curious to note that the term *nei-wai*, which is prominent in the later ritual and instruction books defining proper gender relations and spheres, is not noticeable at all in early canonical texts. In the *Five Classics*, except in the *Liji* (Book of Rites), which was compiled in the early Han, and the commentary of the *Yijing* (Book of Changes), which was probably written in the late Warring States period or in the early Han, the term *nei-wai* is rather marginal and is not correlated with gender.[6] Also, the term *nei-wai* is absent both in the *Shijing* (Book of Songs) and the *Chunqiu* (Spring and Autumn), and is rarely used in the *Shujing* (Book of Documents).[7] As for the *Four Books*, the term *nei-wai* is not in the *Analects*. In both the *Daxue* (Great Learning) and *Zhongyong* (Focusing the Familiar), *nei-wai* is not correlated with gender, instead it is correlated with virtue and wealth, and with various virtues such as *ren* and *zhi* (wisdom). In the *Daxue*, the *junzi* are said to focus on cultivating their virtue first, since "virtue is the root and the wealth is the end result; if *junzi* make the *wai* the root and the *nei* the end result, then they will only be in discord with the masses and teach them robbery."[8] The *nei*, in this passage, signifies the centrality of virtue ethics in the Confucian project of self-cultivation, while the *wai* signifies the external wealth that is merely the end result of a well-governed society. The *nei* and the *wai*, just as the *yin* and the *yang*, are not two opposing, conflicting categories. Instead, they complement and complete each other. As reflected in the following passage in the *Zhongyong*, "Creativity (*cheng* 誠) is not simply the self-consummation of one's own person; it is what consummates events (*wu* 物). Consummating oneself is *ren* 仁; consummating events is *zhi* 智. This is the excellence (*de* 德) of one's natural tendencies and is the way of integrating the *wai* and the *nei*. Hence, whenever one applies this excellence, it is proper."[9]

In the *Mencius*, the complementarity and codependency of the *nei* and the *wai* is also accentuated. In his famous debates with Gaozi on human propensity, Mencius repeatedly repudiated Gaozi's rigid separation between the virtue of *ren* and *yi* (義) and between *xing* (性) and *ming* (命) into two incommensurable categories. To Mencius, the distinction between the *nei* and the *wai* was rather a qualitative one; they differ in degree, not in kind. As he wrote in regard to the misconceived dichotomy between *xing* 性 and *ming* 命 (i.e., between what is given and what is acquired), "The way the mouth is disposed towards tastes, the eye towards colors, the ear towards sounds, the nose towards smells, and the four limbs towards ease is called *xing*, yet therein also lies the *ming*. That is why *junzi* do not describe it as *xing*. The way *ren* pertains to the relation between father and son, *yi* to the relation between ruler and subject, *li* to the relation between guest and host, *zhi* to the wise, and sage to the way of *tian* is called *ming*, but therein also lies the *xing*. That is why *junzi* do not describe it as *ming*."[10] Hence, *xing* and *ming*, just as *nei* and *wai*, are relational categories that overlap one another.

If we keep the co-affectivity and the codependency of the *nei* and the *wai* in mind, then the correlation made between *nei-wai* and gender in the *Mencius* can be more adequately understood. In regard to the golden age of the past sage-king recorded in the *Shijing*, Mencius remarked: "At that time, in the *nei* there were no dissatisfied women, and in the *wai* there were no unmarried men."[11] In early translations, the *nei* and the *wai* immediately are rendered as inside and outside the household. Although this translation is within the limit of the text, it overlooks the codependency of the *nei* and the *wai* where the satisfaction of women in the *nei* is intertwined with the condition of men in the *wai*. There is, in a word, reciprocity between the *nei* and the *wai*. "What is in the *nei* will manifest itself in the *wai*."[12] The correlation between gender and *nei-wai* only appears once in the above passage in the *Mencius* among the Confucian *Four Books*, and its correlation is made rather loosely. Hence, one might infer from this that the term *nei-wai* found in the Confucian *Four Books* is not intended to denote gender relations, but by and large signifies various correlative virtues or forms of conduct in the process of self-cultivation.

The earliest appearance of the *nei* and the *wai* as a binary term is found in the *Shujing* where *nei-wai* is primarily a spatial concept signifying the boundary between the inner, civic sphere of the imperial court and the military sphere of the outside world. In the *"Hongfan"* chapter of *Shujing*, the term *nei-wai* appears in the context of a divination for the state affairs: "If you [i.e., the King] and the tortoise agree, while the milfoil, the nobles and officers, and the common people oppose, the *nei* operations will be fortunate, and the *wai* operations will be unfortunate." The *nei* and the *wai* in this passage signify the internal, civic affairs of the imperial court and the external, military affairs of the outside world respectively, since the ordering of the imperial court depends on the King himself while the success or failure of the military affairs depends on the proper employment of the nobles and the commoners.[13] This usage of the *nei* and the *wai* is also found in the *"Jiuhao"* chapter of *Shujing* where the *nei* refers to the interior domains dealing with the imperial court and its subject and the *wai* refers to the exterior domains dealing with the interstate affairs.[14] The term *nei-wai* in its early usage is nongender specific, primarily signifying the spatial boundary between the orderly imperial court and the chaotic outside world. And that boundary is eventually a boundary between what is civil and what is barbaric. And it is from the early usage of *nei-wai* as a symbolic boundary between civility and barbarism that the later use of the *nei-wai* derives its authority in defining proper gender distinction.

The link between *nei-wai* and ritualization (i.e., the concept of *li* ritual 禮 and *bie* differentiation 別), although it is implicit, is important in understanding the symbolic functions of genderization in terms of the *nei* and the *wai* in the Han's project of civilizing the barbarians. The problem of barbarian invasions began in the Spring and Autumn period (c.722–481 BCE) and culminated in the early Han period (c.206 BCE). Sinologist Yu Ying-shi in his classic study on sino-barbarian economic relations in the Han pointed out that this problem had made the boundary marking between the civil and the barbaric especially pressing in the imperial Han court's self-representation.[15] The boundary markings between Han and barbarians were drawn on several levels. The first dynasty Qin's famous wall building on the northern border in the third century BCE, which was expanded in the Ming around the late sixteenth and early seventeenth century, is a case in point.[16] Besides setting up a physical boundary to prevent barbaric forces from disrupting the imperial order of Han, the boundary of Han's civility was also drawn through the proper differentiation between genders. The barbarians in the Han's representation were characterized, among other things, as making no distinctions between man and woman. In the Han text *Yantielun* (Discourse on Salt and Iron), Xiongnu (匈奴)—the strongest barbaric tribe in the northwest—was said to "live in the desert and grow in the land which produces no food. They are the people who are abandoned by *tian* for being good-for-nothing. They have no houses to shelter themselves, and make no distinctions between man and woman."[17] In the *Hou Hanshu* (the dynastic history of the Latter Han), the southern barbarians, Nanman (南蠻), were characterized in the same fashion; they were said to have both man and woman bathed in the same river and are like birds and beasts (*qinshou* 禽獸) making no distinctions between old and young.[18] Apparently the boundary between barbarians and Han symbolically was drawn on the proper ritual distinction between genders as well as on the differentiation between unequal yet reciprocal social and kinship roles.

Nei-wai as a spatial boundary separating the uncivilized barbarian from the imperial Han not only is a political, physical boundary that is substantiated by walls and gates in the frontiers, but more importantly is a cultural, symbolic boundary that is intrinsically intertwined with the very fabric of the Han order, in which civility is expressed through the differentiation between kinship and social roles. And since gender in the Chinese perception is not anchored in the physical features of the human body or innate gender traits, the process of genderization in the familial kinship system is intertwined with the process of ritualization within which all unequal social roles are differentiated. In other words, gender as a performance of different social roles begins with drawing ritual boundaries of what is proper to each gender. And the very act of drawing ritual boundaries is also the beginning of making distinctions among unequal yet reciprocal social roles through the concept of *bie* (differentiation 別) and the concept of *li* (ritual 禮).

As Chu Tung-tsu cautioned, *Li* doesn't just signify ritual ceremony.[19] The rejection of a simple equation between *li* and observing ritual ceremonies can be traced as far back as to the historical narrative of the late Zhou culture in the *Zuozhuan*. Despite his detailed observance of ritual ceremonies during his visit in the state of Jin, Duke Zhao of Lu (c.536 BCE) was criticized for not knowing *li*: "[What Duke Zhao of Lu did] was deportment (儀), and should not be called *li*."[20] One also finds a similar passage in the twenty-fifth year of Duke Zhao. When Zi Dashu was asked about the rituals of bowing, yielding precedence, and moving from one position to another, he responded, "These are matters of deportment, not *li*."[21] Instead, *li*, according to Ru Shuqi in the *Zuozhuan*, is the basis upon which the order of the state and the people are maintained. "*Li* is that by which [a ruler] maintains his state, carries out his governmental orders and does not lose his people."[22] This understanding of *li* is echoed in another passage of the *Zuozhuan*: "It is *li* that governs the state and clan, gives settlement to the tutelary altars, secures the order of the people and provides for one's future heirs."[23]

Li—not impersonal laws or external regulations imposed from without—is fundamental in governance. As Confucius said in the *Analects*, "Lead the people with administrative injunctions and keep them orderly with penal law and they will avoid punishments but will be without a sense of shame. Lead them with excellence and keep them orderly through *li* and they will develop a sense of shame, and moreover, will order themselves"(2.3). In the *Liji*, Confucius also said, "*Li* is the first thing to be attended to in the practice of government."[24] For, as Xunzi explained, "People without *li* will not be prosper, matters without *li* will not come to completion and states without *li* will not be peaceful."[25] *Li* signifies more than a set of formal rules or ceremonial forms; rather, it is that upon which the order of the state is established and maintained. Therefore, Duke Zhao of Lu in the *Zuozhuan*, whose state was in disharmony due to his inability to lead the ruling house and to correctly employ the people, was said not to know *li* despite his correct observance of ritual ceremonies during his interstate visit. To know *li* hence is more than to know correct ritual forms. At the minimal level, to know *li* is to know how to make and maintain a proper social and political order according to one's station. *Li* is the measurement of the propriety of all social, reciprocal transactions in accordance with one's station. As Xunzi put it, "*Li* is the standards of all measurement of ministers by their ruler; it includes all grades of people."[26]

The basic function of *li* is to make distinctions and to differentiate as opposed to the function of *yu* (music), which is to harmonize. As said in the *Liji*, "The aim of music is to harmonize (*tong* 同), the aim of *li* is to differentiate (*yi* 異); with harmony there comes mutual affection (*qing* 親), with differentiation there comes mutual respect (*jing* 敬)."[27] And, "Music is the harmony (*he* 和) between heaven and earth, *li* is the gradation (*xu* 序) between heaven and earth. From that harmony, all things are then transformed and from that gradation all things are differentiated (*bie* 別)."[28] According to Xunzi, the ability to make distinctions or to differentiate is what distinguishes humans from beasts. And, "No distinction is greater than social distinctions; no social distinction is greater than *li*; and no *li* is greater than [the *li*] of the sage-king."[29] In brief, to make distinctions is to make social divisions where the high is distinguished from the low, the noble from the base, and the senior from the junior.

To have *li* is to make and to maintain social divisions and distinctions among unequal social status and roles. In the *Huainanzi*, one reads, "*Li* is for the purpose of distinguishing the superior from the inferior, and of discriminating between the noble and the humble."[30] Similarly, "*Li* is the interactions between the ruler and minister, between the father and son, through which the noble and the humble, the virtuous and the unworthy are distinguished from each other."[31] The same understanding of *li* as a means to differentiate between unequal social status and roles is also found in the *Hanshu*. "To advance, and to retire within boundaries, to have distinction between the superior and the inferior, this is called *li*."[32] The purpose of making such an unequal, yet reciprocal social division, according to Xunzi, is to regulate human desires and to meet human needs.

> Humans by birth have desires; when desires are not satisfied, they then cannot be without a seeking for satisfaction. When this seeking for satisfaction is without limits, they then cannot be without contention. When there is contention, there will be disorder, and when there is disorder, there will be poverty. The former kings detested disorder, hence they established *li* (禮) and *yi* (義) in order to make proper social divisions, to provide for human desires and to give them a chance to seek satisfactions, so that desire must not be extinguished by material things, nor should material things be exhausted by desire. These two should support each other and continue to grow. This is the origin of *li*.[33]

Li, as a means to differentiate, to draw boundaries, is then understood as originating in the need for social division of labor in order to achieve social harmony and good governing.

Li holds the key to social and political cohesion because *li* is a body of normative expressions and institutions that defines as well as reflects one's unequal yet reciprocal social status and kinship role in relation to others. And among all the social distinctions, the distinction between man and woman is the most primary one that sets humans apart from beasts. Again, Xunzi's explanation is revealing: "The reason why humans are human is ... because they have the ability to make distinctions. Whereas beasts have father and son, they don't have the affection between father and son; and whereas beasts have male and female (*pin-mu* 牝牡), they don't have the differentiation between man and woman (*nannuzhibie* 男女之別). Hence the way of humanity cannot be without distinctions."[34] The ritualized, normative distinction between gender roles as opposed to the physical difference between the male and female bodies is what elevates humanity from brute bestiality. In addition, the proper distinction between genders in the early Han's self-understanding also defines Han's civility as opposed to the neighboring barbaric tribes. *Nei-wai* as a boundary marking between Han and barbarians, or between civility and bestiality, is indeed intertwined with the idea of the differentiation between man and woman (*nannuzhibie*).

The concept of "*nannuzhibie*" is often rendered as a rigid separation between man and woman, but it is better understood as a functional distinction. The Western perception of China as a stagnant civilization inevitably leads to the one-sided understanding of a static separation between man and woman in the Chinese gender system. But one only needs to reflect on numerous socially sanctioned boundary crossings in historical reality as in the case of Ban Zhao—the first and foremost female scholar and court historian—to understand the shortcoming of such a one-sided approach to the Chinese gender system. Although it is true that walls and gates that mark permissible sites for ritual exchanges are visible expressions of boundary drawing, which is fundamental to the Chinese perception of ritual propriety, John Hay in his study of *Boundaries in China* cautioned us not to make an equation between the concrete boundary drawing in the form of walls and gates and the static nature of the human body. The need to draw a physical boundary between a "proper" and an "improper place" on the contrary reflects the fluidity of body in the Chinese perception in terms of *qi* (氣) and *shi* (勢)—that is, the configuration of energy where the physical boundary of the body is easily permeated.[35] It is precisely because the body is not perceived as being static in the Chinese world, that to draw physical boundaries as a visible sign becomes a necessity. Along this line of understanding, the physical separation between man and woman substantiated by walls and gates, although it forms an integral part of the concept of gender propriety, does not denote a static nature of the gendered bodies of man and woman.

More significantly, the proper distinction between man and woman made in several pre-Han and Han texts, as Lisa Raphals has shown, is viewed as a defining feature of human civilization.[36] The presence of a proper distinction between genders signifies a well-ordered state and its absence a state in chaos. Several passages in the *Mozi* have linked the distinction between man and woman to the distinction between the virtuous and the vicious or the civilized and the barbaric mode of life. Mozi argued in chapter 9, "Exaltation of the Virtuous," that if the rulers don't exalt the virtuous and employ the capable in government, they will be surrounded by vicious men who are unfilial toward their parents at home, don't respect the elders in the village, and make no distinctions between man and woman (*nannuwubie* 男女無別).[37] By contrast, in chapter 35, "Against Fatalism," when the sage-kings exalt the virtuous, the common people then are said to be filial toward their parents at home, respectful to the elders in the village, and maintain distinctions between man and woman (*nannuyoubian* 男女有辨).[38] Maintaining a proper distinction between man and woman signifies the sage-king's virtuous, orderly governance. Hence, gender distinction is also a sign of the harmonious order of the state.

The *Guanzi*—a forth-third century BCE text—also addresses the important link between the distinction between man and woman and civility and the order of the state. According to Guanzi, making and maintaining distinctions among unequal social standings and between genders is the beginning of civilized human society. For, "[i]n ancient times there were no distinctions between ruler and minister or superior and inferior, nor did there exist the union of husband and wife or man and his mate. People lived like beasts and dwelt together in herds, using their strength to attack one another. Consequently, the clever cheated the stupid, and the strong maltreated the weak.... On behalf of the people, the wise promoted policies that were beneficial and eliminated those that were harmful. They rectified standards of virtue for the people so the people took them as their teachers. It was because of this that methods of the *dao* and virtuous conduct emanated from worthies, and as adherence to appropriateness (*yi* 義) and reasonableness (*li* 理) took shape in the minds of the people, they turned to the moral way."[39] By making distinctions and drawing boundaries among unequal yet reciprocal social standings the order of the state is achieved.

Like Mozi, Guanzi also equated the absence of the proper distinction between man and woman with chaos and primitive modes of life and viewed the loss of distinctions as the fall of humanity into bestiality. According to Guanzi, if ministers take indulging in pleasures and desires to be caring for their lives, then "they will follow their desires and behave with reckless abandon. There will be no distinction between man and woman (*nannuwubie* 男女無別) and instead they will revert to being animals (*qingshou* 禽獸). Consequently the rules of propriety, righteous conduct, integrity and a sense of shame will not be established and the prince of people will have nothing with which to protect himself."[40] And as did Mozi, Guanzi took the distinction between genders as a sign of a strong, well-ordered state under a virtuous ruler. "If there is no cultivation [of appropriate conduct] within the state, [the prince] will not be able to face distant princes. For this reason, he rectifies appropriate conduct (*yi* 義) between ruler and minister, the superior and the inferior, fosters appropriate conduct between father and son, elder and younger brother, and husband and wife. He also fosters the distinction between man and woman (*nannuzhibie*)."[41] The distinction between man and woman or the distinction between the *wai* and *nei* is a sign of civil order. As Guanzi further elaborated, "When the brilliance of the prince is fully trusted, the five officers are stern, the gentry above corruption, the peasants simple, and the merchants and artisans honest, the ruler and his subject will be as one, and there will be distinctions between the *wai* and the *nei*."[42] In short, the proper distinction between genders is an integral part of good governing, and hence is a defining feature of civilized human society as opposed to the primitive mode of life that makes no distinctions among the unequals.

The boundary between what is civil and what is barbaric in conjunction with the concept of *nei-wai* is not static. The spatial image of the *nei* and the *wai* separating the Han from its neighboring barbarians is not anchored solely in the physical walls and gates in the frontier per se, but more importantly it is anchored in one's relative degree of cultural understanding of the Han imperial order. The shifting nature of the *nei-wai* boundary is well illustrated in the "Five-zone" (*wufu* 五服) theory found in the *Shujing*.[43] Sinologist Yu Ying-shih in his study on "Han Foreign Relations" offered a concise understanding of the relative nature of the *nei-wai* boundary through the five-zone theory. "China since the Hsia dynasty had been divided into five concentric and hierarchical zones or areas. The central zone (*tien-fu* 甸服) was the royal domain, under the direct rule of the king. The royal domain was immediately surrounded by the Chinese states established by the king, known collectively as the lords' zone (*hou-fu* 候服). Beyond the *hou-fu* were Chinese states conquered by the reigning dynasty, which constituted the so-called pacified zone (*sui-fu* 綏服, or *pin-fu* 儐服, guest zone). The last two zones were reserved for the barbarians. The Man and I barbarians lived outside the *sui-fu* or *pin-fu* in the controlled zone (*yao-fu* 要服), which was so called because the Man and I were supposedly subject to Chinese control, albeit control of a rather loose kind. Finally beyond the controlled zone lay the Jung and Ti barbarians, who were basically their own masters in the wild zone (*huang-fu* 荒服) where the sino-centric world order reached its natural end."[44]

In the Han perception, the world was arranged in a series of descending concentric circles where the Han royal domain was the center or the focus with an ever-extending outward field as its surrounding periphery. Under the five-zone theory, the Han world order is inescapably hierarchical, but it is also fundamentally correlative and indeterminate since what counts as the inner or outer circle depends on its relative degree of proximity to the royal center. The *nei-wai* binary is a relational category of proximity and remoteness that changes with context. The relativity of center and periphery can be further substantiated in the following passage found in the *Chunqiu fanlu*. In regard to the correct proceeding of the ruler, "One should proceed from what is near to what is remote.... Therefore one should proceed from what is within the state and then to the lords' region outside, and then proceed from what is within the lords' region to the barbarians outside."[45] Measuring against the royal center, the lords' region is the *wai* relative to the state, but it becomes *nei* relative to the barbarians in the *wai*. In the same way, the five-zone theory that marked the boundary between civil and barbaric relative to the Han center, said Yu Ying-shih, "basically and in realistic terms, described no more than a relative dichotomy between the inner and the outer areas."[46]

The relative division of *nei-wai* measured in accordance with the Han imperial center is also reflected in numerous Han historical narratives. As pointed out earlier, the distinction between the *nei* and the *wai* or Han and non-Han, at the rudimentary level, is drawn through the physical boundary of walls and gates in the frontiers. As official literatus Cai Yong stated in 177 CE, the inner region marked by the Great Wall and the frontier barriers was within the direct Han imperial rule while the outer region was to be left to the barbarians.[47] The *nei* symbolizes the centripetal imperial rule, while the *wai* is where the barbarians who are outside the civil influence of the Han dwell. The *nei-wai* boundary is not immovably fixed along with the physical walls and gates, since the *nei-wai* distinction continues to apply to the inner region of the Han as well. For instance, in the Han dynasty, the interior provinces relative to the imperial royal center were called *neijun* (內郡) while the exterior provinces along the frontiers were called *waijun* (外郡).[48] The exterior provinces were *wai* relative to the interior provinces, however they were also *nei* relative to the outer region wherein the barbarians dwelled.

The *nei-wai* relative division continued to apply to the outer barbarian region as well. Through the tributary system established in the early Han, the conquered barbarians who paid regular tribute to the Han imperial court were called *neiyi* (內夷), while the invading barbarians who paid irregular tribute were called *waiyi* (外夷). The terms *baosai manyi* 保塞蠻夷 (frontier-guarding barbarians) and *neishu* 內屬 (becoming an inner subject) were frequently used to describe conquered barbarians in dynastic histories such as the *Shiji* and *Hanshu*.[49] Since the distinction between the *nei* and *wai* is a qualitative one, the conquered barbarians were viewed as relatively civil in comparison with the invading barbarians, and the frontier Han subjects were relatively barbaric in comparison with those in the interior provinces under the direct influence of the Han imperial court. The *nei-wai* binary describes not an absolute spatial boundary marking two conflicting, mutually incompatible spheres, but rather is a relative, shifting boundary between center and periphery, or, what Roger Ames called, between "focus and field," in a series of descending concentric circles.[50]

As interpreted so far, the *nei-wai* binary first, at the rudimentary level, is a spatial boundary separating the Han from its neighboring barbarians through the physical walls and gates in the frontiers. Second, at the symbolic level, the *nei-wai* boundary between civility and barbarism also signifies the process of ritualization and genderization in which social distinctions and reciprocal obligations between the high and the low, the old and the young, and man and woman are established and maintained, and which in turn is a sign of a civilized society. The *nei-wai* boundary at the symbolic level is also a ritual and cultural boundary where the civility of human society is expressed through making and maintaining proper social and gender distinctions. Since the boundary between civility and barbarism is a cultural one instead of an ethnic one, the boundary between the Han and the non-Han is also a shifting boundary depending on one's relative degree of proximity to the Han imperial center expressed through one's acceptance of Chinese culture. The *nei-wai* binary, in short, in Dorothy Ko's words, is "a relational category that describes a series of nested hierarchies whose boundary changes with context."[51]

NEI-WAI, FUNCTIONAL DISTINCTIONS, AND GENDER HIERARCHY

The acceptance of Chinese culture in accordance with the Han imperial center entailed more than just a formal submission in political, tributary terms; more substantially, it was expressed through the concrete adaptation of Chinese ritualized way of life, which in turn was intertwined with creating and maintaining proper gender distinctions. Having a proper distinction between genders was what separated the Han from its neighboring barbarians. The project of civilization began by drawing a ritual boundary between genders and along with it the gender division of labor where both man and woman were inscribed with two sets of different yet complementary duties and activities. In the traditional account, the gender division of labor is defined in terms of the idea of *nangeng nuzhi* (男耕女織), that is, man plows and woman weaves. The imperial annual sacrificial ceremony in which the emperor's ritual plowing in the fields during the spring is paired with the empress's symbolic act of tending silkworms reflects this traditional account of the gender division of labor. As explained in the *Baihutong* (a Han commentary on ancient rituals and origins) regarding this ritual ceremony, "Why does the King [inaugurate] the plowing of the fields, and the Queen the picking of mulberry-leaves [for the silk worms] in person? It is to take the lead in the work of agriculture and sericulture in all under heaven."[52] Symbolically, the imperial ritual display of *nong* 農 and *sang* 桑 (i.e., agriculture and sericulture), in Susan Mann's words, makes "emperor and empress archetypal father and mother of the realm who serve as examples for the people."[53] The ritual activities of plowing the field and tending the silkworms performed by the emperor and the empress defines as well as reflects the normative gender division of labor where man plows and woman weaves. And since proper gender distinction as a sign of civility, in part, is expressed through the normative gender division of labor, the idea of *nankeng nuzhi* (man plows and woman weaves) then symbolizes not only the process of genderization but also the process of civilization as well.

The hidden link of the normative gender division of labor to the process of civilization, though absurd at the first sight, can be best illustrated through the project of "sinicization" or rather "civilization" during the Latter Han and early Wei period when the conquered barbarians that originally lived a nomadic way of life were encouraged to develop a more settled, labor intensive economy. In the *Hou Hanshu* (Book of the Latter Han), the barbarians in the south were encouraged by the imperial official, Zi Chong, to plant mulberry trees for sericulture and hemp for the production of sandals.[54] Also, according to the *Sanguozhi* (Memoirs of the Three Kingdoms), the Xiongnu 匈奴 (the strongest barbarian tribe in the northwest) who lived under the jurisdiction of the imperial official, Liang Xi, in the early third century CE were encouraged to develop both agriculture and sericulture.[55] Perplexed sinologist Yu Ying-shih noted in his study on the Han's treatment of barbarians that the imperial officials sent to govern the exterior provinces along the frontiers "always assumed it to be their immediate duty to teach the barbarians plowing and weaving."[56] But this is the case, precisely because the normative gender division of labor where man plows and woman weaves forms not only part of the proper distinction between genders, but also the very notion of Han's civility. The Han's labor-intensive economy of agriculture and sericulture wherein both genders assume their distinct yet complementary roles in production is intertwined with the propriety of one's gender and ethnic identity.

In practical terms, such a gender division of labor where man plows and woman weaves contributes to a more settled way of life, which encourages the continuity of familial lineage, develops the cohesion of local community, and facilitates centralized governmental supervision and taxation. In fact, before the tax reform introduced in the mid-Ming of the late sixteenth century, all households were taxed in textiles as well as grains.[57] The normative gender division of labor, exemplified by the emperor's annual plowing and empress's tending silkworms, is reenforced by the centralized taxation system in which both man's and woman's roles as producers in the household economy are equally recognized by the imperial court. In symbolic terms, *nangeng nuzhi* constitutes the moral character of one's own person through which the virtues of diligence, industry, and filial servitude are expressed. The moral import of this normative gender division of labor is made explicit in the *Guliang* commentary—a Qing text—on the *Zuozhuan*. "The emperor himself plows to supply millet for the sacrificial vessels; the empress herself tends the silkworms to supply robes for the sacrificial rites. This does not mean that the realm lacks good farmers and woman workers, but rather that it is not as desirable to serve your ancestors with what others have produced as it is to serve them with what you have produced yourself."[58] The emperor and empress's filial devotion to the ancestor is thereby expressed through performing their distinct gender work of plowing and weaving just like commoners, regardless of their royal status.

The virtue of womanhood, as will be discussed more fully in the next chapter, in part is expressed through the work of weaving, spinning, and embroidering, since *fugong* 婦功 (women's work) is one of the four womanly virtues (*side* 四德) as defined in canonical ritual texts and the four didactic books, *Nusishu*, written for and by women. The normative gender division of labor is not only a practical necessity for cooperative living to meet human needs in a well-ordered society, but also a sign of civility and gender propriety where both man and woman assume their distinct yet complementary roles in the household economy.

Gender division of labor, however, only expresses part of the grand notion of the propriety of gender distinction in which the process of genderization begins from birth through regulating the use of space, body, possession, and ritual items. For instance, in the *Liji*, different ritual items are used to signify the sex of a child at birth. "If the child is a boy, a bow is placed on the left of the door; and if is a girl, a handkerchief on the right of it."[59] The bow signifies the art of archery, which forms part of the Confucian "six arts" education for boys.[60] The passage in the *Liji* goes on to say, "After three days, the child begins to be carried, and some archery is practiced for a boy, but not for a girl."[61] Paralleling the bow, the handkerchief symbolizing the birth of a girl signifies the importance of women's work of weaving, spinning, and embroidering, which is one of the four womanly virtues—that is, *fude* 婦德

(women's excellence), *fugong* 婦功 (women's work), *fuyan* 婦言 (women's speech), and *furong* 婦容 (women's deportment).

According to the *Liji*, Boys and girls begin to self-consciously assume different roles and embody deferential postures at the age seven. "At the age of seven, boys and girls do not occupy the same mat nor eat together; at eight, when going out or coming in at a gate or door, and going to their mats to eat and drink, they are required to follow their elders—the teaching of yielding to others is now begun . . ."[62] Once the process of self-conscious genderization has begun, the demarcation of two proper gender spheres has also taken place; boys and girls reside in two different realms with two different curricula. The boy belongs to the realm of *wai*—the realm of classical learning—where he is taught the six arts, canonical texts, and the deferential behavior of a mindful subject for officialdom; and the girl belongs to the realm of *nei*—the realm of domestic skills and household management—where she is taught women's work of weaving, spinning, and embroidering, food preparation for sacrificial ceremonies, and the humble manner of a wife.[63] The disparity between genders, derived from the *nei-wai* distinction as a functional distinction defining two proper gender spheres for man and woman, in fact underpins the problem of gender in Chinese society. This point will be elaborated more fully in chapter 6. For now, it is sufficient to say that the *nei-wai* distinction as helping to constitute gender distinction entails two distinct spheres for man and woman.

It is apparent that the physical separation of man and woman is prominent in defining proper gender spheres where the *nei* and the *wai* are separated by walls and gates and where man and woman not only should have no direct physical contact in a literal sense, but also should not do, wear, or share the same thing. In the *Liji*, the physical segregation between man and woman is clearly defined:

> "The observances of propriety commence with a careful attention to the relations between husband and wife. They built the mansion and its apartments, distinguishing between the exterior and interior parts. The men occupied the exterior (外); women the interior (內). The mansion was deep, and the doors were strong, guarded by porter and eunuch. The men did not enter the *nei* and women did not come out into the *wai*."[64]

Furthermore, "Men and women should not sit together, nor have the same stand for clothes, nor use the same towel or comb, nor let their hands touch in giving and receiving."[65] The emphasis on the physical separation of men and women substantiated by walls and gates in defining gender distinction can also be extrapolated from the following passage in the *Guanzi* in regard to local administration and national security:

> "The main city wall must be well constructed, the suburban walls impenetrable, village boundaries secure from all sides, gates kept

closed, and residential walls and door-locks kept in good repair. The reason is that if the main walls are not well constructed, rebels and brigands will plot to make trouble. If suburban walls can be penetrated, evil fugitives and trespassers will abound. If village boundaries can be crossed, thieves and robbers will not be stopped. If gates are not kept closed and there are passages in and out, and there will be no distinction between men and women."[66]

In this passage, gender distinction is intertwined with the physical, spatial boundary substantiated by walls and gates, which in turn is linked to the concern for order and security. And this understanding of the *nei-wai* binary is consistent with its early use as a boundary between the inner imperial court and the outer barbarian world, which is marked by walls and gates in the frontiers.

But at the symbolic level the walls as boundaries, as John Hay in his study of boundary in China put it, are "in themselves sites for meaning, having no inherent meaning of their own beyond the bounding function."[67] That is to say, the physical walls and gates used to preserve order and security are in effect ritual boundaries as well, since they must be sustained by ritual and ethical representation of the propriety of the ruler, the mode of production, and gender differentiation. As Guanzi went on to say regarding the national security discussed above, "The preservation of territory depends on walls; the preservation of walls depends on arms. The preservation of arms depends on people, and the preservation of people depends on grain. Therefore, unless a territory is brought under cultivation, its walls will not be secure."[68] The preservation of the state eventually depends not on the physical walls and gates, but the proper cultivation of the field, which ties to the normative gender division of labor where man plows and woman weaves. So one can infer from this that the physical separation between man and woman substantiated by walls and gates is also a ritual representation through which gender propriety is expressed by locating oneself in a proper site without being bound to the actual physical walls and gates.

The symbolic meaning of gender propriety is located in the very act of differentiation, since man and woman from the ritualistic viewpoint, as Patricia Ebrey in her study of women's lives in the Song period wrote, "should do different things, or the same things differently."[69] For instance, in the traditional mourning ritual, man and woman each have their separate garments according to their kinship status, and each then must perform similar mourning obligations in distinct ways.[70] The emphasis here is as much on gender as on the necessity to differentiate duties and roles. And the ability to differentiate is what separates humans from beasts, or civility from barbarianism. "Not to differentiate," according to Xunzi, "causes the greatest injury to human beings, and to differentiate forms the basic advantages of the world" (無分者, 人之大害, 有分者, 天下之本利也).[71] Xunzi went on to explain the importance of differentiation: "Humans cannot survive without living together, yet living together without differentiation will result in contention. If there is contention, there will be disorder and if there is disorder, there then will be poverty."[72] The very act of differentiating man and woman into the two distinct gender spheres in terms of the *wai* and the *nei* is the beginning of a well-ordered, prosperous, and civilized society.

Although gender propriety found in the ritual text of *Liji* is clearly defined along the line of the *nei* and the *wai* as two distinct gender spheres coupled with the physical walls and gates in its ritual representation, the *nei-wai* binary does not correspond to the Western dualistic paradigm of private-public or family-state. This incongruity, however, is often neglected in the discussion of the *nei-wai* binary. Two common misconceptions are often evoked, as Dorothy Ko summarized: first, the absolute seclusion of the woman in the inner chambers with her crippled, bound feet where the walls and gates of her inner compartment marks the limit of her movements and activities; second, the juxtaposition of a female domestic sphere with a male political sphere and consequently the separation of the private from the public or the family from the state.[73] The *nei* and the *wai*, in the Western eye, are often treated as the conceptual equivalent of the dualistic paradigm of private and public, or family and state.

The following often-quoted lengthy passage of Sima Guang of Song in his "Miscellaneous Proprieties for Managing the Family," which laid out strict regulations on family members based on the ritual rules presented in the *Liji*, is usually used to support the claim of the mutual exclusivity of the *nei* and the *wai*.

> In housing there should be a strict demarcation between the inner and outer parts, with a door separating them. The two parts should share neither a well, a washroom, nor a privy. The men are in charge of all affairs on the outside; the women manage the inside affairs. During the day, the men do not stay in their private rooms, neither do the women go beyond the inner door without a good reason. A woman who has to leave the inner quarters must cover her face. Men who walk around at night must hold a candle. Men servants do not enter the inner quarters unless to make house repairs or in cases of calamity. If they must enter, the women should avoid them. If they cannot help being seen, they must cover their faces with their sleeves. Maids should never cross the inner gate without a good reason; if they must do so, they too should cover their faces. The doorman and old servants serve to pass messages and objects between the inner and outer quarters of the house, but must not be allowed to enter rooms or kitchens at will.[74]

The above passage seems to support the belief in the physical segregation between man and woman and the absolute seclusion of women in the inner quarters. However, numerous historical studies on women in China has repudiated the strict segregation between genders. In social and historical reality, women's activities and achievements have extended far beyond the inner quarters and domestic skills, and the female sphere of the domestic world is not treated as a secluded entity separated from the male sphere of politics. Instead, the *nei* is the locus of public virtue.[75] A more appropriate reading of Sima Guang's own family instruction would be treating it as a regulative ideal. The enclosed space designated for man or woman should be interpreted as a ritual space where the representation of gender propriety through deferential gestures and symbolic activities is always more important than the actual segregation between genders bound by the physical walls and gates. The physical boundary between genders as a ritual boundary is flexible and ambiguous. The *nei-wai* boundaries, as Dorothy Ko put it, are "negotiated boundaries where the nei and the wai are situated on a relative continuum, instead of two incommensurable realms."[76] But as a regulative ideal, the normative gender spheres in terms of the *nei* and the *wai* indeed function as a *theoretical* constraint for both genders. (The extent to which the structural limitation imposed on women derivative from the *nei* will be discussed in chapter 6.) This explains why justifications are always required for either sanctioned or unsanctioned transgression of the *nei-wai* boundary, which is inevitable in every day life.

The *nei-wai* binary however is different from the Western dualistic paradigm of private-public or family-state. For firstly, family and state are not treated as two discrete spheres. Secondly, unlike the West wherein family is excluded from the civic discourse of politics in cannonical political theories from Aristotle, Hobbes, Locke, Rousseau, to Hegel, the propriety of the inner sphere in which women are located is central to the political order in Confucian ethics. In Confucian teachings, familial virtues of filial piety and fraternal deference are in effect seen as the root of the public virtue of *ren* (cf. *Lunyu* 1.2). The virtuous conduct of *junzi* in the public springs from their familial virtues of filial piety and fraternal deference at home. As said in the *Mencius*, "People have this common saying—'The world, the state and the family.' The root of the world is in the state. The root of the state is in the family. The root of the family is in one's own person."[77] Or, what is the same, in the *Daxue*, "The ancients who wished to illustrate illustrious virtue throughout the world, first ordered well their own states. Wishing to order well their states, they first regulated their families. Wishing to regulate their families, they first cultivated their own persons."[78] The family wherein one is first situated is the starting point, the focused center of a series of descending "concentric circles" where the family, social milieu, and political order are intertwined with one another.[79]

Since the family is not separated from the political realm of the state, women who are located in the domestic realm of *nei* are neither disconnected from the male sphere of *wai*, nor are they secluded in their separate inner quarters marginal to the discourse on familial virtues as public virtues. Women's virtues and propriety in the *nei*, as repeatedly emphasized in canonical texts and didactic books for women, are centripetal to the concentric circles of family, community, and state. In the *Lienuzhuan* (Biographies of Virtuous Women)—one of the earliest didactic texts for women compiled in the Han period—the propriety of the husband-wife relation among the five core social relations is singled out as the foundation. "The way of husband and wife is the beginning of human relations (*fufuzhidao renlunzhishi*)."[80] In the *Xunzi*, one finds the same prioritization: "The way of husband and wife cannot but be proper; it is the root of the way of ruler and minister, and father and son."[81] In the *Zhongyong*, it says: "The way of the *junzi* in its simplest element is found in the husband-wife relation."[82] What women do in the *nei* has an effect in the *wai*, because the *nei* and the *wai* are intrinsically relational and reciprocal. The juxtaposition of the centripetal wifely virtues with the state is illustrated in the following passage of the *Mencius*, in which the transformation of a state is credited to two skillful wives. "The wives of Hua Zhou and Ge Liang bewailed their husbands so skillfully that they changed the custom of the state. What is in the *nei* will manifest itself in the *wai*."[83] In brief, family and state, or the *nei* and *wai* are relational, instead of contradictory, realms.

The West's insistence on separating the private from the public is reflected in the whole debate on the existence of a "civil society" or a "public sphere" in China's past or future raised by Western historians and philosophers. But the very premise of this debate, as Susan Mann critically assessed, is flawed, since the imposition of the paradigm of civil society separated from the private sphere of family reflects the deep-rooted habit of "Orientalism" in Western scholarship in which the progress and merit of Chinese civilization is often measured according to Western standards.[84] The concept of "civil society" or "public sphere" is an invention of the Western liberal tradition. And in assuming the existence of "civil society" as the norm, one is in effect projecting Western historical reality as an idealized path of development for non-Western societies and consequently foreclosing the possibility of alternative models of development. The West's idealized self-projection in this debate is well captured by William Rowe. As he wrote: "In simply asking this question [i.e., Did China ever possess a civil society?], are we in fact not presuming a 'normal' path of socio-political development, transcending the specificity of local culture? Is what we hope to find simply a projection of our own culturally specific path of development—or, worse, of what we merely idealize our own path to have been? Is our very inquiry tautologically formed around a non-controvertible proposition? That is to say, can we even conceive of a set of developments in China substantially differing from the history of early modern Europe of which we might equally approve?"[85] Indeed, asking the question: "Is there a 'civil society' in China?" is very different from asking, "What kind of society is being developed in China?" The former presumes a normative value of a "civil society" or a "public sphere" separated from the "private sphere" of family and household, while the latter takes into account of the complexity of historical locality and cultural specificity.

What is seen as "public" or *gong* 公 as opposed to "private" or *si* 私 in the Chinese intellectual traditions is very different from the Western liberal tradition in which "civil society" or "public sphere" refers to an autonomous entity as distinct from the state.⁸⁶ The emergence of a "civil society" in the West is closely linked to the emergence of capitalism, to the rise of the urban bourgeois class, and to the free association of intelligentsia. In China there are no parallel developments, since the separation between state and commerce, or state and literati, is never clearly defined and maintained. Any organizational entity, be it religion, commerce, or private academy, not sponsored by the state only enjoys relative autonomy from the state control. In reality, the balance between autonomy and state control is by and large "the result of a process of continual negotiation." As analysts of contemporary Chinese political culture have found, "Organizational autonomy ... is not an all-or-nothing issue"; rather, "it is best understood as a continuum."⁸⁷

In historical reality, because of the civil service examination system, literati in China had always been part of the state bureaucracy. Chinese literati were also state officials for the most part, and the idea of free association among official literati to form an independent voice to counterbalance the state power was virtually nonexistent. Benjamin A. Elman in his study on the factions in Song-Ming politics noted that in the traditional account, only the opinion of the imperial court represented public opinion or *gong* 公, while the opinion of literati not sponsored by the state was seen as private or *si* 私. Literati who formed free associations with people of similar rank and status outside their legitimate state duties were typically criticized as profit and power seekers and were often labeled as factions or *dang* (黨).⁸⁸ There is a long tradition in state politics against the forming of an autonomous intelligentsia party independent of the influence of the imperial court. In state politics, this often-quoted phrase from the *Lunyu* attributed to Confucius—"*Junzi* gather together with others, but do not form factions (*dang* 黨)"—was usually used to undermine the legitimacy of any parties inside or outside the imperial court.⁸⁹ The Confucian political ideal against factions is also grounded in the "*Hongfan*" chapter of *Shujing* where it stresses that political cohesion requires the absence of factions (*wudang* 無黨).⁹⁰

Furthermore, the concept of *gong* and *si* continues to apply to individual households as well; the common ancestral hall is called *gongtang* 公堂, and the outer compartments are designated as a common, public area while the inner compartments a personal, private area. The distinction between public and private or *gong* and *si* in the Chinese world, just as the relational *nei-wai*, is also a relative continuum. One may fairly say that the *nei* and the *wai* are not conceptual equivalents of the private and the public or the family and the state in the Western dualistic paradigm, nor are the concept of *gong-si* 公私 (common-personal) and *guo-jia* 國家 (state-family) two separate realms in the Chinese perception.

When the *nei-wai* distinction does apply to gender, it signifies man's and woman's roles in extrafamilial and familial relations respectively. The *nei*, as a gender sphere for women, signifies the domestic realm wherein through occupying the role of daughter, wife, and mother a woman becomes a socially recognizable "woman," a properly gendered social subject. By contrast, the *wai* symbolizes the extended field beyond the centripetal domestic realm, or, if you will, the "nonfamilial" realm, wherein a man becomes gendered through occupying not only the familial roles of son, husband, and father, but also nonkinship roles in the web of extrafamilial relations, such as acquiring an official post. The disparity between man and woman in the process of genderization is undeniable. However, the confinement of women to the familial realm of the *nei* by no means in itself signifies the natural inferiority or subordination of women to men. On the contrary, the familial realm of the *nei* as well as women's roles as daughter, wife, and mother are the focused center, the foundation upon which the extrafamilial realm of the *wai* is based. Moreover, in the Chinese world, the category of "woman" understood as outside the familial, kinship realm is nonexistent. The process of genderization is in effect coextensive with the process of ritualization within the hierarchical kinship system in which the senior is privileged over the junior. Gender disparity in the Chinese world is inevitably intertwined with and submerged in kinship hierarchy.

The connection between kinship hierarchy and gender disparity has begun to emerge as a critical area in Chinese gender studies; the problem of gender is no longer perceived as a uniform subordination of woman to man in all aspects of life. Instead, gender disparity is situated in the complex web of kinship relations where the disparity between genders forms only part of the social inequality between the senior and the junior kin. Gender by itself cannot determine one's position in life. Gender must also be combined with age, generation, marriage, and class, etc. to amount to anything significant. And the hierarchical kinship system in which one finds one's legitimate social place is also a reciprocal one; that is to say, one's position as a senior or a junior in the kinship system is not determinative. Those unequal kinship roles are what Tani Barlow called "reciprocal inequalities."[91] In the hierarchal kinship system one shifts from being a junior to a senior, or being both at the same time, depending on the relative position that one occupies, and one's status in the kinship system must be calculated across a lifetime.

Some scholars go even farther to claim that Chinese kinship system is "asexual" in the sense that the organizational principle in kinship hierarchy is not based on gender but on genealogical seniority, and hence the problem of gender disparity is in effect a historical problem derived from the problem of kinship hierarchy.[92] In the Chinese kinship system, a man and woman of the same class or status are more akin to one another in terms of social privileges and resources that they enjoy than with persons of their own sex but with different kinship status. In this view, one's kinship status takes precedence over one's gender as a woman or man per se. The claim that one's kinship status is primary while one's gender identity is secondary, in part, is supported by Sherry B. Ortner's anthropological study on gender and sexuality in hierarchical societies. Although her study mainly concentrates on Polynesian societies, the conclusion that she draws has cross-cultural implications. "It is inherent in the nature of hierarchies that certain nongender-based principles of social organization take precedence over gender itself as a principle of social organization."[93] The nongender-based principle of genealogical seniority in fact unites rather than divides men and women of the same class who share common interests in maintaining unequal social standings. A hierarchical society with its nongender-based principle of genealogical seniority, as Ortner concluded, in effect tends toward equality between genders of the same social stratification.[94]

Nevertheless, the problem of gender cannot be reduced to, or explained away, by appealing to the nongender-based principle of genealogical seniority in the kinship system. After all, in Chinese society, just as in other hierarchal societies, as Ortner cautioned, "there is still an overall male-favoring bias in the system," and, "[w]ithin the 'strata,' men are formally superior to women, have near-exclusive access to positions of social leadership, and dominate decision making on issues of importance to the unit as a whole."[95] Although Chinese gender constructions are intertwined with and submerged in the kinship system wherein nongender-based genealogical seniority is the organizational principle, the problem of gender disparity runs deeper than the formal submission of the junior to the senior in kinship hierarchy.

The perplexity of the position of Chinese women in which gender inequality intersects with other forms of inequality is made apparent by the many ironies found in historical and social reality. Rubie Watson pondered those ironies in her anthology on marriage and inequality in Chinese society: "[W]omen may be property holders but have few or no legal rights to property, they may be decision makers without the authority to make decisions, they may have physical mobility but are socially and economically constrained, they may exercise the power of an emperor but have no right to the imperial title."[96] This predicament of the lives of Chinese women, in part, can be explained through the concept of *nei-wai* as a regulative ideal in which the actual transgression across the boundary is permitted insofar as the formal, ritual representation of gender propriety is observed. Since the *nei-wai* distinction is a functional, gender distinction that regulates gender propriety, women may enter the political, social, and literary realm of *wai* only insofar as they are under concealment, that is, without being granted a formal right to do so. And it is with the lack of a formal right or social legitimacy to enter the realm of *wai* that women of all classes are abided by the doctrine of "threefold dependence" (*sancong* 三從), according to which women who are formally bound to the domestic realm of *nei* must depend on their fathers, husbands, and sons at different stages of their lives.

The doctrine of threefold dependence first appeared in the *Liji* and was frequently quoted by subsequent instruction books for women as well as commentaries on canonical texts such as the *Lienuzhuan*, *Baihutong*, and *Kongzi jiayu*. In the *Liji*, the doctrine of "threefold dependence" is explained in the following passage in conjunction with the marriage rite: "In passing through the great gate of (her father's house), the man leads the woman and the woman follows the man. This is the beginning of the proper relation between husband and wife. Women are the ones who follow others: when they are little they follow their fathers and elder brothers, when they are married they follow their husbands, and when their husbands die they follow their sons. 'Husband' denotes supporter. A husband uses wisdom to lead others."[97] The same doctrine is also elaborated in the *Kongzi jiayu*: "Women are the ones who follow the teaching of men and thereby grow in their ability to reason. Therefore, for women there is no appropriateness to be self-reliant but there is the way of threefold dependence. When they are little they follow their fathers and elder brothers, when they are married they follow their husbands, when their husbands die they follow their sons and do not remarry."[98] At the first sight, the doctrine seems to require the submission of woman to man at all three stages of life, and therefore the doctrine of *sancong* is often taken as an indication of women's natural inferiority or subordination to men. In fact, *sancong* is usually rendered as "threefold obedience or subordination," in order to accentuate the submissiveness of women's position regardless of their kinship status in Chinese society.

Yet, the proponents for the rendition of *sancong* as "threefold obedience," according to which women are assumed to be subordinated to men in all three stages of a woman's life, would have to confront the problem of the authority of mothers in Chinese society. In social and historical reality, not only does the mother not subordinate herself to her son in any shape or form, but the reverse is true. The mother, especially if she is widowed, has a tremendous power over the son, even if the son is an emperor. The mother's authority over her son is not limited to childhood; it is fairly common that mothers continue to instruct and admonish their grown sons who might be emperors, military generals, or state ministers regarding familial as well as governmental affairs.

There are countless examples of mother-son instruction recorded in the *Lienuzhuan* as well as other instruction books such as the sixth century text *Yanshi jiaxun* (Family Instructions to the Yan Clan) and various dynastic histories in which accomplished officials often attributed their success to their mother's sage instructions.[99] Mencius's widowed mother is the iconic image of a virtuous mother who not only instructed Mencius in his youth but also continued to instruct and admonish him in matters of ritual propriety and state affairs after he became a well-known Confucian scholar.[100] In the imperial court, maternal authority was further expressed in the institutionalization of empress dowagers since the early Han as regents for child-emperors whose dethronement and spousal selection were all in the hands of the widowed mother-empresses.[101] Powerful empress dowagers populated dynastic histories; their power to control the throne went beyond the original designated purpose of instructing and supporting the child-emperors during their transition to adulthood in the absence of a father. The first empress, Lu of the Former Han, who issued "imperial decrees," which were reserved for emperors alone, was a de facto emperor after the death of her emperor son Hui Di. Empress Wu Zetian of Tang who dethroned her son and later declared herself the founding emperor of a new dynasty, Zhou, was the first and the only female emperor in Chinese history. And the last empress, Cixi of Qing, whose regency symbolized the heyday of a widowed empress's power, practically controlled the Qing empire until her death in the early twentieth century, to name just a few.

Although the institutionalized power of empress dowagers is an extreme case of the enigmatic problem of maternal authority in discussing women's subordination to men in Chinese society, the authority of mothers in everyday life is not limited to the iconic image of a virtuous mother exalted in ritual texts; it was in fact supported by imperial laws that recognized the authority of parents over their children. Chu Tung-tsu in his study on law in Imperial China noted that the law not only recognized the parents' right to punish an unfilial son, but also gave them the right to have their son punished by the local authorities. In the Qing dynastic statute, it clearly stated: "When a father or mother prosecutes a son, the authorities will acquiesce without question or trial."[102] Although the degree to which the parents could inflict physical punishment on their unfilial son varied from dynasty to dynasty, the parental right to punish an unfilial son either at home or at imperial court as well as their right to select and to divorce the son's spouse without his consent had always been recognized throughout dynastic histories.[103]

The reverence accorded to mothers in Chinese society is well captured by the following lengthy comments made by Thomas Taylor Meadows, a British observer in late-nineteenth-century China. Despite his inflated polemics on the inferior status of Chinese women in comparison to the West, Meadows's detailed observation of maternal authority in Chinese society is nevertheless telling:[104]

> Woman is still more of a slave of man among the Chinese than among Anglo-Saxons. The quality of her slavery is, however, much tempered by the great veneration which Confucian principles require sons to pay both parents. The Imperial Government dare not refuse leave of absence to a mandarin if he, as an only son, requires it in order to tend his widowed mother during her declining years; even though the government may know that the real cause of his asking for leave is to escape from some impending official difficulty.... A Chinese will rarely introduce his most intimate male acquaintance to his wife.... Introductions to mothers are, on the other hand, not infrequent. The friend introduced then performs the kow tow to the lady, i.e., he kneels before her and touches the ground repeatedly with his forehead. The son does not prevent him, but he returns the salute by kneeling and kowtowing to his friend. Thus two men, and

often, of course, gray bearded men of high stations, will in China be found knocking their heads against the floor in honour of a women of their own class in society. Add to this that if a mother accuses her son before the magistrate, the latter will punish without inquiry into the specific offence. The reader will conclude that this great social and legal authority of mothers in China must operate to raise the position of females generally; and this it does in fact; though in the contraction of their own marriages each is but a passive instrument.

Because of the hierarchical kinship system in which the junior is subordinated to the senior and the emphasis on the importance of filial piety in Chinese society, a great deal of social respect and legal authority are accorded to mothers. Considering the authority of mothers, it would be inappropriate to render *sancong* as "threefold obedience or subordination." In fact, Chu Tung-tsu went farther to argue that since "there is no evidence to support the theory that a mother was subordinated to her son after the death of the father," the question of mother's subordination must be separated from other forms of subordination of women.[105]

Perhaps a more consistent approach to the problem of women's subordination would be to modify the rendering of *sancong* from "threefold obedience" to "threefold following or dependence." Taking into account of the authority of mothers exalted in ritual texts and supported by laws in Chinese society, what *sancong* inscribes cannot be an absolute submission of women to men regardless of their kinship status. A more probable reading of *sancong* is that it inscribes the necessity for women who are formally confined to the domestic realm of *nei* to follow and to depend on the rank of the most senior man in the household since the most senior man is to function as the woman's legitimate link to the *wai* realm. The doctrine of *sancong*, in Marina Sung's estimation, originated in the dress code for women in mourning rites where a woman's mourning attire must match the rank of her father before marriage, her husband after marriage, and her son in widowhood. The meaning of *sancong* is that "she must accustom herself to the position in society held by the most important male in the household. Her rank was dependent on the rank of her father before marriage, husband after marriage, and son in widowhood."[106] *Sancong* signifies the practical necessity for women to follow and to depend on the highest rank of men in the household rather than women's natural inferiority or subordination to men regardless of their kinship status.

It was a practical necessity for women to follow men, since women in general were without rank (*jue* 爵); their status and position in society depended on the status of their fathers, husbands, and sons. Such a dependency inevitably reflects the structural limitation imposed on women who had no legitimate access to the *wai* realm, and consequently women were without name, title, or rank. The *sancong* doctrine nevertheless provides a sense of gender parity especially between husband and wife. That sense of parity is articulated in the *Liji* immediately after the passage on the *sancong* in conjunction with the propriety of the marriage rites: "Husband and wife eat together of the same sacrificial item and thereby they are equally noble and base [i.e., same rank]. Therefore, while the wife has no rank, she follows the rank of her husband and takes her seat according to the position of her husband."[107] The wife is to be respected as the husband, since she is entitled to the same privileges and status that her husband holds. Although her status is dependent and derivative of her husband's, the husband and wife nevertheless are conceptualized as one single body equal to one another. Etymologically speaking, the word *qi* 妻 (wife), as explained in the *Baihutong*, means *qi** 齊 (equal) since the wife is equal to her husband (*yufuqiti* 與夫齊體). And this meaning of *qi* 妻 (wife) as an equal to her husband, as explained in the *Baihutong*, is used from the son of heaven down to the common people.[108] The ritual parity between husband and wife is deemed as a regulative ideal applied to all regardless of their social status.

The emphasis on the parity between husband and wife, in part, stems from the importance of the role of wife as the successor of the mother in continuing the patrilineal line and in assisting ancestor worship. The propriety of the marriage rite, as explained in the *Baihutong*, shows that functionary aspect of the role of wife. When the groom went to meet the bride in person, the father would admonish the son saying, "Go and meet your helpmate, that [with her] you may succeed me in the sacrifices to the ancestral temple. With diligence lead her, [but also] with respect, [for she is] the successor of your mother after her death."[109] The continuity of ancestor worship and the family line are what accentuates the sanctity and importance of the role of wife. As explained in the *Liji*, "The marriage rites are intended to be a bond of love between two [families of different] surnames, with a view, in its retrospective character, to secure the services in the ancestral temple, and in its prospective character, to secure the continuance of the family line."[110] Since the wife is essential in fulfilling these two purposes of marriage, the husband must treat her with a sense of deference and respect. The passage goes on to say, "When the bride arrives, the groom bows to her as she enters. They then eat together of the same [sacrificial] animal, and join in sipping from the cups made of the same melon; thereby showing that they form one body, are of equal rank and pledge mutual affection."[111] Although not without constraints, the husband-wife relation by and large is conceived of as a deferential parity instead of a one-sided domination.

In summary, the *nei-wai* binary, just as the *yin-yang* binary, is also a correlative, relational binary whose boundaries change with context. But unlike the *yin-yang*, the *nei-wai* distinction is also a *functional* distinction that defines the propriety of two gender spheres and the normative gender division of labor. Although the *nei-wai* boundary is primarily a ritual boundary, the regulative force of the *nei-wai* distinction, according to which women are formally confined to the familial realm of the *nei*—the realm of domestic skills and household management and men are assigned to the extended field of the nonfamilial realm of the *wai*—the realm of literary learning, culture, and remembrance—is not a merely theoretical ideal separated from social reality. In order to understand the regulative force of the *nei* and the *wai* in defining the proper and the limiting sphere for women regardless of their social status or literary accomplishments, we now turn to the representation of virtuous women found in the literary tradition of China—virtuous women's biographies in dynastic histories and the didactic books written for and by women. Women are both the subject that defines and transmits women's culture and at the same time the object that is defined by and confined to the limited, nonliterary realm of the *nei*, the women's sphere proper.

CHAPTER FIVE

DIDACTIC TEXTS FOR WOMEN AND THE WOMANLY SPHERE OF *NEI*

The *nei-wai* binary is a nondualistic, nonoppositional, complementary binary whose boundaries change with context.[1] However, when the *nei-wai* distinction refers to gender, it denotes a necessity to distinguish two distinct functions and spheres for men and women respectively. Women belong to the narrow realm of *nei* as the inner focused center, while men occupy the broader realm of *wai* as the extended field of the outer. The demarcation between genders is also a demarcation of two distinct functions in two distinct, but complementary spheres. Yet, the assumption conventionally made in feminist writings is that the womanly sphere of *nei* is marginal and that Chinese women are typically characterized as submissive, oppressed, and illiterate. In order to challenge this, we will begin our journey into the literary representation of virtuous women in the realm of *nei* by examining two important literary genres: first, the *lienu* 列女 tradition in imperial histories whose records of virtuous women's biographies formed part of the official history; second, didactic texts, especially the *Nusishu* (Four Books for Women) that defined the propriety of women's conduct and was written for and by women.

The *lienu* 列女 tradition that forms part of the official dynastic history since the Latter Han attests to the importance of the role of woman and the correct ordering of the womanly sphere of *nei* as the representation of good governance to the imperial court and Confucian literati. In contrast to the West where women's history must be constantly reinvented due to the lack of systematic, historical records of women's past, Chinese *lienu* tradition starting with court historian Liu Xiang in the Former Han down to the last dynasty Qing has in a sense created "a female sphere of historical memory."[2] Unlike the West, the *lienu* tradition of imperial China has assigned women a distinct place of their own in historical records and hence has provided a sense of solidarity for women in history. And unlike the West where women's voice in the literary world was virtually mute in premodern times, the legitimacy of female authorship in defining the propriety of women in the realm of *nei* was not only recognized but also socially sanctioned by official literati. The four canonical didactic books—the *Four Books for Women*—not only were written for women but more importantly were written by women themselves. The womanly sphere of *nei* not only signifies the centrality of women's role in the discourse on ethics and good governance; but more importantly it paradoxically legitimizes the authority of female authorship as well as readership in the world of letters, despite the constraints of *nei* that relegate women to the realm of strict household management.

However, despite the occasional boundary crossing that enables women to achieve in the political, military, and literary realm beyond the familial realm, the normative force of the *nei-wai* distinction as gender distinction nonetheless deprives women of a legitimate access to a full personhood in the *wai* where a person is not only filial and proper but also fully learned and cultured. The limited gender roles for women can be illustrated by examining the literary representation of virtuous women both in the *lienu* tradition and the didactic instruction books for women. The criteria for virtuous women in the imperial history evolved from the early non–gender specific virtues such as *ren* (humanity; authoritative conduct) and *zhi* (wisdom) to the later emphasis on spousal fidelity and filial devotion as the defining "womanly" virtues. The didactic books for women, although they were written by learned women themselves, reinforce the purely functionary roles of women as daughter, wife, and mother confined to the nonliterary realm of household management that renders women's literary skills superfluous. Literary learning (*wen* 文) is in effect exclusively a male privilege enforced by both learned male and female authors in the Chinese literary tradition.

LIENUZHUAN, *GUIFAN*, AND THE TRADITION OF VIRTUOUS WOMEN'S BIOGRAPHIES

Whether literate or not, Chinese women first and foremost were remembered for their virtuous conduct throughout imperial histories. The earliest record of women's biographies is Liu Xiang's *Lienuzhuan* (Biographies of Virtuous Women), compiled in the Former Han. It laid the foundation for later dynastic records of women's biographies and later popular didactic texts for women and family instructions. The *Lienuzhuan* consists of 125 life stories of women ranging from peasants to empresses. It was initially compiled as an admonition to the Han emperor Cheng Di to recognize the importance of women, whose virtuous and vicious conduct were viewed as intertwined with the rise and fall of both prominent families and states. According to the *Hanshu* (Book of Han), Liu Xiang's intent in compiling the *Lienuzhuan* was that "Liu Xiang believed the teaching of kings must proceed from inner to outer, beginning with those who are closest [i.e., empress and concubines]. Therefore he selected from the *Book of Songs* and *Documents* virtuous concubines and chaste women who could be taken as models for making their countries prosper and their families illustrious. He also selected pernicious favorites who caused disorder and ruin. He put them in order and compiled the *Lienuzhuan*, originally in eight volumes, in order to put the emperor on guard."³ In order to exalt the virtuous; Liu Xiang devoted six chapters to six virtuous forms of conduct and one chapter to the "pernicious and depraved" women, which was omitted in later dynastic biographies of women.

The six virtues praised by Liu Xiang are: (1) *muyi* 母儀 (maternal rectitude); (2) *xianming* 賢明 (sage intelligence); (3) *renzhi* 仁智 (benevolent wisdom); (4) *zhenshun* 貞順 (purity and deference); (5) *jieyi* 節義 (chastity and appropriateness); and (6) *biantong* 辯通 (skill in argument). In contrast with later dynastic biographies of women in which women were mostly praised in accordance with their gender roles as daughter, wife, and mother, especially during the Ming and Qing periods, the six virtues praised in the *Lienuzhuan* are not strictly "female virtues" per se. Virtues such as *xianming* (sage intelligence) and *renzhi* (benevolent wisdom) in particular are also frequently used to assess the worth of men as well. The terms *xianming* and *renzhi* appear regularly in Warring States and early Han texts such as *Lushi chunqiu* (Springs and Autumns of Master Lu), *Hanfeizi*, *Zhanguoce* (Strategies of the Warring States), *Mengzi*, *Guanzi*, *Huainanzi*, and *Xunzi* and are used to describe the virtue of a *junzi* or a ruler.⁴ In other words, in early literary representation, women as virtuous agents are not limited to their gender roles of daughter, wife, and mother. The representation of women as intellectual agents of moral and political virtue in the *Lienuzhuan* is particularly illuminating when contrasted with the later dominant representation of women as either filial daughters, chaste wives, or self-sacrificial widowed mothers in dynastic biographies of virtuous women and popular instruction books. There are two inferences that can be tentatively drawn from the early representation of virtuous women: first, there is no fundamental inconsistency between Confucian virtue ethics and the representation of women as intellectual agents of moral and political virtue; second, the change of the representation of women as agents of particularly "female virtues" of widow chastity and motherhood in later dynasties is a problem of historical development that must be contextualized rather than being seen as a natural fallout of Confucian teachings.

To begin with, Lisa Raphals in her study on the textual matrix of *Lienuzhuan* has demonstrated that the representation of women as intellectual agents of virtue found in the *Lienuzhuan* is not an invention of Liu Xiang in the early Han. They are found in numerous pre-Han texts as well, such as *Zuozhuan* (Zuo Annal) and *Guoyu* (Discourse of the States). All the following stories recorded in the *Lienuzhuan*—the story of "Ding Jiang of Wei" (1.7) who correctly observed the fault of her husband's heir and consequently predicted the inevitable ruin of the state of Wei; the story of "Ji of Lu" (1.9) who instructed her son including an analogy between weaving and statecraft, and was praised by Confucius for her knowledge of the rites; the story of "Deng Man of Chu" (3.2) who correctly predicted future events and effectively counseled her husband to avoid military disaster; and the story of "The wife of Xi Fuji of Cao" (3.4) who was able to recognize her husband's talent and successfully saved both her husband and her state—also appear in the *Zuozhuan* and *Guoyu* with similar narratives.⁵

The virtue of *biantong* or "skill in argument" praised in the *Lienuzhuan*, in particular, is at odds with the assumed passivity of Chinese women. In the chapter "*Biantong*" of *Lienuzhuan*, women are presented as active agents who turn a dangerous situation in their favor through constructive arguments. For instance, in the story of "The Wife of the Bow-maker of Jin" (6.3), the bow-maker's wife fearlessly intervened with Duke Ping of Jin when he intended to kill her husband for making a useless bow for the duke. She boldly admonished the Duke for his poor shooting skill that rendered the bow useless, and furthermore instructed him in archery—one of the six arts preserved for men only. As a result, she not only saved her husband, but also brought in handsome rewards from the duke as he improved his archery skill. The authenticity of the story is not clear, yet Liu Xiang's deliberate representation of a woman in the pre-Han period as a courageous agent fearlessly admonishing the superior through intellectual means nevertheless can be viewed as a "historical" precedent to repudiate the common perception of the passivity of Chinese women.

Similarly, in the story of "The Discriminating Woman of the Chu Countryside"(6.5), commoner Zhao's wife was threatened with a beating when her cart collided with that of the envoy of Duke Jian of Zheng in a narrow road. Instead of submitting to the envoy, she argued that the envoy's servant was at fault for monopolizing the already narrow road. Now if the envoy instead of punishing his own servant beat her, he would add a second fault to himself and hence ruin his own goodness. The envoy was embarrassed and had nothing to say to respond to her argument. In this story, a woman with inferior social status argued her way out of danger instead of submitting to her social superior. Women in the early literary representations are anything but passive. Another skillful argument made by a woman in the inferior position to turn an unfavorable situation in her favor is the story of "Xuwu of Qi"(6.14). In this story, the neighbors of a poor woman, Xuwu, intended to exclude her from their weaving gathering at night, because Xuwu could not afford to bring in her fair share of candles. Xuwu argued that precisely because she was poor and unable to bring in enough candles to share, she always came in early and stayed late to clean up the place, and always sat in a far corner so as not to inconvenience others. Besides, as she argued, the presence of one more person in the room would neither increase nor diminish the light. Afterward, no one objected her presence. Women are praised not for their passivity or submissiveness; instead, in the early literary representation of women, one way to be "virtuous" is to be skillful in argumentation.

However, in later editions of *Lienuzhuan* as well as later dynastic biographies of women, the representation of women as intellectual agents of virtue was replaced by emphasis on strictly familial virtues and specific "female concerns" such as spousal fidelity, widow chastity, and motherhood. The shift in the representation of virtuous women in history is especially telling when one compares the Han/Song edition of *Lienuzhuan* with the Ming/Qing edition. The organizational scheme in the Han/Song edition is "virtue" oriented; that is, women are exalted according to six virtues regardless of their defined gender roles. In the *Guifan*—a Ming expanded edition of *Lienuzhuan*—the organizational scheme is "role" oriented. "Virtuous women" praised in this Ming edition are organized into three female life cycles—daughter, wife, and mother. In other words, virtuous women in late imperial China were by and large understood as filial daughters, chaste wives, and self-sacrificial widowed mothers.

The *Guifan* consists of four books. Book one is devoted to locating relevant passages on gender propriety in canonical texts throughout history; books two, three, and four are devoted to illustrating "virtuous women" according to their three life cycles and familial roles. For instance, book two is mainly devoted to illuminating the proper way of an unmarried girl (*nuzizhidao* 女子之道); and fourteen out of thirty stories are listed in this section under the title of *xiaonu* 孝女 (filial daughters). Book three deals with the proper way of a married woman (*furenzhidao* 婦人之道), and more than one-half of the stories recorded (thirty-nine out of seventy-one) are devoted to exalting ritual propriety and chastity under titles such as *fufu* 夫婦 (husband-wife), *xiaofu* 孝婦 (filial wives), *sijie* 死節 (die for chastity), *shoujie* 守節 (protect chastity), and *shouli* 守禮 (protect the rites). Lastly, in book four, the way of motherhood is discussed (*mudao* 母道); in addition, at the end it also touches on the way of sisterhood, the way of sister-in-law, and the way of female servants, etc.

As Lisa Raphals observed, in the *Guifan*'s Ming edition of virtuous women's biographies, two nongender-specific virtues praised in the *Lienuzhuan*—*renzhi* (benevolent wisdom) and *biantong* (skill in argument)—in particular are either lost or reclassified.[6] Nongender-specific virtues are replaced with wifely fidelity and ritual propriety. For instance, the story of "The Wife of the Bow-maker of Jin" (6.3) in the *Lienuzhuan* is classified under the virtue of *biantong* (skill in argument); yet in the *Guifan* it is reclassified under the title of *sijie* (die for chastity) as part of the wifely virtue in book three. The bow-maker's wife, her eloquent skill in argument against the incompetent Duke of Jin, in the Ming edition, is construed as the role of a virtuous wife begging for her husband's life as part of her undying fidelity to her husband. The story of the "Xuwu of Qi" (6.14), where the poor woman, Xuwu, argued her way out of her neighbors' objection to her participation in the weaving gathering at night despite her inability to contribute her fair share of candles, in the *Guifan* is reclassified as *shouli* (protecting ritual propriety). In other words, the virtue of Xuwu's conduct is now seen as derived from her knowing the proper ritual, instead of her skill in argument.[7]

The rising emphasis on filial piety and female chastity in the representation of virtuous women during the Ming and Qing is also reflected in the dramatic increase of the number of virtuous women's biographies in the dynastic records. Departing from the organizational scheme of Liu Xiang's *Lienuzhuan*, women in later dynastic histories are not classified separately under any specific virtues. Without classifying women under any specific virtues, the dynastic *lienu* history allows for a more flexible criterion for "virtuous women" in each dynasty. In the Later Han dynastic history, there are only eighteen entries of virtuous women's biographies including a detailed biography of Ban Zhao—the first and foremost woman scholar and court historian—as well as her entire literary work—"*Nujie.*" In the subsequent major dynasties—Sui, Tang, and Song—the number of virtuous women's biographies ranges roughly from sixteen to fifty-five.[8]

In the Yuan dynastic history, the number of women recorded increased drastically to 187. The dramatic increase in the number of virtuous women's biographies compiled in the late Yuan and early Ming periods is probably a byproduct of the institutionalization of widowhood in the early fourteenth century by the Yuan imperial court. With the institutionalization of widowhood, virtuous women were increasingly defined by the gender-specific virtue of female chastity and spousal fidelity. In the Ming, there were nearly three hundred women's life stories preserved in the *Lienu* section of the imperial history. In the Qing, an unprecedented number of women's biographies were recorded; there were more than four hundred entries listed as virtuous women in the Qing dynastic history.[9] It is true that the drastic increase in population between the 1400s and 1600s from 50 million to 150 million, and to 300 million in the 1800s, must be taken into account when considering the increase in the number of women's biographies. However, court historians' deliberate attempt to seek out and compile virtuous women's biographies from local histories in large numbers is an indication of the imperial court's interest in the literary representation of virtuous women perhaps as part of its conformity to the popular sentiment of its time, or perhaps as part of its self-conscious representation of good governance reflected in its virtuous subjects.

In the Qing, the criteria for virtuous women in the "women's biographies" focused on filial piety, female chastity, and spousal fidelity. In the Qing dynastic introduction to the "Women's Biographies," women were mainly praised for being *xiaonu* (filial daughters), *xiaofu* (filial wives), *lienu* (daring daughters), *liefu* (daring wife), *shoujie* (protecting chastity), *shunjie* (dying for chastity), and *weihuan shoujie* (protecting chastity before marriage), etc.[10] On the one hand, the dramatic increase in the number of women's biographies in the Ming and Qing can also be interpreted as a heightened awareness of the centrality of "virtuous women" in state politics; on the other hand, the emphasis on filial daughters, chaste wives, and self-sacrificial widowed mothers reduced the representation of "virtuous women" to specific "womanly virtues" of chastity, fidelity, and widowhood.

From the dramatic increase of the number of women's biographies recorded in the Ming and Qing dynastic histories, and the reclassification of *Lienuzhuan* in the popular Ming instruction book, *Guifan*, the shift in the historical perception of what constitutes a "virtuous woman" and her place in society is evident. The heightened interest in the discourse on "female virtues" of chastity and fidelity in the Ming should also be seen in the context of the rise of the discourse on men's political loyalty. During the turbulent time of the late Ming when the Han people increasingly lost ground to the strong invading Manchu barbarians, men's loyalty to the Ming court became especially pressing. The classical, Warring States' analogy between the fidelity of a chaste wife to her husband's familial lineage and the loyalty of an official to his righteous ruler received a revival in the late Ming. Widow chastity and suicide, exalted in the Ming and Qing dynastic histories, are socially sanctioned forms of self-sacrifice and violence used to bring women honor, just as the death of a knight for his lord brings the knight honor. The pairing of chaste women in the domestic realm with loyal ministers in the political realm is clearly shown in the early Han text, *Shiji*. "A noble man dies for one who recognizes him, just as a beautiful woman adorns herself for the one who pleases her." And "If a family is poor then it seeks a good wife. If a state is chaotic it seeks a good minister."[11] Hence, the shift of the emphasis to female chastity and spousal fidelity in both the popular instruction books and dynastic histories can be attributed, in part, to the increasing emphasis on male loyalty in the political realm during the late Ming, since the familial bond between husband and wife is traditionally deemed parallel to the political bond between ruler and minister.

Besides the changes in the political climate, other social changes also contributed to the increasing discourse on female fidelity to patrilineage. One noticeable change occurring during the late Ming was the rise of commercial activities and the printing culture with its woodblock illustration. Prosperity in the economy translated into a luxurious lifestyle for the gentry that demanded entertainment not only from the world of courtesans but from the literary world as well. The popularity of fictional writing ranging from romance and adventure to historical fiction during the Ming attests to the growing printing culture at the time.[12] With the rise of commercial printing and the help of woodblock illustration, printing was no longer a domain of high culture. As Katherine Carlitz noted, Ming publishing industry ranged from government publishers that printed, standard canonical texts to commercial ones that printed everything "from connoisseurship to domestic worship at one end of the scale ... and at the other, paper gods and ritual money."[13] Due to its ability to reach a semiliterate public, illustration helped the printing industry reach new heights during the Ming. The popular predrawn, predesigned woodblock illustrations used in commercial printing for fiction, drama, and even didactic books, in turn, also blurred the line between entertainment and virtue. Carlitz observed that the same illustration used to portray a lovesick maiden in a fiction was also used to portray the faithful widow of Liu Changqiu in the Ming edition of an illustrated *Lienuzhuan*.[14] Furthermore, the supposedly moral messages of a didactic book sometimes also seemed to get lost in the visual appeal of illustration. In the portrait of a ritually proper empress in an illustrated *Lienuzhuan*, instead of being on the empress who is hiding her face to conceal the improper sight in the corner, the visual focus ironically is on the bold, half-naked dancing girls at the ruler's drinking feast.[15]

The dramatic effect of illustration, on the one hand, helped to disseminate social virtue praised in ritual and instruction books to the semiliterate public and hence strengthened the conservative "gendered" virtues. Yet, on the other hand, the popularity and interchangeability of illustration between fiction and didactic texts created ironies around the representation of "virtuous women" in didactic texts, in which the illustration of virtuous women was used as much for its didactic value as for entertainment value. The visual appeal of illustration facilitated the dissemination of the didactic messages to their targeted audience—unmarried young girls and new brides—who were by and large without formal schooling. The popularity of instruction books during the late Ming and early Qing, in part, can be attributed to the rise of illustration in commercial printing, which blurred the line between the literate, gentry class and the semiliterate reading public. The visual representation of virtuous women also made drawings with dramatic content, such as a self-mutilated widow or a self-sacrificial filial daughter, far more appealing than drawings of a wise mother instructing her son, or an eloquent young girl debating the emperor.

The omission of intellectual virtues such as *biantong* and *renzhi* and the shift in the motifs to filial devotion and widow fidelity in the representation of virtuous women during the late Ming and early Qing, as Lisa Raphals proposed, might just simply have been facilitated by the emotional appeal of illustration with tragic content rather than by deliberate conservatism.[16] In other words, the shift in the early representation of virtuous women as agents of intellectual and moral virtues to the later dynastic representation of virtuous women as bearers of specific "gendered" virtues such as fidelity, chastity, and motherhood might not have been a natural fallout of the so-called "neo-Confucianism" in the Ming and Qing. Nor was it a one-sided, conspicuous imposition of male orthodoxy onto women in general. Instead, it might have been a byproduct of the popular sentiment shared by both men and women in the age of printing and illustration.

Surprisingly, the normative "four virtues" or *side* 四德 that later became the authority in measuring the worth of a "good woman" was elaborated and formulated by learned and talented women themselves, who supported the conservative discourse on the proper sphere of woman and her limited functional gender roles. But, at the same time, through their writing and presence in the literary world, they also subverted the conservatism by legitimizing female authorship as well as readership in the illiterate realm of *nei*—the realm of pure household management. Paradoxically, the shift of the motifs from "virtuous women" in the early time to "womanly virtues" in late imperial China was sanctioned and facilitated by learned and talented women themselves, who conformed and at the same time subverted the conservative familial discourse on the womanly sphere of *nei*.

THE FOUR BOOKS FOR WOMEN AND BY WOMEN

Paralleling the authority of the Confucian canonical *Four Books*, which dominates the literary realm of *wai*, the authority of the *Four Books for Women* (*Nusishu* 女四書) dominates the womanly sphere of *nei*. Since men are supposed to be in charge of the affairs of *wai* and women the affairs of *nei*, it is not surprising to note that the *Nusishu* as the standard text for women's education were not just written for women but also written by women. The *Nusishu* is composed of four different instruction books written by learned and talented women in four different historical times. It was first compiled as an anthology by Wang Xiang (1789–1852) in the mid-Qing. The widespread influence and popularity of the *Nusishu* as part of the proper education for women in the gentry class can be attested by its mention along with other women's classics in the popular Qing novel *Hongloumeng* (Dream of the Red Chamber), as well as by several well-preserved Japanese editions of the anthology.[17] Given the canonical status of the *Sishu* (Four Books) in men's education, the titling of the female-authored instruction texts as the *Nusishu* (Four Books for Women) by a male editor apparently alludes to the parity between the *nei* and the *wai*, that is, the parity between the authority of male and female authorship in regard to the education of men and women in their proper spheres respectively. Just as the *Sishu* signifies the Confucian exemplary person—*junzi*—in the realm of *wai*, the *Nusishu* represents ideal womanhood in the realm of *nei* as defined by learned and talented women themselves.

The first and foremost instruction book included in the *Nusishu* is Ban Zhao's *Nujie* 女誡 (Admonitions for Women), which laid the foundation for later didactic texts and was frequently quoted by both male and female authors in this literary genre. It is the oldest extant instruction text and is fully preserved in the dynastic biography of Ban Zhao (45–120 CE) in the *Hou Hanshu* (Book of the Latter Han). According to the *Hou Hanshu*, Ban Zhao was "broadly learned and highly talented" (博學高才) and observed the propriety of widowhood. After the death of her brother Ban Gu, Ban Zhao was then commanded by Emperor He (88–105 CE) to complete the dynastic history of the *Hanshu* (Book of Han).[18] Her contributions to the *Hanshu* include "The Treatise on Astronomy" and "The Eight Tables," which recorded the chronology of the nobles and the high officials of the pre-Qin as well as the House of Han. Besides the *Nujie* and the *Hanshu*, Ban Zhao's literary works preserved today also include two memorials—one to the emperor and one to the empress—three short poems, and a long essay that recorded her journey to the eastward frontier with her son to his post.[19] Her profound erudition was highly respected by both men and women of her time. Ban Zhao was not only the mentor of Empress Deng, whom she had instructed during the empress's twenty-year regency, but also the mentor of numerous male court historians.[20] Contrary to the ritually proper women that were confined to the nonliterary realm of *nei* prescribed in her instruction book, *Nujie*, Ban Zhao was a talented official actively participating in the state politics as well as in the literary world, both belonging to the realm of *wai*. The irony of a conservative instruction book written by the first and foremost woman court historian whose work was later used to justify female servitude and her lowly status in subsequent instruction books seems appalling. However, there is more to the apparent conservatism in Ban Zhao's *Nujie* than first meets the eye.

Ban Zhao's *Nujie* is composed of seven chapters entitled "Base and Weakling" (*beiruo* 卑弱), "Husband and Wife" (*fufu* 夫婦), "Respect and Tolerance" (*jingshun* 敬順), "Women's conduct" (*fuxing* 婦行), "Undivided Attention" (*zhuanxin* 專心), "Bending and Following" (*qucong* 曲從), and "Harmony with Junior Brothers- and Sisters-in-Law" (*heshumei* 和叔妹). Chapter 1, "Base and Weakling" begins with the discussion of the humble position of a girl indicated by ancient rites observed for the birth of a baby girl as recorded in the "*Sikan*" of the *Shijing*; and concludes that woman's primary function is to serve and to humble herself before others. In chapter 2, "Husband and Wife," the way of *yin-yang* is said to be analogous to the way of husband and wife and therefore husband should lead and wife should serve; however, the text also stresses the reciprocity between husband and wife who must be worthy of each other. Ban Zhao's understanding of the *yin-yang* is entirely consistent with our characterization of the *yin-yang* in conjunction with Han cosmology, which is hierarchical but also complementary. Chapter 3, "Respect and Tolerance," advises young girls to avoid confrontations and to make generous allowance to others. In chapter 4, "Women's Conduct," there are four areas of conduct that must be observed by a virtuous woman—women's virtue (*fude*), women's speech (*fuyan*), women's comportment (*furong*), and women's work (*fugong*); they are also called the "four virtues" (*side*). Chapter 5, "Undivided Attention," stresses the wife's fidelity to the husband and advises girls to be moderate in their appearance. Chapter 6, "Bending and Following," advises girls to follow their in-laws' wishes. Similarly, in the last chapter girls are urged to cultivate a harmonious relationship with their brothers- and sisters-in-law to avoid disharmony in the family.

The most influential chapter of *Nujie* is chapter 4, on the propriety of women's conduct, in which Ban Zhao's humble and conservative reading of the four female virtues was frequently used, especially during the Ming and Qing, to justify the exclusion or limited involvement of women in literary arts. The first mention of the four virtues (*side*) is in the chapter on the "Meaning of the Marriage Rites" in the *Liji* as part of the proper training of a bride-to-be three months before the marriage ceremony. In Ban Zhao's humble and conservative reading of *side*, women's virtue (*fude*) signifies one's adherence to ritual propriety expressed in a manner of tranquility rather than a colorful display of one's talent and brilliance. In the same humble manner, women's speech (*fuyan*) signifies not one's persuasive skills or eloquence but one's ability to be circumspect. Women's comportment (*furong*) focuses on the clean and proper presentation of oneself instead of the attractiveness of one's appearance. Lastly, women's work (*fugong*) consists in the practical skills of weaving and spinning for textile production and the domestic skill of food preparation for feasts or ancestral sacrifice.

In Ban Zhao's rendering of *side*, a virtuous woman is defined by, first and foremost, her adherence to ritual propriety that inscribes the *nei*—a sphere of domestic skills and wifely servitude—as the proper sphere for women. In the Ming and Qing periods, learned women of the gentry class that took Ban Zhao as a model of female virtue and respectability, however, asserted a more progressive reading of the four virtues. Learned women of Qing strongly rejected the Ming popular saying, "A woman without talent is virtuous," and reconciled Ban Zhao's conflicting reading of virtue and talent by making the possession of literary talent a prerequisite for the correct observance of ritual propriety. Moreover, Ban Zhao's literary achievement as a historical precedent and object of aspiration enabled learned women of subsequent generations to extend the virtue of "women's speech" (*fuyan*) from spoken words to written words, and thereby justify women's involvement in the literary world of *wai*.

Conservative or not, the *Nujie*, according to Ban Zhao's own introduction, was originally written as a family instruction text for the female members of her family in order to educate them with proper rites. Given her highly visible position as a court historian and a close advisor to Empress Deng (d. 121 CE), Ban Zhao's *Nujie*, published during Empress Deng's early regency—a turbulent time in the Han court history—inevitably carried with it a public and political function. The excessive humility and conservatism displayed in the *Nujie*, in part, as Yu-shih Chen suggested, might be a deliberate strategy to avoid the potential danger entailed in the close relationship between Ban Zhao and Empress Deng during the empress's regency, during which the possibility of usurpation by the empress was always under close scrutiny.[21] The deliberately conservative sentiment in the *Nujie* is necessary if one takes into account the dangerous precedent set by the powerful first empress dowager, Lu, of Han who dominated the Han court throughout the entire reigns of her son, Emperor Hui (r. 195–188 BCE), and two subsequent child emperors until her death in 180 BCE. The conservative reading of the limited womanly sphere and her humble, lowly position stated in the *Nujie*, in other words, was a public statement by Ban Zhao and Empress Deng to display their loyalty to the patrilineal Han court under the watchful eye of their male counterparts.

Yu-shih Chen in his study of Ban Zhao's *Nujie* attributed Ban Zhao's conservative propensity to her possible Daoist roots. Given the Daoist affiliation in Ban Zhao's family background as well as her knowledge of *yin-yang* cosmology demonstrated in "The Treatise of Astronomy" in the *Hanshu*, Ban Zhao's *Nujie*, which accentuates the virtues of lowliness (*bei* 卑), meekness (*ruo* 弱), following (*shun* 順), and yielding (*rang* 讓), according to Yu-shih Chen, reflects the deep-rooted Daoist concerns of self-preservation and practical survival in an unstable world.[22] Although Chen's reclassification of Ban Zhao's *Nujie* as a Daoist instead of a Confucian text is overstated given the canonical status of the text in the tradition of virtuous women's biographies and instruction books, the affinity between Ban Zhao's excessive humility in the *Nujie* and the Daoist virtue of "yielding" is rather appealing.

Despite its deliberately conservative overtone, the *Nujie* is also the earliest text surviving in Chinese history that explicitly advocates female literacy. Ban Zhao forcefully argued in chapter 2, on the parity between husband and wife, that: "Yet only to teach boys and not to teach girls, is that not ignoring the essential relation between them. According to the *Rites*, it is the rule to begin to teach children to read at the age of eight years, and by the age of fifteen years they ought then to be ready for cultural training. Only why should it not be (that girls' education as well as boys' be) according to this doctrine?"[23] In effect, Ban Zhao was trying to extend the parity and reciprocity between *yin* and *yang* to the parity between the education of boys and girls under the banner of the canonical text of the *Rites*, which explicitly preserves literary education for boys only. The radicality of her argument for female literacy seems to set itself apart from the overall conservatism in the *Nujie*, and that inconsistency invokes some difficulties for scholars in constructing a coherent interpretation of Ban Zhao's intent in writing the *Nujie*.

One possible interpretation, according to Lily Xiao Hong Lee, is that, contrary to what is stated in Ban Zhao's own humble introduction, Ban Zhao wrote the *Nujie* with the intention of establishing a normative, prescriptive standard for all women as her contribution to the Han Confucian movement, which aimed at restoring proper rites in a post-Qin society.[24] In Lee's view, Ban Zhao's advocacy for female literacy was but a means to bring women under control in order for them to conform to the passivity that she prescribed in the text. Given Ban Zhao's highly visible position at the time, it is probable that the *Nujie* was written with the intent to reach a much larger audience than the female members in her family, or her pupil Empress Deng alone. But unlike all other canonical texts that prescribe ritual propriety for both men and women, Ban Zhao's *Nujie* explicitly addresses women's need for literacy. Considering Ban Zhao's own background—both men and women in her prominent gentry family were all highly learned and talented—it is not surprising to see why she, as the first female court historian and close advisor to the dowager empress, sought to legitimize female literacy despite the overall conservatism in the *Nujie*. Alternatively, Lisa Raphals proposed that Ban Zhao's *Nujie* can be interpreted as "primarily an argument for female literacy, rendered in terms acceptable to a conservative male audience."[25] In any case, both the conservative and the progressive readings of the *Nujie* greatly influenced later writings on gender propriety.

Ban Zhao herself became both a conservative icon of widowhood and a progressive exemplar of a respectable female who was not only virtuous but also talented and learned, especially during the Ming and the Qing periods when the compatibility between female literacy and womanly virtues was seriously contested. The indeterminacy of Ban Zhao's intent in the *Nujie* along with her visible literary achievement have rendered two somewhat conflicting views of gender propriety: on the one hand, according to the *Nujie*, literary talent is irrelevant to, or can be even distracting for, virtuous women carrying out their gendered duties of household management, but on the other hand, female literacy exemplified by Ban Zhao can be used as an indication of the compatibility between literary talent and womanly virtues in the realm of *nei*.

Following Ban Zhao's *Nujie*, the second book in the *Nusishu, The Analects for Women* (*Nulunyu* 女論語) was written by Song Ruoxin and Song Ruozhao of the Tang dynasty and it offers similar practical advise for young girls in their dealing with their future in-laws and in carrying out household management. Unlike Ban Zhao's *Nujie*, the *Nulunyu* does not appeal to the canon in defining gender propriety. Instead, its brief twelve chapters are entirely composed of simple verses of four characters, which might be intended to facilitate learning and reciting by semiliterate young girls. The book's simple style of writing and straightforward instructions contrast greatly with its ambitious title, which compares itself with the foremost Confucian canon, *Lunyu* (Analects). The ambitious title of the book had upset some literati such as Lan Dingyuan and Zhang Xuecheng who denounced the intended parity between the *Nulunyu*, a simple handbook, and the *Lunyu*, the foremost Confucian classic.[26] But precisely because of its simple language and accessible four-character verses to the semiliterate female population, the *Nulunyu* was also one of the most widely circulated handbooks in early China.[27]

The colloquial style of the *Nulunyu* contrasts greatly with the profound erudition of its authors, the Song sisters of Tang. The book was originally authored by Song Ruoxin, the eldest of the five learned daughters of the Tang official literatus, Song Tingfen. It was later extended and annotated by her sister Song Ruozhao, the most talented and learned among the five sisters. Taking Ban Zhao—a learned young widow—as her inspirational model, Song Ruozhao was determined to lead a solitary, literary life. While all of her four sisters were requested by the emperor to the palace and later became imperial concubines, Song Ruozhao declined the imperial favor and remained unmarried. Her determination was later honored by the emperor who put her in charge of literary affairs in the inner court and assigned her a share of the duty of teaching the prince and princess, along with male official literati in the outer court. The similarity between Song Ruozhao and Ban Zhao is striking. Song Ruozhao often compared herself with Ban Zhao.[28] Ban Zhao's early widowhood and her literary achievement inspired later learned and talented women in the gentry class who saw early widowhood as a means to a solitary, literary life—a respectable alternative to the socially sanctioned gender roles for women as dependent daughters, wives, and mothers. Despite the conservative overtone in these two instruction books, which prescribe limited roles for women in the familial realm of *nei*, both authors—Ban Zhao and Song Ruozhao—led rather solitary, literary lives that were beyond the reach of most illiterate, common women.

The effect of female literacy as first advocated by Ban Zhao indeed had a transformative impact on women in the gentry class, who in their writings continued to support the conservative orthodoxy of gender propriety but in their conduct implicitly subverted those conservative values they advocated. The subversion, or, if you will, the expansion of the womanly sphere of *nei* to include literary talent was especially telling during the late Ming and the early Qing periods. The rise of the publication and circulation of conservative didactic texts during the Ming and Qing periods was accompanied by the rise of female literacy, which in turn invoked a heated debate on the compatibility between womanly virtues and female literacy.

Despite the popularity of the common Ming saying, "A women without talent is virtuous," which denounces women's pursuit of literary talent, the third book of *Nusishu—Neixun* 內訓 (Instruction for the Inner Quarters)—written by Empress Wen of Ming, who demonstrated her erudition by grounding her arguments in traditional canonical texts such as the *Shijing, Shujing, Liji,* and *Yijing,* shows otherwise. Following Ban Zhao's *Nujie* and Song sisters' *Nulunyu,* Empress Wen's *Neixun,* composed of twenty chapters, also offers practical advice to women to properly perform their gender roles. Unlike the previous two, the *Neixun,* according to its introduction, was written specifically for the imperial members of the Ming court in the palace. It was intended to groom future empresses and high court ladies, and hence the scope of its concern, unlike the previous two, went beyond the traditional female virtues and servitude in the familial realm; it also was concerned with court politics and management, including the qualifications and virtues of past empresses, the treatment of imperial servants in the court, and dealing with the empress's relatives.

Although its style and content differed greatly from other instruction texts, which usually aimed at educating the general public, the *Neixun,* like Ban Zhao's *Nujie,* also strongly advocated female education and literacy. Empress Wen wrote in the introduction that according to the *Rites,* boys eight years old must receive elementary education, girls ten years old must model their mother's words and deeds, and yet for boys there is Zhu Xi's *Xiaoxue* or *Elementary Learning* that they can begin with, while in comparison there is no comprehensive text for girls. As she benefited from her mother-in-law's teachings (i.e., Empress Ma of Ming, a self-educated former peasant with natural feet)[29] Empress Wen composed the *Neixun* to pass on the teachings of her mother-in-law as part of girls' comprehensive education. In other words, Empress Wen intended to elevate female education in the *nei* to the same level of respectability as male education in the *wai,* as the hinted parity between Zhu Xi's *Xiaoxue* 小學 (Small Learning) for boys and Empress Wen's *Neixun* (Instruction for the Inner Quarters) for girls implies.

The debate on the compatibility between female virtue and female literacy reached its height during the Qing period, which paradoxically saw a volume of publications of women's writings unprecedented in Chinese history.[30] The rise of female literacy during the late Ming and early Qing periods is evident not only in the mention of *Nusishu* as part of the proper education of women in the popular Qing novel *Dream of the Red Chamber* but also in the mention of the issue of female literacy in popular instruction books and literary essays such as the *Guifan*, the *Nufan jielu*, and the essay *"Fuxue"* (Women's Learning) by the Qing official literatus, Zhang Xuecheng.

The visibility of female literacy and the intensity of the debate during the Qing is also reflected in the last book of *Nusishu*—*Nufan jielu* 女範捷錄 (Concise Selection of Model Women)—written by the compiler Wang Xiang's widowed mother, Liu, who devoted one entire chapter specifically to dealing with the issue of the compatibility between female talent and virtue. In the last chapter, "Talent and Virtue," woman Liu began by pointing out the inappropriateness of the common saying that trivializes the importance of virtue in women by equating the lack of talent with the possession of virtue. Possessing virtue by cultivating oneself should be the priority for both men and women. She then appealed to the authority of *Shijing*—the majority of the songs were written by women—to demonstrate that in ancient times women from all walks of life were learned as well as virtuous. She also cited numerous famous learned and talented women in history such as Ban Zhao of Han, the Song sisters of Tang, and Empress Wen of Ming as models of female respectability and virtue. In contrast, she argued, when women were illiterate they tend to overlook the rites, and hence they were neither learned nor virtuous. She then concluded that only when women were educated could they be proper in their conduct and be virtuous. Contrary to the common belief, literacy, in her view, made the observation of ritual propriety possible; female literacy brought out female virtue. In short, talent and virtue were not just compatible; they were, in fact, intertwined.

Just like Ban Zhao, woman Liu strongly advocated women's education. But unlike Ban Zhao, she had a strong sense of female agency and refused to hold women to a lower standard. A visible difference between Ban Zhao's *Nujie* and Liu's *Nufan jielu* is that the latter does not much concerned itself with household management, nor is it immersed in excessive humble rhetoric that naturalizes the lowly position of women. Instead, the *Nufan jielu*, which is composed of nine chapters, focuses more on the cultivation of virtues, with specific virtuous women in history as examples. For instance, in chapter 1, "Comprehensive Discussion" (*Tonglun*), she not only advocated women's education, but went further to say that girls' education was more important than boys' since one must proceed from the *nei* to the *wai*. Citing learned and talented empresses throughout history to demonstrate the importance of *nei* in sustaining a successful empire, woman Liu not only justified the appropriateness of female literacy, but furthermore elevated the status of *nei* by designating it as the necessary foundation of *wai*.

The same prioritization of *nei* over *wai* also appears in chapter 2, "Maternal Rectitude" (*Muyi*) which argues that maternal rectitude must precede paternal admonition since the youth is first educated by the mother. Chapter 3 discusses the nongender specific virtue of filiality and refuses to hold women to a lower standard, and argues that although men and women are different, as far as carrying out the virtue of filiality is concerned they are the same. Chapter 5, "Loyalty and Appropriateness" (*Zhongyi*), points out that these virtues should be applied to women as well, since, like men, women are the lord's subject. In sum, what the *Nufan jielu* demonstrates is a subtle change in women's own perception of themselves and the impact of female literacy justified in the form of conservative instruction books and women's biographies. Although the conservative "female texts and biographies" were a source for reenforcing orthodox values of gender propriety in women, they were also a source of empowerment through which women became self-affirmative in their historical consciousness.

The rise of female literacy and engagement in reading, writing, and publishing implicitly challenged orthodox gender propriety in the realm of *nei*, since in the traditional account the true calling of a virtuous woman primarily rested on her self-sacrifice and fidelity to patrilineage rather than on her personal need to explore her literary talent. Unlike her male counterpart in the realm of *wai*, her literary talent in the *nei* was inconsequential. In other words, without a legitimate access to the civil service examination system, which ultimately led to officialdom, women's pursuit of literacy was at best superfluous to their gender identity. Yet the increasing commercial publication of illustrated instruction books and romance in fiction aimed at female readers and the increasing demand for private tutors for women in the gentry class during the late Ming and early Qing periods sparked an intense debate on the propriety of female literacy and its compatibility with the orthodox four virtues (*side*), especially the virtue of women's speech (*fuyan*). It is in this debate that we see the conservative reading of the canonical tradition on the one hand, and women's own interpretation and justification for female literacy without overstepping the bound of ritual propriety, on the other.

THE QUESTION OF FEMALE LITERACY AND THE VIRTUE OF WOMEN'S SPEECH (*FUYAN*)

Perhaps the most influential essay written on the question of female literacy is "*Fuxue*" (Women's Learning) by the Qing official literatus, Zhang Xuecheng (1738–1801 CE). The popularity of this essay reflects, among other things, the visibility of female literacy and a shared conservative sentiment among official literati against some progressive yet unorthodox literati, such as the poet Yuan Mei, who freely admitted and intermingled with female pupils and actively sought out women's poems for publication. Before venturing into the details of Zhang Xuecheng's argument, one thing should be pointed out: Zhang's "*Fuxue*" was as much an essay on the propriety of women's learning as a bitter, personal attack on Yuan Mei. He was a popular poet-critic who saw the function of poetry as merely an entertainment without any moral import and who daringly admitted a fair number of talented female students into his poetry writing and publishing circle, and at the same time crossed the boundary of gender propriety by getting involved with at least three of his female students.³¹ Keeping the provocation of Yuan Mei's unorthodox literary theories and his unconventional, hedonistic lifestyle in mind, the aim in Zhang's "*Fuxue*" to restore classical learning and gender propriety becomes more understandable.

Zhang's intent to restore classical learning as opposed to Yuan Mei's "women's learning" is, first of all, shown in the title of his essay. The term *fuxue* (women's learning) was first used by Yuan Mei to signify the study of women's poetry, which took the *Shijing* (Book of Songs) as a model.³² By implication, Yuan Mei seemed to reduce women's learning to poetry writing alone without properly understanding the moral import of *Shijing* embedded in its historical contexts and commentaries throughout history. It was Yuan Mei's unorthodox approach to women's learning and to learning poetry in general that Zhang was most strongly objecting to. In Zhang's "*Fuxue*," he began by pointing out that, in ancient times, women's learning referred to four different areas: virtue, speech, comportment, and work (i.e., the four virtues, *side*); in contrast, contemporary women's learning had been reduced to literary arts alone (i.e., poetry writing and reading). But in ancient times, only those women who were well versed in classical ritual and accomplished in letters could be considered as learned.³³ By implication, Zhang was attacking Yuan Mei's literary theory, which dismisses the relevance of historical contexts and ritual propriety in the study of poetry. Zhang as an official Confucian scholar intended to bring back classical study in women's learning where in one's correct understanding of ritual must precede one's engagement in literary arts.

The main issue for Zhang on the question of female literacy, just as for most Qing scholars,³⁴ was not so much whether women should be educated, or whether women had the intellectual ability to receive classical training, since he repeatedly appealed to numerous talented and learned women in history, such as Ban Zhao of Han, and the famous Song poets and painters—Li Qingzhao and Guan Daosheng—as examples of female respectability and virtue. The question for Zhang, rather, was more what constitutes learning and for what aim. The literary trend of expressing personal emotions and romantic feelings through poetry, compounded with the institutionalized palace culture of dancing girls and courtesans since the Tang dynasty, had in Zhang's eye, devalued women's learning into entertainment and triviality. The popularity of the courtesan culture where top courtesans were often well versed in poetry had helped blur the line between the respectable and the base, especially if women's respectability was measured according to their literary talent alone. Yuan Mei's teaching, which emphasized free expression of one's inner feelings through poetry writing without first observing ritual propriety, was, to Zhang, not worthy of bearing the name of "women's learning." Yuan Mei overlooked the normative distinction between men and women—that is, *nei-wai* distinction—by freely admitting and being improperly involved with his female students, and that in Zhang's eye had rendered Yuan Mei into the level of bestiality undeserving of the name of an erudit.³⁵

Genuine women's learning, according to Zhang, must encompass the four virtues—virtue, comportment, speech, and work (*de, rong, yan, gong*). Among the *side*, sage *de* is too elusive, and *gong*, expressed in weaving and spinning, is too commonly obtained. It is *yan* (speech) and *rong* (comportment, conduct), according to Zhang, that are the most important female virtues to be cultivated. These two virtues, in turn, are interwoven with the two classics, the *Book of Songs*, and the *Book of Rites*. According to the traditional commentaries the *Songs* provides a basic training for literacy and the *Rites* for ritual conduct. And of these two, according to Zhang, learning proper ritual conduct must take precedence over the study of poetry:

> As for women's speech (*fuyan*), its emphasis is on the mastery of speech (*ciming* 辭命). [Yet] in ancient times, words do not pass from the inner quarter to the outside world. [Hence] what is called the mastery of speech (*ciming*) is also a fundamental characteristic of ritually correct literary art. Confucius once said: 'Without learning the *Book of Songs*, one has nothing to say.' This means there is no one who is good at mastering speech without having a deep understanding of the *Book of Songs*. And this makes it clear that in women's learning one must begin by learning ritual and then move to comprehending poetry.... The women's learning of ancient times always begins with the rites and then poetry. The women's learning of today is the reverse; it uses poetry to destroy the rites.[36]

In other words, without understanding ritual propriety, one's learning of poetry only leads one astray. The virtue of *fuyan* to Zhang, unlike to Yuan Mei, is not limited to one's mastery of literary arts and techniques, but, more importantly, it signifies one's mastery of rites, since only within rites can one's erudition in the classics as well as literary arts be properly expressed without overstepping the bound of gender propriety marked by the distinction between the *nei* and the *wai*.

The question of women's learning in the late Ming and early Qing is really a question of gender propriety. And, according to the normative distinction between genders marked by the *nei-wai* distinction, literacy in the realm of *nei*—a woman's sphere proper—is marginal if not inconsequential to women's gender identity. The realm of *nei*, as Susan Mann characterized it, is really a realm of silence,[37] since women's words, according to the rites, must stop at the door of the inner chambers. The seclusion of *nei* as well as women's functionary gender role not only makes literary learning inaccessible to women, but also makes it unnecessary from the ritual viewpoint. Although it is true that mothers are traditionally responsible for providing basic education for their young, women's education is often limited to a basic and practical training for domestic skills of weaving and cooking, rather than a comprehensive study of the canon, six arts, and statecraft. The limited scope of women's education is a logical fallout of the *nei-wai* distinction as a functional distinction, if one takes into account the fact that without a legitimate access to the civil service examination system, which ultimately leads to officialdom in the realm of *wai*, women's advanced literacy is destined to triviality. Learning and writing, according to the orthodox view, must have a public and ethical function. Unlike their male counterparts, talented and learned women have no legitimate access to the *wai* realm where their talents can be utilized by the state and hence their advanced literacy can be justified. Due to the lack of justification, women's advanced literacy is often viewed as a useless social surplus irrelevant to their gender identity or to the public good.

The possession of literary talent by women is indeed tragic in nature. Women with advanced literacy surpassing their brothers or husbands, yet without a legitimate outlet to utilize their talents, bring sorrow rather than honor to the family. The tragic nature of women's advanced literacy is a shared sentiment among learned women whose surplus literary talent is an obstacle rather than a means to contentment in life. Liang Lanyi—a Qing poet—in her poem "Teaching My Daughter" (*kenu* 課女) wrote: "How unhappy and unfortunate a life has your mother been leading?/ I have been suffering from knowing and learning too much./ Four virtues *(side)* and three followings *(sanchong)* are forever the most important guidance for women./ That's why I have been teaching you these sorts of conduct industriously./ You should learn to be gentle and tender, act in a womanly way./ All other insignificant skills should be given up."[38] Learned and accomplished women poets, such as Liang Lanyi whose poem eventually was published in *Guixiu zheng shiiji*—a Qing anthology of women's poetry—were torn between the fame of poetry writing and their gender sphere of *nei*, where advanced literacy served no practical purpose at all.

The conflicting feeling of learned women toward their own "insignificant" literary skills is a sign of the unspoken conflict between women's gender identity in the realm of *nei* and the pursuit of literary learning in the realm of *wai*. It is plain that literacy and writing in general properly speaking belong to the realm of *wai*. *Wen* 文 (literary learning), which ultimately leads to one's engagement in *zheng* 政 (governance), is a male privilege proper. The constraints of the *nei* and the *wai* imposed on women as gender beings ultimately underpin the problem of gender disparity in premodern China where women of all classes must constantly yield to the wish of the patrilineal family. The *nei-wai* gender division of labor not only reduces women's function in the patrilineal family to their reproductive capacity, but also denies women of all classes a legitimate access to vital cultural resources that are needed for the cultivation of the consummated Confucian personhood, which marks the substance of being one's own person in the world.

Since the realm of *nei* symbolically is also a realm of concealment, Zhang's objection to Yuan Mei's teaching and publishing women's poetry can be interpreted as the orthodox defense of the normative gender boundary according to which literacy in the realm of *nei* must be concealed from the public eye. Due to the silent and nonliterary nature of *nei*, the ultimate model of a virtuous and respectful woman for Zhang is a woman at rest; that is, a woman that is secluded in the familial realm of *nei* and is concealed in the literary, public realm of *wai*: "A woman who is good is called a 'woman at rest' (*jingnu* 靜女). To be at rest is close to learning. Today those that are so called 'talented women' (*cainu* 才女)—how they move about! How they make a dreadful racket."[39] In other words, female virtue and respectability, first and foremost, are measured in accordance with gender propriety, which is marked by the seclusion of *nei*, not one's literary skills. And since writing and publishing belong to the realm of *wai*, they are not the true calling of a virtuous and respectable woman. By implication, although Zhang, like most of his contemporary scholars in the early Qing, did not object to women's learning and writing per se, a respectable woman should then concentrate on ritual propriety in the nonliterary realm of *nei*, and be silent about her literary talents, which properly speaking belong to the public realm of *wai*.

Despite the popularity of Zhang's "*Fuxue*," the number of women's publications reached an unprecedented, historic height during the Qing dynasty. It might be difficult to imagine how learned women during this time reconciled the conflicting demand between the public act of poetry writing and publishing and the seclusion of the nonliterary realm of *nei*. First of all, learned women such as woman Liu—author of the didactic text *Nufan jielu*—repudiated the conflicting nature of talent and virtue in women as indicated in the common Ming saying, "A woman without talent is virtuous." In the learned women's eye, to be virtuous, that is to be within the bounds of ritual propriety, one must be literate at the minimal level. Without being literate and being aware of ancient rites recorded in the canonical texts, as woman Liu argued, one is also ignorant about ritual propriety as well. Secondly, although advanced literacy is not required of women to carry out their domestic roles, learned women, by taking the female poets in the *Book of Songs* as their models, extended the traditional understanding of the virtue of *fuyan* (women's speech) from spoken words to written words. And the cultivation of *fuyan* as one of women's four virtues justifies women's engagement in literary learning. For just as women in ancient times recorded in the *Book of Songs* were both talented and virtuous, women of today can also be virtuous while at the same time possessing literary skills of poetry writing.

Women's use of the *Book of Songs* as a theoretical justification or "historical" precedent to legitimize their engagement in literary arts is demonstrated in the preface of the *Guochao guixiu zhengshi ji*, an anthology of Qing women's poetry. Yun Zhu, a female Qing poet, boldly wrote: "Long ago when Confucius edited the *Book of Songs*, he did not eliminate writings from the women's quarters. But teachers of later times have spoken of women's highest role as limited to ritual acts, such as the pouring of libations.... They do not understand that in ancient ritual texts... women's learning and women's attributes were transmitted by women's speech (*yan*). To be sure, speech does not refer explicitly to essays and written phrases, but it must not depart far from written words. If view the problem this way, what could we find wrong with women studying or writing poetry?"[40] First, Yun Zhu rejected the traditional ritual notion that "women's words do not pass the gate of the inner quarters," and hence she also rejected the silent nature of realm of *nei*. Second, by appealing to women's voices preserved in the *Book of Songs*, she extended *fuyan* (women's speech) from its traditional understanding as spoken words to written words. In so doing, she justified the act of studying and writing poetry in the realm of *nei*. Advanced literary learning was thereby made compatible with female virtue and respectability.

But for some, the talented, learned model of womanhood shown through the transmission of women's poetry in the *Book of Songs* seems to be in conflict with the ritually bound womanhood praised in the *Book of Rites*. Since unlike their male counterparts whose consummated personhood encompasses the familial as well as the political realm, women of all classes must, first of all, derive their normative womanhood from their conformity to ritual propriety in the realm of *nei*. That is to say, the true calling of a virtuous woman must reside in her gender roles confined to the functionary, familial realm of *nei*. The proper distinction between genders where man is in charge of the *wai* and woman the *nei* marks the boundary between civility and barbarianism. When such a normative, ritual boundary between man and woman is violated, one consequently falls below socially sanctioned humanity and into bestiality. For instance, the lack of proper gender distinctions in his dealing with female pupils as an animal behavior was exactly what Zhang criticized Yuan Mei of.[41] The controversy in Zhang's essay is not so much concerned with women's learning or their intellectual ability as with what defines genuine womanhood. Apparently, women and men of high power during the Qing period appealed to two different models of womanhood found in the *Book of Songs* and the *Book of Rites* and thereby justified or objected to the popular trend of women's writing and publishing poetry in their time.

In any case, for both men and women the orthodoxy of the ritual boundary of the *nei* and the *wai* remains unchallenged. In other words, whether learned or not, women must first and foremost derive their gender identity from the familial roles in the *nei*, and only by extension can women's engagement in literary arts be justified. The weight of the ritual boundary of the *nei* and the *wai* in assessing female virtue and respectability is evident not just in theory but also in historical reality. Ban Zhao is a perfect example. Ban Zhao's literary achievement and her political engagement in the Han court are well documented. At first sight, Ban Zhao seemed to violate the ritual boundary of the *nei* and the *wai*, since unlike the virtuous woman who was bound to her limited familial roles in the realm of *nei* prescribed in the *Nujie*, Ban Zhao traversed the gender boundary into the realm of *wai*—that is, into the male domains of literature and politics, or the realm of *wen* (culture) and *zheng* (governance). Yet, instead of condemning her, conservative official literati as well as learned women throughout imperial histories took Ban Zhao as the ultimate model of female virtue and respectability. This is so because in the eye of the conservative literati, Ban Zhao's womanhood was first secured by her early widowhood, which conformed to the ancient virtues of female chastity and wifely fidelity to the patrilineage. Second, her contribution to the completion of *Hanshu* was justified as a filial act, that is, as carrying out the family project after the death of her brother Ban Gu, rather than a personal search for fame in the literary realm of *wai*. Third, her requested assistance to Empress Deng during the empress's twenty-year regency on behalf of the child emperor was viewed as an act of political loyalty to the Han court from Ban Zhao's prominent family, rather than a search for personal gain during the fragile transition of power. In sum, Ban Zhao's involvement in literature and politics were justified through an extension of her gender roles in the realm of *nei* as a filial daughter who illuminated her family literary tradition and a chaste widow who remained faithful to her husband's family despite her early widowhood. But unlike her male counterparts, her achievement in the literary and political realm could not be justified solely on the ground of personal fulfillment fundamental to her gender identity in its own right.

It is, then, clear that although the ritual boundaries between the *nei* and the *wai*, demonstrated in numerous works, overlap and are subject to negotiation in different contexts, they also mark the beginning of one's humanity and civility; women are identified with the limited realm of *nei*, and men the all-comprehensive realm of *wai*. The womanly sphere of *nei*, by and large, is a realm of practical household management, wifely servitude, and undying fidelity to the patrilineage. Although advanced literary skills as demonstrated in numerous women's biographies, didactic texts written for and by women, as well as the unprecedented number of publications of women's writings in the late Qing, are not incompatible with the demand of ritual propriety, they are superfluous and inconsequential to women's gender identity, which must, first and foremost, be grounded in functionary, familial kinship roles.

The possession of literary talent in women is tragic in nature, since, unlike men, who are located in the realm of *wai* in which nonfamilial, public roles may be realized, women's literary talent has no legitimacy. Consequently, a woman might possess de facto recognized talent, yet her talent, because of her gender role, cannot be legitimately utilized by the state on its own behalf without first being disguised as an extension of her gender and familial roles, as shown in the case of Ban Zhao. Viewed in this light, the problem of gender disparity in imperial China can be said to be derivative from the functional gender distinction of the *nei-wai*. The disparity between the realm of *nei* and the realm of *wai* is therefore also the beginning of gender disparity between men and women. However, one thing must be borne in mind: unlike the West where the category of "woman" in the dominant philosophical tradition from Aristotle, Augustine, Kant, to Nietzsche is marked by her insufficient intellectual capacity,[42] womanhood in China is not marked by lack of rationality or will. Instead, a Chinese woman is marked by her limiting womanly sphere of *nei*, which conceals her intellectual capacity and renders it into a superfluous skill. Hence, women, whether learned or not in imperial China, are essentially nameless ones who are outside the realm of culture, that is, outside of the realm of rememberence in which one's name and one's good name are remembered and passed on.

CHAPTER SIX

CHINESE SEXISM AND CONFUCIANISM

Given the complexity and ambiguity of *Ru* or "Confucianism" discussed in chapter 2, how is it possible to identify a definitive connection between Chinese sexist practices and Confucianism as a polysemous symbol of Chinese high culture? Early feminists' portrait of Confucianism as a unified, sexist ideology through and through is surely a misappropriation and oversimplification of *Ru*. The link of Confucianism to sexism in early scholarship is mostly focused on a few statements made either by Confucius himself or by *Ru* literati. Most notably, Confucius's analogy between young girls and morally deficient "small persons" is said to be a statement about women's nature. Han *Ru* Dong Zhongshu's base *yin* and venerable *yang* is taken to be an indication of the inferiority of the feminine and the superiority of the masculine. Song *Ru* Chen Yi's statement on widow chastity is treated as an absolute doctrine. In the *Liji*, passages dealing with the *nei-wai* distinction are interpreted as a rigid separation between private and public or a physical segregation between genders. There might be some truth in feminists' accusation of the sexist nature of Confucianism, given the coexistence of Confucianism as the emblem of Chinese high culture with the persistent patriarchal and patrilineal tradition in Chinese society. But by equating some ritual texts or some *Ru*'s sexist comments with Confucianism as a whole and then Confucianism with sexism, one arrives at two dangerous conclusions: first, one is in effect making the removal of Confucianism a necessary and sufficient condition for gender equality in China, and second, one is committing oneself to a logical fallacy that negates the worth of a philosophy based on a few statements made by the philosopher.

As regards the logical fallacy, it is important that one separates the philosophy from the philosopher at least at the theoretical level in order to assess the worth of a philosophy. Feminists' and sinologists' assessments of the worth of Confucian ethics by and large focus on the lack of a positive model of woman in historical narratives. Lisa Raphals in her essay "A Woman Who Understood the Rites" went a step farther; she attempted to point out the subtle sexist nature of Confucianism even in the context of Confucius's praise for two virtuous women. She cited Confucius's encounters with two virtuous women, one prominent older woman—Jing Jiang—from the powerful family of Ji in the state of Lu, and one poor servant-girl—the girl of Agu—as examples. Despite Confucius's repeated praises for both women found in pre-Han and Han texts, Raphals argued, in the historical narrative Confucius and those virtuous, learned women did not stand in a benefactor/beneficiary relation, which was reserved for his male disciples only.[1] In other words, Confucius only talked about women by using them as objects for moral instruction, but did not talk to women who were not proper subjects of instruction. Based on these two examples, Raphals, despite her own caution about deriving any certainty from them, went on to say that "they do provide the uncomfortable suggestion that Confucius' views on human perfectibility and self-cultivation may have spanned social class, but not gender."[2] Yet the absence of a benefactor/beneficiary relationship between Confucius and women in the historical narrative by itself does not need to be interpreted as indicating the impossibility of self-cultivation for women to achieve virtuous personhood. In other words, the worth of Confucian ethics should not be decided based solely on the lack of an explicit reference to women as virtuous *junzi* in historical narratives. Otherwise, the same critique can be applied to almost all prominent Western philosophers, such as Aristotle, Kant, and Nietzsche, to name a few, whose ethical theories are nonetheless by and large assessed independently of their obvious sexist attitude toward, as well as writings on, women.

For instance, Aristotle wrote in the *Generation of Animals*: "[T]he female is as it were a deformed male," and in *Politics*, woman's rationality is said to be less effective than man's.[3] Based on these remarks, one might say that a woman due to her defective nature is incapable of exercising intellectual contemplation in the Aristotelian world. The same exclusion of the possibility of female participation in the realm of ethics is also present in Kant's writings. Kant in his *Observations on the Feeling of the Beautiful and Sublime* made the distinction between genders where in woman is said to be the fair sex who has a beautiful understanding that deals with concrete appearance and man the noble sex who by nature has a deep understanding that deals with abstract reasoning. A woman, due to her nature, according to Kant, should learn no geometry, physics, or philosophy. "A woman who has a head full of Greek ... or carries on fundamental controversies about mechanics ... might as well even have a beard." And of the principle of sufficient reason, as Kant advised, "she will know only so much as is needed to perceive the salt in a satire ..."[4] Since woman by nature is incapable of having a deep understanding and exercising abstract reasoning, woman is also incapable of understanding Kant's ethics of principle. And hence Kant's deontology can be said to preclude the possibility of female participation in the realm of ethics as well.

Likewise, in Nietzsche's writings, where will power is deemed as the basis of self-transformation, woman is perceived as lacking the will power that can be exercised by man. As stated in the essay "Of Womenkind, Old and Young": "Man's happiness is, I will. Woman's happiness is, He will."[5] Woman's desire to become equal to man, according to Nietzsche, is "one of the worst developments of the general *uglification* of Europe." Furthermore, Nietzsche was unconvinced that woman can will her enlightenment: "Whatever women write about 'woman,' we may in the end reserve a healthy suspicion whether woman really *wants* enlightenment about herself—whether she *can* will it—"[6] (emphasis original) Hence, woman, the weaker sex, as Nietzsche called it, should be treated as a possession, as property that can be locked up, the way they are treated by the *Orientals*.[7] (emphasis original) In this, one might say, not only is Nietzsche's writing sexist but also racist as well. Yet despite the obvious sexist components in all three philosophers' writings, scholars continue to affirm the validity of Aristotelian virtue ethics, Kantian deontology, and Nietzsche's existential ethics. Therefore, by the same token, the validity of the Confucian virtue of *ren* that signifies the ideal personhood through self-cultivation can also be assessed independently of the lack of benefactor/beneficiary relationship between Confucius and women or explicit sexist remarks made by *Ru* scholars in historical narratives.[8]

As for the first commitment to making the removal of Confucianism the necessary condition to achieve gender equality, Confucianism has been an easy target and a scapegoat for the oppression of Chinese women. This view is shared by both Western feminists and the Chinese gentry in the late Qing period and the early days of the Republic. Anti-Confucian sentiment ran high during the May Fourth movement in 1919, which was an intellectual movement for a new literary style turned political, or rather a political movement of literati urging replacement of the old literary style, which was for them symbolic of the sickness and the corruption of the Qing imperial court. The purge of Confucianism continued in Communist China during the 1940s, and reached its height during the Communist Cultural Revolution of the late 1960s to the early 1970s. The renewal of the study in Confucianism did not emerge until in the late 1980s and early 1990s. After the fall of the last imperial dynasty, Qing, Confucianism was no longer the dominant intellectual force in state politics. Yet early feminists generally agree that Communist China is far from being a sexually egalitarian society, even though, in its political rhetoric, it explicitly rejects Confucianism in favor of an egalitarian communist utopia. The removal and purge of Confucianism, as if it were a fixed, sexist, feudal ideology frozen in time in the political arena, did not result in gender equality in China.

The root of women's oppression in China runs deeper than Confucianism as a state ideology. Confucianism is more than a state ideology for the learned social and political elites; its connection, if there is any, with gender oppression in everyday life must be found instead in the institution of the family where the Confucian emphasis on the familial virtue of filial piety, the continuity of the family name, and ancestor worship are more of a way of life. The Confucian virtue of familial continuity is a regulatory ideal that underpins the very concept of civility and hence humanity. In other words, the root of gender oppression in China must be sought within the institution of the family where the convergence of these three cultural imperatives reinforced in Confucian familial virtue ethics—the continuity of the family name, filial piety, and ancestor worship—serves as a powerful basis for generating, sustaining, and justifying the social abuse of women. In the following, we will begin our journey into the connection between Confucian virtue ethics and Chinese sexism by examining specific social practices such as female infanticide, child-bride/child-servant, concubinage, widow chastity, and footbinding, where the complex intersection among patrilineage, ancestor worship, filial piety, and the power of *wen* forms the cultural basis for gender oppression in China.

GENDER OPPRESSION AND CONFUCIAN VIRTUE ETHICS

Despite the obviously "sexist" orientation of social practices such as female infanticide, child-bride/child-servant, and concubinage in the eyes of modern readers, our starting point in the study of gender oppression in China will go beyond the simplistic "gender conspiracy" theory that views all men as the oppressors and women the oppressed. We begin with the assumption that those social practices have substantial cultural and social meanings to all the participants in a given community, and the continuation of a "sexist" practice is sanctioned by both men and women, despite its general negative effect on and implications for women. In other words, in what follows women are not seen as mindless victims uniformly oppressed by men: both women and men are perceived as active participants in justifying, sustaining, and perpetuating identifiable "sexist" practices to conform to social and cultural ideals. By keeping the three cultural imperatives in mind—the continuity of the family name, ancestor worship, and filial piety—the social practices of female infanticide, child-bride/child-servant, and concubinage may become more intelligible. Because the male is privileged as the sole bearer of the family name in a patrilineal system, which is coded with the religious practice of ancestor worship and the virtue of filial piety, the importance of the female is reduced to her success in perpetuating the family line by producing a male heir. The purely functional role of women in relation to the whole cultural scheme of prioritizing male descendants is especially illuminating in the case of female infanticide and concubinage.

Although it is uncertain how widespread the practice of female infanticide was in Chinese society in comparison with others,[9] the cultural preference for a boy is evident in the symbolic gesture of instituting different ritual items to symbolize the birth of a boy and a girl in the canonical text *Liji*. The social practice of female infanticide can be found as early as in the late Qin and early Han text, *Hanfeizi*: "[I]f a boy is born, the parents congratulate each other, if a girl is born, they kill her. [Both boys and girls] all come from the same parents, yet boys are celebrated, girls are killed; this is because they [i.e., the parents] consider the benefits (of having a boy) in the long run."[10] The regularity of the practice of female infanticide can also be inferred from "*Family instructions for the Yan Clan*"—a sixth century text—written by prominent *Ru* official-scholar Yan Zhitui (531–591). He strongly condemned such practice: "Nowadays people do not want to raise girls; how could those who kill their own flesh and blood still expect blessings from heaven?"[11] Widespread or not, female infanticide, as hinted in the *Hanfeizi*, is a strategy to enlarge the possibility of acquiring a male child and reserving limited family resources for the upbringing of the male heir whose survival is directly linked to the survival of one's lineage and the aged parents.

For the same reason, taking a concubine when the original wife is infertile or fails to produce a male heir is not just socially acceptable; it is, rather, a cultural imperative. Failure to produce a male heir, according to Mencius, is the most unfilial deed. "There are three unfilial things, and having no descendants is the worst."[12] The importance of having a male heir is also reinforced in the legal/customary law of the "Seven Reasons for Expelling One's Wife" (*Qichu* 七出) sanctioned in Han texts such as the *Kongzi jiayu* and *Lienuzhuan*, according to these texts the failure to produce a male child constitutes a legitimate ground for expelling one's wife.[13] In theory, the only ethical reason for taking a concubine when one already has a legal wife is to produce a male child. The origin of concubinage, as explained in the Han text *Baihutong*, is to ensure the continuity of one's lineage. "Why is it that high officials (are entitled to) take one wife and two concubines? It is to honor their worthiness and to emphasize the importance of continuing their descendants." The number of concubines allotted to people of status is then hierarchically ranked: nine for the lord, two for high officials, and one for common officials.[14]

In practice, the wealthy often departed from such an ethical rationale. But concubinage was more than a sexual privilege of the rich and the powerful. The importance of having a male heir was considered an integral expression of the virtue of filial piety sanctioned by the state law. As early as in the Northern Wei (386–534), a state official even proposed making it an imperial decree that those without a male heir must take a concubine, or they must bear "the crime of being unfilial (不孝之罪)."[15] And later in the Yuan and Ming dynasties, the imperial law clearly stated that all commoners over forty years of age without a male heir must take a concubine for the sake of lineage.[16] Concubinage, hence, as sinologist Florence Ayscough wrote in the late 1930s, is a logical fallout of the family system and social structure that requires male descendants to conduct ancestor worship.[17] In this light, gender oppression in premodern China might be interpreted as being interconnected with filiality, patrilineality, and ancestor worship.

The intersection between gender oppression and Confucianism lies in the mutual reinforcement of these three cultural imperatives and Confucian virtue ethics, which takes the familial virtue of filial piety as the root of civic virtues. Filial piety is a recurring theme in ancient literatures such as the *Shujing* and *Shijing* as well as the Confucian *Four Books*. Filial devotion to one's family is inseparable from one's reverence toward one's forefathers—that is, one's lineage. At the minimum level, to be filial is to carry on the work of one's meritorious ancestors, to honor one's parents, and to continue one's lineage. For instance, the "Book of Shang" of *Shujing* says: "O King zealously cultivate your virtue; regard the example of your meritorious ancestor. At no time allow yourself in please and idleness. When honoring our ancestors, think how to prove your filial piety (奉先思孝)."[18] Also, the "Book of Zhou" of *Shujing* says: "Uncle Yihe, you render still more glorious your illustrious ancestor. You are the first to imitate the example of Wen and Wu [i.e. Zhou sage-kings], collecting the scattered powers, and continuing the all-but-broken line of your sovereign. Your filial piety goes back to your accomplished ancestor, and is equal to his . . ."[19] In the same vein, King Wu was praised for walking in the ways of his forefathers in the *Shijing*: "Successors tread in the steps [of their predecessors] in our Zhou; for generations there had been wise kings . . . and King Wu was their worthy successor in his capital. . . . He secured the confidence due to a king and became the pattern of all below him, ever thinking how to be filial, his filial mind was the model. . . . Ever thinking how to be filial, he brilliantly continued the doings [of his forefather]."[20] In the *Classics*, filial piety and the continuation of one's meritorious lineage are viewed as inseparable.

It is important to note that, for Confucius, filial piety is not just a private virtue limited and only applicable to the institution of the family. For instance, in the *Analects*, filial piety is perceived as the root of the moral character of exemplary persons in the political realm. "It is rare for someone who has a sense of filial and fraternal responsibility to have a taste for defying authority. And it is unheard of for those who have no taste for defying authority to be keen on initiating rebellion. Exemplary persons concentrate their efforts on the root, for the root having taken hold, the way will grow therefrom. As for filial and fraternal responsibility, it is, I suspect, the root of *ren* (仁)" (1.2). Filial piety in the familial realm is the basis for one's moral capacity in the political realm. This connection is also demonstrated in the case of King Wu in the *Shijing*, quoted earlier, where King Wu's filial piety was directly linked to his moral capacity to carry on the meritorious works of his forefather in securing the kingdom. It is true that the focus of one's filial devotion must start with one's parents; the field of filial piety, however, extends far beyond the family into the state. Filial piety in the Han classic *Xiaojing* (Book of Filial Piety) begins by serving one's parents in the familial realm and culminates in one's service to the state in the political realm in order to honor one's parents and to illuminate one's lineage.[21] In short, filial piety is the training ground for the broader political virtue of doing one's utmost in serving the state.

Furthermore, filial piety does not require an absolute obedience or submission to the will of one's parents. For instance, the sage-king Shun defied his wicked father in marriage, yet King Shun is considered exemplary in the virtue of filial piety.[22] Being filial has more to do with doing what is proper and good in serving one's parents than doing what one is told regardless of the consequences. Contrary to the marriage rite, King Shun did not inform his wicked father of his marriage to King Yao's two daughters, and his act of defiance was justified on the ground that the father would have opposed the marriage, and then the Shun lineage would have had no one to carry on. King Shun did what is proper and good instead of adhering to the wish of the wicked father, and therefore he was most filial of all.

A filial son has a duty to defy the wishes of his parents, just as a good minister must defy the commands of the ruler in times of impropriety. As Xunzi wrote in regard to the proper way of being a son, "There are three reasons why a filial son should not follow the parents' command: first, if it endangers the parents; second, if it brings shame to the parents; and third, if it renders one's parents beast-like [i.e. uncivil]." As Xunzi explained, great filial piety consists in this: "Following the way (of the sage and worthy) instead of the ruler, following what is proper instead of the father."[23] Similarly, in the *Xiaojing*, we learn that to admonish one's parents when they are at fault is the duty of a filial son, just as a good minister has the duty to admonish his ruler.[24] Great filial piety, as illuminated in the case of King Shun, noted Mencius, consists in King Shun's ability to reform his wicked father to find delight in what is good and thereby transform the whole empire so that both father and son are able to fulfill their respective duties (i.e., father affectionate, son filial).[25]

Filial piety, whether familial or political, is construed as a fundamental virtue. As stated in the *Shujing* and echoed in the *Xiaojing*, being unfilial toward one's parents or disrespectful toward elder brothers is considered the greatest crime.[26] To be filial to one's parents and to one's deceased ancestors is seen as the minimal qualification of personal moral worth. As stated in the *Mencius*, "One who could not get the hearts of his parents could not be considered a person; one who could not get to an entire accord with his parents could not be considered a son."[27] One's filial devotion to one's parents is indicative of one's humanity. To be filial to one's parents, however, means more than one's ability to provide them with food. As Confucius said, "Those today who are filial are considered so because they are able to provide for their parents. But even dogs and horses are given that much care. If you do not respect your parents, what is the difference?" (*Lunyu* 2.7). The meaning of filial piety consists in complying with the rite in serving one's parents when they are alive, complying with the rite in mourning them, and complying with the rite in sacrificing to them, when they die (cf. *Lunyu* 2.5). Similarly, in the *Liji*, one reads, "As for a filial son to serve the parents, there are three ways: provide them when they are alive, bury them when they die and worship them after the burial."[28] A similar account of filial piety is also stated in the *Xiaojing*.[29] All in all, one's filial piety, as the root of one's humanity, is in effect intertwined with the mourning ritual as well as the sacrificial ceremony of ancestor worship.

The importance of ancestor worship and the three-year mourning ritual is evident in the marriage rite where the purpose of marriage as explained in the ritual text, *Liji*, is to ensure, first, the sacrificial ceremony in the ancestral temple and, second, the continuation of the family line.[30] Given these two as the chief purposes for taking a wife, it is not surprising to note that the status of a wife is also defined by them as well. In particular, the status of a wife, who is different from a concubine, is chiefly marked by the wife's ritual duty to assist her husband in preparing for a sacrificial ceremony in the ancestral hall. A concubine is construed as a helper of the principal wife, since the only ritual required of a concubine when entering the household of her master is to serve tea to the principal wife.[31] Symbolically, a concubine is the extension of the principal wife, and therefore she shares the function of the principal wife in perpetuating male descendants. In some cases, it is the principal wife who arranges the purchase of a concubine for the sake of the husband's lineage. For instance, prominent Song *Ru*, Sima Guang, whose principal wife and her sister, despite his indifference, acquired a concubine for him since he had no sons.[32]

However, a concubine is not allowed to replace the principal wife in handling the sacrificial ceremony in the ancestral hall, neither is she allowed to directly serve the husband's parents, since both duties belong exclusively to the legal wife who is considered part of the patrilineage proper.[33] Ancestor worship is the chief duty of the principal wife, whose status is in turn defined by her participation in the worshipping. In fact, according to the traditional account, the consummation of a marriage is marked by the ritual act of presenting one's wife to the ancestors in the temple. As explained in the *Baihutong*, "After the wife has been in [her husband's home] for three months, she takes part in the sacrifices [to the ancestors of her husband].... If a woman dies before she has been presented to [the ancestors of her husband in] the ancestral hall ... the body is returned to be interred in [the cemetery of] her kindred, which indicates that she has not yet become his wife in the full sense."[34] Moreover, according to the customary law—"Three Grounds that a Wife Cannot Be Expelled" (*Sanbuchu* 三不出)—stated in the *Kongzijiayu*, the wife's participation in the three-year mourning ritual for the in-laws constitutes one of the three compelling grounds that override the "Seven Reasons for Expelling One's Wife" (*Qichu* 七出).[35] In other words, the wife's participation in ancestor worship and the mourning ritual for the in-laws marks the permanent bond between the wife and the husband, and thereby her permanent status in the patrilineage. It is only by acquiring a permanent status in her husband's lineage that a woman finds her legitimate social place.

Without entering into a marriage, a woman is in fact without a permanent social place of her own. Given the importance of continuing one's lineage, marriage is the most important rite of passage not just for women alone but also for men. However, marriage defines the *only* legitimate social place for women, while this is not the case for men. This is to say, marriage is not just a marker of adulthood for both man and woman; but more specifically, it is also a marker of womanhood. For as argued in the *Yin-yang* chapter, in Chinese society, the category of "woman" describes the role of a wife and mother, and the role of a wife and mother are, in turn, perceived as constitutive of a woman's gender identity. These kinship roles are not external additions to the "core" concept of woman. It is only through occupying these roles that a woman becomes a socially recognizable woman. Marriage is the definitive marker of womanhood, and hence by definition an unmarried girl is, in a sense, not fully gendered. A daughter's staying in her natal family prior to her marriage is characterized by its temporality; she is, in a word, a woman-in-waiting, a person in transition.

A married woman is not allowed to worship the ancestors of her natal family. She is now like a stranger to her natal family and she is considered a kin of her husband's lineage instead. In marriage, her permanent status in her husband's lineage, in turn, is defined by her participation in ancestor worship and in giving birth to a male heir. Given those cultural constraints, it is clearly in women's best interest to participate in these social practices such as female infanticide and concubinage to ensure their permanent social place in their husband's lineages. By the same token, women must also participate in the practice of child-bride/child-servant where a mother-in-law typically takes in a young girl to be the future bride of her son thus ensuring the loyalty of her future daughter-in-law who, in turn, is destined to take over her role in producing a male heir for the patrilineage of which she is now a part. These three cultural imperatives—filial piety, ancestor worship, and the continuity of lineage—in Chinese sexist practices, in effect, converge into one basic demand placed on both genders.

Women's participation in prioritizing the production of a male heir to secure their place in a patrilineage inevitably reflects the nameless aspect of women's personhood, the aspect that is altogether outside the realm of *wai*, namely, the realm of literary learning, the realm of *wen*, the realm of ethical-political accomplishments, and the realm of remembrance, wherein one's family name and one's good name are passed on and remembered. The *nei-wai* distinction as gender distinction, together with the *Liji*'s definition of the purpose of marriage, renders a woman's presence in the family structure purely functional and substitutable. A woman's gender role as a wife and mother within the realm of *nei* bears no distinct mark of her own person; she is merely functional for the perpetuation of a male heir. Unlike her male counterpart who is a bearer of his family name and his own good name, a woman is a bearer of her kinship titles or general categorical terms in her husband's lineage. For instance, Ban Zhao of Han, despite her prominent natal family and her own literary and political accomplishments, is usually referred to as "Cao Dajia" (曹大家), in which her husband's surname Cao replaces her surname Ban, and her given name Zhao is then superseded by the honorary kinship title "*Dajia*" or "*Dagu*"—i.e., aunt.[36] In the end, a woman is referred to and remembered as a kin of her husband's lineage, and nothing more.

Yet, names in the Chinese world, as Rubie Watson observed, have a transformative power, since the process of naming provides an important social transition for men whose social growth is marked and expanded by naming.[37]

One's birthname marks the parent-child relation in which one's place in the lineage is first located; one's stylename signifies one's style in the world of letters; and one's official and posthumous titles indicate one's political accomplishments beyond the familial realm. Names mark one's outward relations with others and expand the field of one's personhood. The more names one has the fuller his achieved personhood becomes. In contrast, a woman as a person of *nei* or "*neiren*" 內人—a customary term that a man uses to refer to his wife—is nameless. Because of the confinement and the concealment of *nei*, women in general are outside the realm of personal achievements, and therefore the realm of remembrance. Whether as a daughter, wife, or mother, her social standing is entirely dependent on her male counterpart and she bears no distinct mark of her own person. Judged against the standard of men, as Watson argued, "women do not, indeed cannot, attain full personhood."[38]

The nameless aspect of women's personhood is not just limited to illiterate peasant women. Women since ancient times regardless of their social status are the ones who are without ranks (i.e., official titles). As explained in the *Baihutong*, "Why is it that a wife has no rank (or title)? It is because the lowly *yin* has no business in the *wai*. For this reason, it is proper for her to have the 'threefold following.' When she is not yet married she follows her father; once married she follows her husband; after the death of the husband she follows her son. Therefore when the husband attains honor at court, the wife [also] attains glory at home; she follows in the wake of her husband." This is why in the *Liji* it says, as the *Baihutong* goes on to explain, "The wife has no rank, she takes her seat according to the position that belongs to her husband." Those without rank during their life do not receive a posthumous title after their death either.[39] Consequently, women are entirely dependent beings that are not allowed any formal means to acquire social honors in the realm of *wai*, including *wen* which, in turn, can be seen as the privilege of the male.

Wen 文 (the way of culture) as opposed to *wu* 武 (the way of force) is an exclusively male privilege. Kam Louie and Louise Edwards in their theorization of *wen* and *wu* as Chinese masculinity have made clear that, unlike in the West, *wu* (martial art) is not an index of "maleness."[40] In comparison with *wen* (a civil and refined way of being), *wu* is a lesser form of masculinity, if you will. Although there is a persistent emphasis on the balance between *wen* and *wu* in the self-cultivation of exemplary person according to *Ru*, the preference for *wen* over *wu* is evident in the traditional representation of Confucius, the first and foremost sage teacher, as the cultural icon of *wen*. *Ru* learning is understood as a learning of the sages and worthies whose virtuous governance in the narratives of the ancient tradition relies not on *wu* (physical force) but rather on *wen* (humane governing). *Ru* learning, like *wen* learning that models itself after sagely humane governance, reinforces the complex correlation between *wen*, governance, and the realm of *wai*. *Wen*, in short, is a male privilege proper.

Wen as a male privilege is most noticeable in the institution of the civil service examination system that excludes all women whether learned or not from the participation in an exam that is by and large based on the literary learning of the *Five Classics* and the Confucian *Four Books*. But in comparison with *wen*, *wu* (the mastery of martial art) is in fact more accessible to women, a marked contrast to the situation in the West. In Chinese historical narratives, there are numerous celebrated female generals or heroines recognized by the imperial court, such as Princess Pingyang of Tang, Liang Hungyu of Song, Shen Yunying and Qin Liangyu of Ming, Lin Puqing of Qing. The legends of Hua Mulan of the sixth–seventh century, and Mu Guiying of the tenth–eleventh century are popular tales told and retold through dramas and plays even today.[41] However, there has been no female prime minister—the highest civil post in the imperial court—in Chinese history. Even Ban Zhao, who served as master to the subsequent male court historians and mentor to the high court ladies including the empress, was never granted an official title in the outer court; her contribution to the completion of the dynastic history of the Former Han after the death of her brother was also unrecognized. The exclusion of women from the realm of *wai* not only conceals women's involvement in state affairs, but also renders women's literary talent superfluous, a social surplus, without any ethical-political functions. And that concealment in turn reinforces the purely functional role of woman as wife and mother—as producer of male descendants—in order to fulfill these three cultural imperatives: filial piety, ancestor worship, and the continuation of patrilineage.

CASE STUDIES: WIDOWHOOD AND FOOTBINDING

At first sight, the cult of widowhood, which reached its height during the Ming and Qing periods, and the practice of footbinding, which lasted for a thousand years, seem incidental to the whole cultural scheme of prioritizing the production of a male heir for the sake of one's lineage. In the case of the cult of widowhood, especially the canonization of a sonless widow, or a young bride-to-be widowed before marriage, would seem to be contradictory to the cultural imperative of continuing the family line. To affirm the widow's own determination not to remarry in fact challenges the customary parental authority, the hierarchical power of the senior over the junior in the kinship system. Especially during the Ming and Qing, the will of a widow not to remarry took precedence over the socially and legally sanctioned authority of the senior in the kinship system. In a word, the cult of widowhood, which serves no formal purpose in perpetuating a male heir and instead challenges parental authority, seems to destabilize rather than to reinforce the assumed patriarchal and hierarchal structure of the Chinese family system. In the case of footbinding, the connection between a pair of bound feet and the perpetuation of a male heir is even more obscure. And even with the threat of severe penalty imposed onto the practitioners of footbinding repeatedly issued by the Qing court from 1636 to 1902, this practice not only continued to thrive among the Han people but also further spread to the non-Han population and even as far as Korea. As late as 1997, old Chinese women with bound feet could still be found in rural China.[42] How should we make sense of these social practices, these socially sanctioned forms of violence against women that serve no formal purposes in the perpetuation of patrilineage? And what connection, if any, exists between Confucian virtue ethics and the widely accepted social practices of widow chastity and footbinding?

To begin with, widow chastity did not really become a regulatory, social ideal until the Yuan period, and it reached its height during the Ming and Qing periods. And despite the alleged correlation between neo-Confucianism and the observance of widowhood, the emphasis on widow chastity is entirely absent in the Confucian *Four Books*. Among the *Five Classics*, only in the *Liji* and the later commentary of *Yijing* does one find an explicit mention of maintaining one's chastity and fidelity after the death of one's husband as part of wifely virtue.[43] In ancient times, widow remarriage was a common practice. In fact, after the death of Confucius's son, his widow was remarried and moved to the state of Wai, and after her death, Zisizi—Confucius's grandson—still mourned her.[44] In the pre-Qin period, there was no social stigma attached to a widow's or widower's remarriage. Instead, it was a social policy of each state that there should be no widows or widowers since no one should be left behind uncared for. The *Guanzi*, a forth-century BCE text, makes the policy explicit: "Each state has an official matchmaker, those men without wives are called widowers, those women without husbands are called widows, [the matchmaker] takes widowers and widows and then match them up ... so that it is called harmonizing singles (合獨)."[45] A similar view is also stated in the *Mencius*. Mencius advised King Xuan of Qi to make it a social policy that both men and women are able to find their respective mates, so that in the *wai*, there is no man without a wife, and in the *nei* there is no woman without a husband since marriage is a common desire for both genders.[46]

The purpose of marriage, as explained in the *Liji*, is linked to the continuation of one's lineage and ancestor worship; both in turn are integral expressions of the foundational virtue of filial piety. Through the marriage rite the groom assumes the role of the father and the bride the mother, and thereby one enters the adulthood. Marriage, in other words, provides a social occasion for both genders to assume their legitimate social places and roles. A widow or widower, who is neither married nor unmarried, occupies an ambiguous social place and serves no formal social function in the hierarchal kinship system, which is entirely structured based on marriage. Given the importance of having a male heir, both widowers and widows, especially the sonless ones, naturally were encouraged to get remarried. Indeed, there is no shortage of examples in history of prominent historical figures whose widowed mothers or daughters were remarried.

Nonetheless, widowhood that expresses the life-long bond between a husband and a wife has been recognized as a social virtue since the Han. The traditional analogy between widow chastity/fidelity and the political loyalty of a virtuous minister to his righteous ruler accentuates the dignity of widowhood. This long recognized womanly virtue, however, received unprecedented attention during the late Ming and early Qing periods in which not only was widowhood glorified, but so too were extraordinary acts of self-sacrifice and suicide committed in the name of safeguarding one's integrity. As will be discussed in detail, the increased attention to the cult of widowhood in the realm of *nei* during the late Ming and early Qing is intertwined with the rising emphasis on political loyalty in the realm of *wai*.

The first written prohibition denouncing remarriage appeared in the Qin when the First Emperor commanded that those who had children and were remarried would be subject to punishment for being unchaste. However, the First Emperor's emphasis on spousal fidelity applied to men as well as women, since the edict also said that killing an unfaithful husband was not a crime.[47] The first imperial honor bestowed on chaste widows was in 58 BCE of the Former Han when widow fidelity, among other socially recognized virtues such as filial piety, household harmony, women's sexual purity, and even longevity, was, for the first time, honored by the imperial court with a "testimonial of merit" (*jingbiao* 旌表).[48] Two Han court-scholars, Liu Xiang of the Former Han in the *Lienuzhuan* and Ban Zhao of the Later Han in the *Nujie*, also advocated, among other things, female chastity and widow fidelity as part of feminine virtue. However, widow remarriage was not uncommon, even among the royalty and high officials during the Han. After the fall of the Han dynasty, the state was divided into three contesting city-states, and, coincidentally, all three founders married widows.[49] One can infer from this that although widow fidelity and chastity have been recognized as social virtues since the Han, widowhood in social reality was not yet widely practiced.

The first imperial prohibition against widow remarriage appeared in the Sui dynasty (581–618). The imperial edict issued in the late sixth century prohibited the remarriage of the wife of the ninth ranking officials and the concubine of the fifth ranking officials.[50] The ban on widow remarriage, according to the dynastic history of Sui, was intended to correct the declining public morality exemplified by the practice that after the death of high officials, their concubines or maids were usually sold in remarriage by their sons or grandsons.[51] The severity of the social problem of selling wives and daughters in exchange for money or silk in the sixth-century culture was noted and condemned by *Ru* scholar Yan Zhitui (531–591) in his family instruction, *Yanshi jiaxun*.[52] The imperial ban issued by the founding emperor of Sui on widow remarriage can therefore be interpreted as a *protection* for women against the increasing treatment of women as a commodity in the patrilineal family. This imperial ban was later reversed by the notorious Sui emperor, Yang, who collected widows and married them off to soldiers on the frontier.[53]

While widow remarriage might seem progressive to contemporary readers since it seems to conform to our modern conception of sexual freedom, it might not, in reality, have been beneficial to women in traditional Chinese society, since marriage, for the most part, was arranged by the senior member of the family with or without consent. The apparent "freedom" of widow remarriage in early times might, in fact, only reflect the subordinate status of women in the kinship system and the dependent nature of women's gender roles as wife and mother. Indeed, the commonality of widow remarriage in early China reflects neither women's own agency nor their possession of sexual freedom, but rather women's vulnerable position in a society in which women of all classes had no right to refuse marriage and their legitimate place in society entirely depended on their marital status. In this light, the later dynastic law prohibiting forced widow remarriage was, in fact, a step *forward* in recognizing women's own agency in their voluntary widowhood.

The Tang statute, for the first time in dynastic laws, prohibited forced widow remarriage arranged otherwise than by the widow's own grandparents or parents, and the punishment imposed on offenders depended on their degrees of kinship to the widow. For those who were not the widow's relatives, the punishment was a one-year jail term; for the widow's relatives, the punishment was two degrees less.[54] In this statute, although the widow's "right" to refuse marriage was protected, the absolute parental authority over their children was still the overriding concern of the imperial court. That is to say, the wishes of the grandparents or parents still took precedence over the wishes of the widow in regard to marriage.

Despite this legal protection, during the Tang period widows were still by and large encouraged to marry, even daughters of prominent families. For instance, in the *"Lienu"* section of the Tang dynastic history, when a daughter of a prominent clan was widowed and intended to stay widowed, her brothers and sisters tried to persuade her to remarry by pointing out that for someone like her—a young widow without children—remarriage is consistent with "ritual propriety and regulation (禮儀常範)."[55] One can infer from this that in the Tang, widow remarriage was still a social norm. In fact, widow remarriage was well accepted even in the royal family; among the 211 Tang princesses, twenty-eight were remarried, and three were married three times![56] At first glance, this number of remarriages might not seem extraordinarily high. But it should be noted that after the Tang, apart from one princess of Song, none of the princesses in the subsequent dynasties remarried. Again, remarriage by itself doesn't necessarily signify any sort of freedom for women. Remarriage in the royal house, in fact, was often intertwined with the problem of incestuous relationships among kin. For instance, the well-known love affair between Tang emperor Xuanzhong and his beloved Yang Guifei, was in fact an incestuous relationship between father and daughter-in-law. Similarly, Empress Wu Zetian of Tang, the only female emperor in Chinese history who took over the state after the death of Tang emperor Kaozhong, was a court lady of the emperor's father.

Well into the early Song, widow remarriage was still the norm. Prominent Song *Ru* Fan Zhongyen, who followed his widowed mother to her remarriage, later on set up a fund to help widows get married. After the early death of his son, Fan also remarried his daughter-in-law to his disciple.[57] However, compared to the Tang, widow chastity did have a greater impact on the Song and Ming royal houses where of more than eighty Song princesses only one remarried, and none in the Ming.[58]

The rise of the cult of widowhood is often attributed to the infamous statement made by Song *Ru* Cheng Yi and reiterated by Zhu Xi in his *Jinsilu* (Reflections on Things at Hand) regarding the importance of widow fidelity. When asked about the propriety of a man marrying a widow, Cheng Yi responded: It is improper to marry a widow, since a marriage is a match and if one takes someone who has already lost her integrity, he would also lose his. When asked about the propriety of remarriage for an impoverished widow with no one to depend on, he responded, "This is only because people of later generations are afraid of hardship and starving to death, therefore there is such a saying. But to starve to death is a very small matter; to lose one's integrity is a very serious matter."[59]

Obviously this is an elite discourse where to safeguard one's integrity must override the practical concern of staying alive. Even Zhu Xi acknowledged the gap between widow fidelity as a regulative social ideal and widow remarriage as a practical necessity. Zhu Xi remarked in his commentary on Cheng Yi's statement, "Although to remarry after the death of one's husband would result in losing one's integrity, there are also people who do it out of necessity and sages cannot prohibit that..."[60] The gap between widow fidelity as an elite morality and widow remarriage as a common social practice is demonstrated in Cheng Yi's own personal life. Despite his strong stand on the ideal of widowhood, both his niece and his nephew's wife remarried.[61] And the story of Cheng Yi's father who housed and later gave his widowed grandniece in marriage was proudly retold by Cheng Yi himself. When Zhu Xi was asked about whether Cheng Yi's father's act contradicted the teaching of widow fidelity, Zhu Xi responded: "Generally speaking that should be the case. But people cannot follow that absolutely."[62] Cheng Yi's statement on widow fidelity hence must be understood as an elite discourse of virtue-ethics, a regulative ideal not an absolute doctrine.

Cheng Yi's analogy between widow remarriage and the loss of one's integrity mirrors the traditional analogy between a virtuous wife and a loyal minister. An early Qing commentator wrote, "The injunction not to marry a widow is intended for morally superior men. How can morally inferior commoners on the street be asked to do so? Some people question that Master Cheng's words are too extreme, but they are not. They only express a constant propriety." For, "If a widow who loses her integrity out of the fear of hardships and hunger, how is she different from a minister who surrenders to a bandit out of the fear of battle?"[63] In other words, just as a courageous minister has a duty to serve his righteous ruler without the fear of death, a virtuous widow must also rise above the immediate concern of staying alive in order to safeguard her integrity as a married woman. The extraordinary sacrifice of the widow is often compared with the extraordinary sacrifice of the soldier in battle, since both value the virtue of *yi* 義 (appropriateness) according to their station, more than their lives.

In discussing Cheng Yi's stand on widow fidelity, scholars often overlook the fact that Cheng Yi also advocated the equal worth of husband and wife since for him marriage is a match between two equals; that is to say, they must be equal in terms of their virtues. Cheng Yi's injunction regarding the impropriety of remarriage after the death of one's spouse applies to men as well. When he was asked about the propriety of *widower* remarriage, he responded, "Those high officials and above [i.e. those who already have concubines] have no justification to remarry." He went on to explain that once people are husband and wife, they are husband and wife forever. How can there be such a thing when if one dies early the other would remarry?[64] The lifelong bond between a husband and a wife demands mutual spousal fidelity. But, according to Cheng Yi, there is an exception to this ideal of spousal fidelity; that is, after the death of one's wife, if there is no one to serve one's parents and to continue the sacrificial ceremony in the ancestral temple, then a widower taking another wife would be permissible.[65] This exception is consistent with our proposed hypothesis of the three cultural imperatives—the virtue of filial piety, ancestor worship, and the continuity of the family name—as an explanatory account of Chinese sexism.

Widow fidelity, despite the popularity of Cheng Yi's statement, did not become a major social force until the succeeding dynasty, Yuan, where widowhood was first institutionalized by the Mongol whose native custom, ironically, sanctioned the incestuous relationship between a son and a widowed stepmother, or a nephew and a widowed aunt.[66] In the Yuan dynasty, widow chastity, among other social virtues, continued to be honored by the state as part of the dynastic tradition of honoring the virtuous and punishing the vicious. In 1304, the Yuan imperial court furthermore set up a clear standard for honoring chaste widows. In the Yuan's regulation, a chaste widow who was eligible for the imperial honor must be widowed before age thirty and for at least twenty years by age fifty. And once recognized, the household of the chaste widow would receive a testimonial of merit to be displayed on the door to set it apart from other common households, and it would be exempted from labor services.[67] Widow chastity in the Yuan thus became a means through which women of common households were able to acquire the highest social honor because of their own doing instead of the doings of their father, husband, or son. To put it another way, the virtue of widow chastity reflects the determination of women themselves since they are honored not by association with their male counterparts, but by their own virtuous doing.

Just as the civil service examination was the primary means through which learned men of all classes acquired imperial honors for themselves as well as their lineages, the institutionalized widowhood of Yuan can be seen as a means through which women of all classes could, in a sense, freely compete for imperial honors, which were traditionally beyond their reach.

With Yuan's award system, widow chastity was elevated to the same level as the civil service examination through which successful candidates were able to bring the highest social honor—imperial recognition—to themselves as well as their kin.

The popularity of widow chastity as a normative ideal among commoners is reflected in the dramatic increase of the number of biographies of virtuous women in the Yuan dynastic history to more than 160 entries from the sixty entries in the previous Song dynastic history, with 90 percent devoted to chaste women.[68] The dramatic jump in the number of virtuous women's biographies in the Yuan is a clear indication of the popularization of female virtue, or what Mark Elvin called a "democratization" of the virtue of widow chastity, that is, a social virtue democratized among and made accessible to the masses.[69] The imperial honor bestowed on chaste widows was, by and large, intended for commoners, not for the wives of high ranking officials, since they already had been granted honorary titles through their husband's official status.[70] Institutionalized widowhood, hence, can be seen as a means through which social capital and privileges were redistributed; it was a means through which commoners were able to achieve social mobility. Interestingly, the popularity of widowhood also coincided with the declining mobility rates for learned men through the civil service examination during the Ming and Qing periods. This decline was, in part, the result of population growth. And the declining mobility rates for learned men through civil service examination might have also contributed to the rising popularity of widowhood as a mark of status, an alternative means to gain social mobility, in late imperial China.[71]

Yuan's award system for chaste widows continued in the succeeding dynasty, Ming. The 1368 edict issued by the founding emperor of Ming clearly stated that all filial sons, obedient grandsons, righteous persons, and chaste widows once recognized should be honored with a testimonial of merit to be displayed outside the doors of the family home. But only the households of chaste widows were awarded with the exemption from labor services.[72] Clearly, widow chastity was elevated above all other social virtues or achievements; it became an alternative route for families and local communities to acquire status and imperial honors. The popularity of widow chastity as a means to social advancement is also reflected in the Ming imperial edict of 1465 in which the court found it necessary to impose punishment on sponsors making fraudulent claims to chaste widowhood in the local community, in order to cope with the large number of applications.[73] In 1511, Ming emperor Wuzhong further expanded the avenue through which women could receive a testimonial of merit for being a chaste widow to include those who committed suicide to avoid rape or forced remarriage. It is tempting for modern readers to infer from this edict some sort of sexist motivation to restrict women's sexual freedom. But the 1511 edict should be understood within the context of the declining Ming imperial court resisting the rising power of the Manchus, who eventually established a Manchu state in the north in 1559. It is not surprising to note that the 1511 edict was originally issued to honor those chaste Ming women residing on the frontiers who chose death instead of losing their integrity to invading barbaric tribes, or bandits.[74]

In the late Ming and early Qing periods, the practice of widow suicide further took on a political meaning. It came to symbolize the Ming loyalists' resistance movement against the barbaric force of the Manchu state. The case of Gu Yanwu is especially illuminating. Gu Yanwu was a late Ming loyalist and his foster mother starved herself to death in protest of the Manchu invasion of her home region in 1645. Gu as a filial son and a loyal subject of Ming followed the example of the extraordinary sacrifice made by his mother and also refused to serve the Qing dynasty.[75] Because of the association between widow suicide and the resistance movement of the Ming loyalists against the Qing court, during the early Qing period, widow suicide, in fact, was repeatedly discouraged by Qing imperial court.[76]

Widow chastity and widow suicide in the late Ming however was taken to the extreme. Now widowhood not only was practiced among married women but also among young girls who upon receiving the news of the death of their future husband began their lifelong widowhood prior to the consummation of marriage. Several late Ming and early Qing literati such as Gui Youguang (1506–71) and Mao Qiling (1623–1716) objected to widowhood prior to marriage as well as widow suicide. Widowhood prior to marriage, they reasoned, is contrary to the propriety of the marriage rite that marks the legitimate union between a husband and a wife. Consequently, without the sanction of the marriage rite, widowhood that symbolizes the lifelong bond between a husband and a wife cannot take place. Widow suicide, besides lacking historical precedent, is contrary to one's filial devotion to one's family, since to serve and provide for one's parents is the beginning of filial piety.[77] Their opposition had little impact, if any, on the popularized social practice of widowhood, which nevertheless, in practical terms, was an alternative route for the wives of commoners as well as their families to acquire social honors and to elevate their social status in the local community sanctioned by the imperial court, whose legitimacy, in turn, was supported by the commoners and the gentry class through their participation in the institutionalized widowhood. The reciprocal benefits between the state and the commoners inevitably reenforced the popularity of institutionalized widowhood and widow suicide despite the objections made by some *Ru* literati.

In the Qing, widow chastity became a cult, a religious expression that enshrined and worshipped chaste widows. In the Qing's detailed procedures and regulations for conferring imperial honors, eligible women were divided into three categories: first, "chaste widows" (*jiefu* 節婦) who remain widowed for twenty years at age fifty, or widowed for at least ten years if they die before reaching fifty; second, "daring women and girls" (*liefu, lienu* 烈婦, 烈女) who die to avoid rape, die while resisting rape, or commit suicide out of shame after being sexually assaulted, or die to avoid forced remarriage, or die while resisting premarital advances of their intended spouse; third, "virtuous girls" (*zhennu* 貞女) prior to marriage, who upon receiving news of the death of their fiance commit suicide, or remain widowed in the husband's family. The width and depth of Qing's system for bestowing imperial honors on chaste women surpassed all previous dynasties.

The families of those chaste women of Qing, unlike in all previous dynasties, were also given monetary support to construct memorial arches. Upon receiving testimonials of merit, those chaste women were eligible for enshrinement in the temple of integrity and filial piety (節孝祠) constructed at the capital as well as local districts where virtuous women were worshipped at spring and autumn sacrifices.[78] With the construction of a monumental arch and the enshrinement in the temple of integrity and filial piety, chaste widows were elevated into the same level as orthodox *Ru* who were enshrined and worshipped in the temple of Confucius at spring and autumn sacrifices conducted both at the capital as well as local districts. The parity between widow chastity in the *nei* for women and literary learning in the *wai* for men—both were means through which social honors were acquired—is apparent.

It is true that the emphasis on widow chastity, in part, derived from the assumed loyalty required of women to the patrilineage and hence strictly speaking it could not be reflective of women's own agency. However, widow chastity in reality could also be disruptive to the patrilineal family. For a closer look at the Qing imperial law against forced widow remarriage by one's kin shows that a widow's legal right to voluntary widowhood often overrode the patriarchal structure of the kinship system in which the senior had an absolute authority over the junior. According to the Qing law, unlike the Tang law that exempted parents and grandparents from the punishment imposed on forced remarriage, all offenders were punished according to the degrees of their kinship relationship to the widow. The senior was punished less harshly than the junior offender, and the closer the offender's kinship relationship to the widow the lesser the punishment would be.[79] This statute again expresses a basic deference one owes to the senior members of one's family. Yet, what is new and radical in the Qing law is that even one's grandparents and parents were also subject to punishment when exercising their customary right to arrange marriage for the junior relative. The daughter's determination not to get remarried, according to the Qing law, took precedence over the parental authority. The radicality of the Qing law cannot be fully appreciated, if one fails to take into account the dependent nature and the subordinate status of women's gender roles, especially as daughters and daughters-in-law in relation to their parents and in-laws. In a society where selling one's wife and daughter due to poverty had always been tolerated, the Qing law against forced widow remarriage, in effect, gave sanction to the junior's disobedience against the senior's wish; and thereby it affirmed and legally sanctioned women—the subordinate beings—in their own agency through voluntary widowhood for the first time in Chinese history.

Another point one should take into consideration is that, from the widow's viewpoint, remarriage in fact might bring more harm than good since it entailed a loss of the right to inherit the property of her late husband on behalf of her sons and the right to the custody of her children. Widow remarriage benefited nearly everyone in the family except the widow herself, who in a new marriage must again assume the lowly status of a new bride in the hierarchical kinship system organized on the principle of seniority. Given such a structural limitation, it is not surprising that women themselves came to embrace widowhood as an expression of their virtuous intent of spousal fidelity and loyalty to their husband's lineage, which marked the only permanent social place for women.

All in all, widowhood, with its encoded layers of social meaning, symbolized, first and foremost, the ancient virtue of spousal fidelity in which the lifelong bond between a husband and a wife was analogous to the ethical-political relation between a loyal minister and a righteous ruler. The Confucian virtue of *yi* 義 as the governing principle in the minister-ruler relation, in the case of a woman who was confined to the realm of *nei*, was actualized in the husband-wife relation, and a virtuous wife safeguarding her chastity and fidelity to the patrilineage in the *nei* was equivalent to a loyal minister serving a righteous ruler in the *wai*. Second, voluntary widowhood protected in imperial statute since the Tang signified women's own agency since women's moral intent in safeguarding their integrity as married women took precedence over the parental authority that emphasized the power of the senior over the junior. Third, with the bestowal of imperial honors on and the exemption of labor services for the households of chaste widows, widowhood was also a social virtue with practical consequences. Comparable to the civil service examination for men, widowhood was a means of social mobility for women, that is, a means through which women were able to acquire the highest social honor—imperial recognition—due to their own virtuous actions instead of the actions of their father, husband, or son. Lastly, widowhood in the late Qing was also a religious expression in which chaste widows, comparable to orthodox *Ru* enshrined in the temple of Confucius, were also worshipped and remembered in the local temples of integrity and filiality. That is to say, chaste widows canonized during the Qing, whose virtuous conduct was emulated and remembered beyond the familial realm of *nei*, had their virtue recognized by analogy with that to Confucian exemplary persons. In a society where women had no names, had no legitimate access to official titles, and were outside the realm of remembrance, the canonization of chaste women in the Qing was the ultimate honor for women. In short, widowhood, as part of women's own agency, was a means through which women were able to participate in the Confucian discourse of virtue ethics in the realm of *wai* where one's name and one's good name were passed on and remembered.

As for the notorious practice of footbinding, it has captivated the imagination of the West as an erotic practice of the Chinese as well as the ultimate sign of the backwardness and the barbarianism of Old China. From Howard

Levy's *Chinese Footbinding: The History of a Curious Erotic Custom* in 1966 to Beverley Jackson's *Splendid Slippers: a Thousand Years of An Erotic Tradition* in 1997, footbinding in the Western eye is termed as an erotic tradition.[80] Footbinding is seen as a purely sexual oppression of women by men for the sake of male desire, and that, in turn, enables feminists and alike to mark footbinding as the ultimate sign of the sexist nature of Chinese society. The image of a victimized Chinese woman hobbling around with bound feet becomes the horrific symbol of Old China in the West. Yet this sort of reductionism is a rather simplified understanding of such a complex history of footbinding, which was practiced across different social classes, historical times, ethnicities, and regions. As will become clear, the practice of footbinding was intertwined with the concept of gender propriety, civility, and lastly the ethnic identity of the Han people.

Western scholarship on third world women, as Chandra T. Mohanty in her anthology *Third World Women and the Politics of Feminism* stated, mostly has focused on women as victims in "their own 'traditional' sexist cultures," instead of as subjects or agents. In this neocolonial discourse embodied in early feminist writings, third world women are often taken as objects to be theorized and rescued by their white sisters in the West, who in turn are presumed to be autonomous, moral subjects not beholden to any local traditions.[81] In order to go beyond such a false dichotomy between "liberated" Western feminists and the rest of the "traditional," "sexist" cultures, we will have to go beyond the simple picture of footbinding as a mere sexual oppression of women by men. We will have to take into account possible cultural meanings that were embodied in the practice of footbinding in which women were not just sexual objects; instead, they were active participants in transmitting the practice of footbinding as women's work, women's knowledge, and women's culture under the privation of *wen*—that is, literary culture.

In the traditional account, the practice of footbinding began around the mid-tenth century as a practice employed by court dancers to achieve a certain dancing technique, comparable to a technique of modern ballerinas.[82] Scholars generally agree that prior to the Tang dynasty (618–906), there is no historical evidence of the practice of footbinding. Judging from the attire and activities of the Tang women, horseback riding and wearing boots were quite common among women, so it is safe to say that the practice of footbinding was nonexistent then.[83] Well into the early Song, the practice of footbinding was still by and large limited to court courtesans, since prominent Song poets were still writing about the beauty of women's natural feet.[84] The much popularized tale of Zhu Xi of Song's involvement in promoting the practice of footbinding in the South as a way to promote womanly docility and chastity, as Patricia Ebrey argued, is probably fictitious.[85] During the Song, male literati were more preoccupied with widow chastity and spousal fidelity as a sign of female virtue than with the practice of footbinding. The Song's preoccupation with widow chastity is attested in the Song literati's attack on the famous female poet Li Qingzhao, whose often blunt and harsh criticism of her contemporary male poets eventually inspired the rumor that she remarried in her old age.[86] In the Song, widow fidelity rather than a pair of bound feet was indexical of gender propriety.

However, in the late Song, the practice of footbinding gradually spread from court courtesans to the gentry class and it was during this time that the earliest criticisms of footbinding were found. Che Ruoshui in the late Song wrote: "The practice of women binding their feet is not known when it began. Little children not yet four or five years old who have not done anything wrong are nevertheless made to suffer the unlimited pain. What is the use of binding the feet small?"[87] Indeed, it is perplexing to ponder why parents were so willing to subject their young daughters to such an excruciatingly painful process of physical mutilation in which the four little toes were forcefully bent inwardly and the heel bone turned vertical in order to condense the foot size to the three-inch ideal at such a young age. What is even more perplexing is that, unlike all other sexist practices discussed so far, footbinding required direct and exclusive involvement of women themselves, especially between a mother and a daughter or an aunt and a niece, since footbinding only took place in women's inner quarters; and in the initial stage—the first two years— it required persistent enforcement from the mother to bind her young daughter's feet, usually starting between age five and seven.[88] In other words, without the persistent active involvement of women themselves, footbinding would be impossible. Of course, there is no doubt that the practice of footbinding was, in part, supported by male sexual desire that the female body embodied feminine beauty with a pair of bound feet. And that standardized feminine beauty in turn became a mark of a woman's marriageability. A mother's willingness to bind her young daughter's feet, despite her cries of pain and the countless health risks involved, was really an expression of a mother's care for her daughter's future in married life where the daughter's self-sacrifice and absolute obedience to her husband and her in-laws were required. Anthropologist Fred Blake interpreted footbinding as "a voluntary ordeal undertaken by mothers to inform their daughters of how to succeed in a world authored by men."[89] In other words, footbinding was a mother's purposeful disciplining her daughter so that she was prepared for the life of servitude required of her by men.

In practical terms, the physical mutilation and impairment inflicted on women through footbinding greatly limited the range of activities that women were able to engage in. Footbinding thereby helped confine women to the inner quarters, and to reinforce women's limited and subordinated gender role as a wife—that is, neiren 內人 or a person of the inner quarter. Confinement to the inner quarters also helped enforce the conservative virtues of female chastity and docility. This sentiment is expressed in the Nuerjing (Classic for Girls)—an instruction book for women by an unknown author. "For what reason is it that women have bound feet? It is not because bound feet that look like an arched bow are good looking. It is from the fear that women would be easily walking out of their quarters, so that there are tens of thousands of wraps and bindings to constrain them."[90] The physical constraint imposed on women through the practice of footbinding ensured gender propriety, and it further symbolized the spatial seclusion of *nei*, the woman's sphere proper.

The severe physical limitation and confinement imposed on women through footbinding also limited women's ability to contribute to the household economy. Especially in the formative stage of footbinding, due to the excruciating pain, young girls spent most of their time sitting and lying on the bed, and some even required a maid's assistance in walking. Hence a pair of mutilated, useless, bound feet also symbolized the wealth of the family that could afford the idleness of its female members in the household economy. With its required daily medical care in the formative stage, footbinding was a substantial family investment in the daughter whose unproductive, deformed feet represented not only her inner strength but also more importantly the reputation and the gentry status of her family.

In the Yuan and Ming periods, the practice of footbinding spread from the gentry class to theater actors and commoners. The widespread phenomenon of footbinding was commented on in the dynastic history of Ming: "In the early Song, women still did not bind their feet...nowadays it is extreme." And, "[A]s for the arch-shaped small feet, nowadays even a small child knows how to envy them."[91] Footbinding during the Ming was no longer an exclusive privilege of the gentry class; it was a shared feminine ideal, an aesthetic object admired by many. A pair of bound feet signified more than just feminine beauty; it was also a sign of status, a sign of social acceptability, since men of beggar households were prohibited from literary learning and women from footbinding.[92] Beggars occupied the lowest stratification of social class, and their lowly status excluded them from participating in the normative, social activities of literary learning for men and footbinding for women. The importance of footbinding for women in this prohibition was equated with literary learning for men, since only through these activities did both men and women become properly marked as recognizably normative, social beings. In other words, just as literary learning marked the civility of the male, footbinding marked the civility of the female. As Fred Blake put it, footbinding can be interpreted as women's subverted Confucian way of being civilized.[93] Without legitimate access to literary learning where the civility of the male was cultivated, women cultivated their civility instead through disciplining their body. That is to say, the Confucian project of self-cultivation (*xiushen* 修身), in footbinding, was taken literally as reshaping one's own body, a strict management of one's own flesh, just as the term *xiu* 修 as shaping or trimming and *shen* 身 as one's body or one's whole person suggest.[94]

However, the Confucian concept of self-cultivation (*xiushen* 修身), which is fundamental to one's moral personality, must begin with the learning of *wen* and *li*, that is, the learning of the literary and ritual traditions of the sages. Confucius once said to his son: "If you do not study the *Songs*, you will be at a loss as to what to say," and, "If you do not study the *Rites*, you will be at a loss as to where to stand"(*Lunyu* 16.13). Through learning the *Songs*, which comprises one of the earliest written records of Chinese civilization, one comes to learn not only the virtuous deeds of the sages, but also an aesthetic, poetic style of expressing one's intentions, and hence it is through learning the *Songs* that one learns to speak with substance as a fully cultivated cultured being. One's familiarity with the literary traditions of the sages must be complemented by one's appropriation of the ritual traditions. For without embodying the ritual traditions of the sages and the worthies, one is also at a loss as to where to stand. The wisdom of the past sages must be reappropriated, that is, actualized through one's kinship as well as social roles in one's particularized situations, otherwise one's knowledge of the *dao* of the sage-kings is merely an intellectual curiosity. In sum, in the Confucian world, the learning of *wen* and *li* are the beginning of the lifelong process of one's self-cultivation as a cultured, moral being. The learning of *wen* and *li* is an integral part of the Confucian lifelong project of self-cultivation, yet at the same time, as we have discussed so far, *wen* is also a male privilege proper. The gender disparity is reflected in the two different curriculums for boys' and girls' education stated in the *Liji*. The process of self-conscious gender marking begins at age seven and the proper education for the boy comprises a comprehensive learning of ritual deference as well as six arts and literature, and that in turn prepares him for officialdom later on.[95]

By contrast, the proper education for the girl comprises only practical household management in preparation for her life of servitude as a wife. "A girl at age 10 ceases to go out. Her governess teaches her the skills of making agreeable and pleasant speeches and the ways of listening and following, to learn to handle the hempen fibers, to deal with the cocoons, to weave silks and form fillets, to learn women's work (*nugong* 女功), how to furnish garments." She is taught to observe the sacrifices and to assist in preparing for the ceremonies. "At age 15, she assumes the hairpin [i.e. adulthood]; at twenty she is married..."[96] The disparity between boys' and girls' education is apparent, and their aims differ as well. The process of gendering coincides with the process of civilizing in which the boy through the comprehensive learning of *wen* and *li* becomes a fully integrated cultured being while the girl through the learning of practical household skills is prepared for her life of servitude as a wife.

Paralleling the boy's lifelong project of self-cultivation through literary learning and ritual observation, the girl cultivates herself through shaping and trimming her flesh in the lifelong project of footbinding. Age seven—a normative age when boys and girls begin to assume their self-consciously separate gender identities and spheres—is also the normative age when girls are marked with bound feet. While her brother is cultivating himself through literary learning in the process of acculturation, she cultivates herself through wraps and bindings. Women's subverted Confucian way of becoming civilized through an intentional bodily mutilation is also a silent testimony to the sub-person aspect of women's existence in the cultural perception. In other words, in order to become a fully cultured being, women must first of all be mutilated, marked through human means. Women's natural body symbolize an untamed animal in the wild, and by altering the natural body, just as bodily mutilation is applied to tamed oxen or horses, one brings the natural body of women into the realm of men—that is, the realm of *wen*, the realm of culture. The purposeful alteration applied to tame animals as a mark of man is illustrated in the following passage in the *Zhuangzi*. When Zhuangzi was asked what he meant by heavenly and human, he responded: "Oxen and horses having four feet is what is meant by 'heavenly.' Putting a halter over a horse's head or piercing an ox's nose is what is meant by 'human.'"[97] In the same way, one might say that the natural state of a woman's body, like the body of wild animals, is brought into the realm of men through the process of footbinding, a purposeful mutilation. A pair of deformed feet thus is a mark of woman's civility under the privation of *wen*, which is the genuine mark of man's civility in the realm of literary culture.

Although footbinding took place in women's inner quarters, it was not just a private, family affair. To the contrary, the date for commencing the first binding for the young girl was also a date of great importance, and the mother often sought divine blessings prior to the commencement. It was a celebratory, festive event for the family's female friends and relatives who with their tiny bound feet often traveled long distances to attend since it marked the beginning of "womanhood" for the young girl.[98] The technique of binding varied just as the pattern and the shape of the so-called "golden lotus" shoes varied greatly from region to region, family to family, as well. Footbinding was a sort of knowledge and work that was passed on from mothers to daughters, and from aunts to nieces. The making of the unique pattern of the bindings as well as the shoes not only expressed women's own tradition but also was women's work proper. In footbinding, women made their own cultural patterns and traditions through wraps and needles, while men made their literary cultural patterns through brushes and words. The parity between man's literary culture and woman's culture of bodily inscription is attested by the meaning of the term *wen*, which interestingly enough signifies both literary culture, which is a male privilege proper, and colorful patterns, which is usually associated with women's needlework or artifacts. *Wen* 文, as defined in the *Shouwen*, means crossing drawings (i.e., patterns). Footbinding was exclusively women's culture whose patterns were made not with words or brushes, but with wraps and needles. In footbinding women were both the objects that were bound and the subjects that did the binding, the pattern making; women were the ones who appropriated and transmitted the culture of their foremothers.

In times of foreign invasion such as in the Yuan and Qing periods—two dynasties founded by non-Han tribes—footbinding also took on a political meaning; it became a marker of the ethnic identification of the Han people who were distinguished from the uncivilized, big-foot barbarians dominating the imperial courts. Both Mongols and Manchus were prohibited by their own ruling minorities from participating in footbinding.[99] In conjunction with the prohibition, footbinding signified more than gender identity; more importantly, it signified the ethnic identity of the Han and their civility. Footbinding—a purposeful bodily inscription, a cultural pattern making—was considered part of women's correct attire, that is, the way in which an acculturated body was properly presented. Dorothy Ko in her study on footbinding argued that in the Chinese perception correct attire was what separated humans from beasts, or the civilized from the uncivilized.[100] Correct attire as a sign of civility expressed the grand notion of *wen* whose meaning encompasses not only literary patterns of words but also aesthetic patterns of artifacts and clothing. Footbinding in seventeenth-century China, as Ko summarized, was regarded as: first, an expression of Chinese *wen* civility; second, a marker of ethnic boundaries separating the Han from the Manchu; and third, an ornament of the body, that is, the correct, cultural concealment of the female body.[101]

Footbinding, along with Ming-styles (i.e., Han styles) of attire, clothing, hairdressing, and headgear, was repeatedly prohibited by the Qing court with a threat of severe punishment. The founding Qing emperor commanded in his edict of 1636: "All Han people, be they official or commoner, male or female, their clothes and adornments will have to conform to Manchu styles. Males are not allowed to fashion wide collars and sleeves; females are not allowed to comb up their hair nor bind their feet." In 1638, he reiterated the ban on footbinding and Ming styles of attire for both men and women.[102] In the formative stage of the new dynasty of Qing, Han attire used by the surviving subjects of the previous dynasty, Ming, certainly signified one's political loyalty to the fallen dynasty of Ming. In order to purge any remaining Ming influence, the Qing founding emperor found it necessary to impose Manchu styles of attire onto his Han subjects; in particular, Han males were to adopt the Manchu hairstyle by shaving their head leaving only a queue in the back and Han females were to unbind their feet. Although there were numerous rebellions against the Qing "head-shaving" edict throughout the Qing rule, it is safe to say that by the end of the seventeenth century the uniformity of the Qing hairstyle of queue among officials and commoners was by and largely completed.[103]

While Han males were forced to conform to the new style of hairdressing as a sign of political submission to the Qing court, Han females, however, continued to defy the imperial ban on footbinding despite severe punishment imposed on bound-foot women and their parents. In 1645, women with bound feet were barred from the imperial inner court. In 1664, Emperor Kangxi further decreed that all girls born after 1662—the beginning of his reign—were prohibited from binding their feet and the offender's father would be subject to flogging and exile.[104] As late as 1902, anti-footbinding edicts were still being issued by the Qing court.[105] However, the prohibition on footbinding issued in the 1664 edict, along with numerous edicts issued before and after it, was in vain. Although it is true that, being exposed in public, man's hairdressing was a public statement, women's bound feet by comparison were relatively private concerns. Nevertheless, without the sanction of the Han people, the practice of footbinding would not have persisted in the face of severe punishment imposed by the Qing court.[106] Hence, footbinding during the Qing was also a means of political resistance, a means through which the Han majority were able to defy the authority of the ruling barbarians.

All in all, footbinding, as a cultural practice that lasted for a thousand years and survived numerous imperial prohibitions, should be understood beyond the obvious—that is, beyond its being a sign of sexual oppression of women by men and a sign of the victimization of women by the patriarchal family structure. Instead, footbinding can be interpreted as follows: first of all, as a sign of Chinese *wen* civility; that is, women made and transmitted the unique culture and tradition of their foremothers through wraps and needles. Second, it was a sign of gender propriety; that is, "womanhood" was marked through a pair of bound feet, through a purposeful concealment of the female body. Lastly, it was a sign of ethnic identity; that is, Han civility was expressed through the persistent defiance against the authority of the Qing court. These cultural meanings of footbinding became inverted by the end of the nineteenth century in the face of countless defeats by the rising imperial power of the West in China. Footbinding in women, like the queue in men, was then transformed into the most visible sign of Chinese barbarianism and backwardness. A victimized Chinese woman with deformed, bound feet became the horrific image of China in the West, from missionary writings in the late nineteenth century to feminist discourse on sexism in China in modern times.

However, to say this is not to undermine the cruelty of footbinding as a sanctioned act of social violence against women. Young girls at age six or seven were subjected to a violent act of mutilating their natural body, accompanied by dangerous infections and endless pain from literally trimming their raw flesh and rearranging their foot bone structures in order to achieve the normative ideal of "three-inch golden lotus." After enduring the shocking pain of the first two years of binding done by their mother or the senior female member of the family, young girls then assumed the responsibility of binding themselves for the rest of their lives. Footbinding, unlike modern cosmetic beautification inscribed onto the female body, was a lifelong process that required a persistent effort by women themselves to keep binding their feet. To reverse the result of bound feet to their previous, "natural" condition was not entirely impossible, but it was not any less painful than the initial process of binding itself. To force the deformed foot of an adult woman back to its previous "natural" state was just as brutal, if not more, as the first rearrangement of the foot bond structures imposed on the child. This in part explained why in the late nineteenth century or even early twentieth century when the opinion of the social elite began to shift away from the normalcy of footbinding, women continued to bind their feet and the feet of their daughters.[107]

Besides its brutality, footbinding was also a timely practice, because once the child passed the proper age for footbinding she could never be properly bound. Whether to bind their daughter's feet was thus not just a decision that the parents would have to eventually make on behalf of the child, but also a decision that, if not made in a timely fashion, they would have to bear the social consequences of, by depriving their daughter for the rest of her life from participating in this feminine ideal. And that was a consequence that few parents wanted to bear despite knowing the enormous health risks involved in footbinding and despite hearing the cries and the mercy pleas from their young daughters. Footbinding, paradoxically, despite its brutality, was an expression of parental love and care for the future of their daughter.

The infamy of footbinding, as a custom of Old China, is well publicized in the West; yet few have reflected on the infamy of cultural inscriptions still imposed on the female body in modern times. The point here is not so much to make an apology for the practice of concubinage, widowhood, or footbinding by explaining away its "sexist" components or excusing them under the banner of "cultural diversity." After all, most of these practices no longer exist as normative, social ideals within the Chinese cultural boundary encompassing China, Taiwan, and Hong Kong. Rather, the intent here is to take modern readers beyond the simple, false dichotomy of the West where people are autonomous, moral subjects and the rest of the world where people are victimized objects to be rescued, liberated, or made conscious of their "sexist," "traditional" society. Such an assumption imposes a unspoken cultural as well as racial hierarchy in which the West is viewed as the supplier of ethical theories and the rest of the world as a moral problem to be solved. This assumption not only precludes other possible ethical theories from emerging but also limits our understanding of the social practices of an alien culture whose encoded symbolic meanings are often hidden from the eye of the outside observer. It is only through decoding those cultural meanings embodied in social practices that we come to see women as subjects, and come to understand women's own agency in not only embracing but also actively participating in those practices in order to achieve some sort of shared cultural ideals given the structural limitation imposed on them. Without such a cultural understanding, women in the third world remain frozen in time as mere victims whose liberation can only be justified by Western ethical theories that are supposed to rise above parochial, "cultural" moralities.

In order not to fall prey to such a neocolonial assumption, we now turn to Confucianism, the most prominent emblem of Chinese high culture, in order to construe Confucianism not just as a viable ethical theory comparable to dominant Western ethical theories such as liberalism, utilitarianism, existentialism, etc., but more radically as a feminist theory as well. In other words, if we are to reject the assumed monopoly of ethical theories by the West, and if we are to reject the highly inflated rhetoric of Confucianism as a fixed, sexist ideology through and through, we must then dare to affirm the possibility of Confucianism as a feminist alternative. In the concluding chapter, we will go beyond the assumed incompatibility between Confucianism and feminism by proposing viable Confucian theoretical components for a future construction of a hybrid, feminist theory—"Confucian feminism"—as a theoretical foundation for gender parity.

Chapter Seven

TOWARD A CONFUCIAN FEMINISM—FEMINIST ETHICS IN-THE-MAKING

In feminist discourse, the term *Confucianism* appears more as a term of reproach than a possible theoretical ground for women's liberation. In the early feminist imaginary, "Confucianism" signifies a systematic oppression of Chinese women, in theory as well as in practice, because of its emphasis on male supremacy, its support for patriarchal family structure, and its gendered sphere of *nei*. The only theoretical salvation for Chinese women wanting to achieve gender parity seems to lie exclusively in adopting Western theories. Some contemporary feminists have explored the possibility of making Daoism an ally of feminism by pointing out its prioritization of feminine attributes. But this possibility is often accompanied by the assumption that Daoism works within the Cartesian duality where *yin* and *yang*, femininity and masculinity are treated as equivalent concepts. However, in previous chapters we have called this assumption into question. Feminists, sinologists, and the like often suppose, as Margery Wolf did in her critique of Tu Wei-ming's reappropriation of neo-Confucianism, that "Confucian personhood" coincides with the male self, and make Confucianism as a whole fundamentally incompatible with feminism. In other words, Confucianism and feminism are viewed as conceptually incommensurable. Yet, to suppose that Confucianism and feminism are incompatible is to impose a racial hierarchy under the guise of feminism, with the West being the sole supplier of ethical theories and the rest of the world a moral problem waiting to be solved. In order to reject such a neocolonial assumption, we must reject the misappropriation of Confucianism found in feminist discourse. More importantly, we must go beyond feminists' negative assessment of Confucianism by outlining a future project of constructing a feminist theory from within the Confucian framework. However, this is not to say that Confucianism cannot benefit from feminists' critiques, especially criticism of gender-based division of labor in terms of the *nei* and the *wai*. But to admit that there are elements in Confucianism that need rectification is not the same as saying that Confucianism as a whole is essentially sexist and antifeminist, just as one would not say that Aristotelian virtue ethics,

Kantian deontology, or Nietzschean existentialism is essentially sexist and antifeminist because some elements of it need rectification.

In the following, we will concentrate on key Confucian ethical concepts, in particular the concept of *ren*—a virtue-based achieved personhood—the virtue of filial piety as the beginning of humanity, and the complementary correlation of *yin-yang* and *nei-wai*. The assumption here is that a hybrid feminist theory of Confucianism or Confucian feminism is possible; not only is Confucianism able to meet the challenges of feminism and to address feminist concerns about women's oppression without going beyond its theoretical framework, but, more importantly, it is able to expand the theoretical horizons of feminism. In other words, despite its emphasis on reciprocal inequalities of social roles and its emphasis on the familial virtues of filiality and continuity, Confucianism is assumed to be able to inform feminism with an alternative theoretical ground for women's liberation. A fully articulated Confucian feminism will be reserved as a future project in order to do justice to contemporary feminist theories. For now, to provide an outline for this future project shall be sufficient to demonstrate the possibility of the convergence between feminism and Confucianism, or that a possible "feminist space" can be created within the Confucian tradition.

THE PROBLEMS OF GENDER AND THE POLITICS OF FEMINISM

As an analytic category, "gender" has troubled feminists greatly, especially since the existentialists' deconstruction of traditional accounts of the "essence" or "nature" of a woman. The category of "woman" no longer signifies a set of inborn biological facts that supposedly give support to a naturalized gender division of labor and social roles, nor does it signify a set of distinctively feminine psychological and/or behavioral traits. In the existentialists' deconstruction, "woman" signifies a social construct, a phenomenon sustained by one's participation in the process of genderization, that is, a process of acquiring and embodying a set of socially recognizable gender norms. As de Beauvoir boldly declared, "One is not born, but rather becomes, a woman." There is no "woman" as a natural being out there, but rather each woman as a socially and culturally recognizable "woman" is made in accordance with each cultural conception of what constitutes a proper "woman." This existential deconstruction, in part, frees women from the traditional "biological determinism," where women are taken to be natural beings with a set of natural roles, duties, and capacities rooted in their biological differences from men. The existential emphasis on the authentic self defined by its freely chosen projects, instead of by its predetermined essence, opens up a new possibility for women to be free from the patriarchal tradition that defines them. Existential feminism offers a new ethical as well as epistemological ground for women's liberation.

Such a deconstruction however also poses a difficulty for feminists. Namely, how can feminists continue to use the category of "woman" as a collective term to talk about gender oppression across cultural, racial, and class boundaries, since there is no "woman" as such beyond a specific social construct?[1] In other words, in the existentialist's world, the phenomenon of being a "woman" is coextensive with one's participation in the process of genderization sanctioned by a specific society as a whole, and nothing more. Hence, in principle, one can only speak of American women, Chinese women, Latino women, etc. but not "woman" as a being that transcends all cultural, racial, or class specificity. There is not, as it were, an original idea of "woman" to function as the essence underlying each peculiar, cultural conception of "woman," and in virtue of which each cultural conception of "woman" is seen as a particular example of that comprehensive, original idea of "woman." If it is true that a "woman" as a specific cultural phenomenon is made not born, then any cross-cultural attempt to understand women's condition must also begin with the study of culture. In the case of Chinese women, the concept of "woman" signifies a set of kinship roles and a ritually proper sphere and division of labor within the hierarchical kinship system. In other words, genderization coincides with ritualization and civilization in Chinese society, where a gendered being is also a being that embodies ritual propriety and hence civility. The inquiry into what constitutes a Chinese woman, therefore, should also begin with the concept of culture, instead of a set of transcultural characteristics of the original idea of "woman."

The need to affirm the cultural differences among women, as it were to preserve a room of one's own, is well articulated by third world feminists such as Chandra Mohanty and Caren Kaplan in response to the mainstream feminist discourse that tends to naturalize the analytic category of "woman," and yet at the same time totalize both the categories of "third world women" and "Western women."[2] The politics of location has emerged as an important part of postmodern feminist discourse in the cross-cultural study of gender since the term was first coined by Adrienne Rich in the 1980s.[3] Empirical locality is important in discussing gender in a cross-cultural context, but empirical locality signifies more than just one's physical presence in that particular region that one is addressing. That is to say, one's understanding of the position of Chinese women whether past or present will be limited if one hasn't had the necessary linguistic skill to navigate the rich cultural resources of China and has never set foot in China, although by merely being in China, one's observations of the position of Chinese women are not automatically valid, since empirical observations must be guided by a conceptual framework. And as long as her familiar conceptual framework remains intact, her empirical observations will reflect more of her own cultural categories than those of the subjects that she is trying to represent. The instance of Margery Wolf pressing her Chinese informant to describe the attributes of a good woman outside of her kinship roles is a perfect example. Hence, to recognize the empirical differences among women requires more of a shift in one's theoretical imagination, in which one's familiar cultural categories are no longer the normative reference points. To deconstruct the centrality of Western theories—a critical practice in postmodern feminist discourse—as Caren Kaplan cautioned, should not amount to superficial inclusion of theories from the margins, by which the privileged position of "whiteness" remains intact.[4] In other words, what that amounts to is really no more than an act of domination and marginalization of the "third world women" who, ironically, are marginalized and dominated through their very inclusion in Western feminist discourse.

In Western feminist scholarship, a fair amount of work has been devoted to the analysis of the issues of race and class. But the element of culture in cross-cultural gender studies is relatively neglected, and this is in part due to the neocolonial assumption that women in other parts of the world are merely passive victims of their uniformly "sexist" traditions, which should be discarded without reservation. Yet without a genuine understanding of culture, feminists also erase the very subject matter and the agency of the subject that they intend to understand. The same pattern of marginalization found between white man and white woman is thereby perpetuated in the transnational feminist discourse in which the agency and modernity of "Western women" is contrasted with the victimization of the tradition-bound "third world women." However, the imposition of one's cultural framework onto the world of the Other reflects only the limitation of one's conceptual horizon, instead of an approximation of the reality of the Other. Western authors often adopt the pose of a moral theorist coming to the rescue of the victimized third world women. Through this lens, the global feminist movement can then only be conceived of on a simple "impact-response" model, according to which changes in a "sexist," "traditional" society can only come about by importing Western ethical theories and ways of life. This implicit yet imperialistic dichotomy embodied in cross-cultural studies must be rejected by affirming the moral agency of the Others who are able to rectify themselves from within their own cultural resources. In the case of Chinese society, Confucianism would appear to be the most important cultural resource for self-rectification, where rectified Confucianism is also a newly hybrid feminist ethical theory for women's liberation. However, by concentrating on Confucianism, this project does not intend to preclude the possibility of constructing Daoist feminist ethics, or Buddhist feminist ethics, both of which are important in Chinese cultural narratives. But since most feminist critiques have focused on Confucianism and most sinologists have agreed that Confucianism underpins the foundation of Chinese civilization, it seems fitting that Confucianism be our point of entry into the new world of a hybrid feminist theory in transnational feminist discourse.

OUTLINE OF A CONFUCIAN FEMINISM: A HYBRID IDENTITY

In previous chapters, we have discussed the possible causes of women's oppression in China and its connection with Confucianism. The convergence of three cultural imperatives—the familial virtue of filial piety, ancestor worship, and the continuity of the family line—work as a theoretical, ethical ground to justify and sustain social practices—most noticeably concubinage, child-bride/servants, and female infanticide. To a large extent, Chinese sexism can be interpreted as the logical fallout of the emphasis on familial continuity coupled with the assumption that this continuation is possible only through the male line. This in turn is interlocked with the Confucian familial virtue of filial piety, and the ritual-religious-civil practice of ancestor worship. The *nei-wai* distinction as a gender distinction, based on which men are assigned to the realm of *wai* (the realm of *wen*, personal accomplishment, and extrafamilial relations) and women the *nei* (the realm of concealment, practical household management, and familial, kinship relations), helps to substantiate the limited functionary roles and sphere allotted to women. Besides being groomed to be daughters, wives, and mothers for the sole purpose of perpetuating the patrilineal line, women are also deprived of an access to the *wai* realm of *wen* (culture) and *zheng* (governance), where one's literary talent has an explicit ethical, public use and where one's name and one's good name are passed on and remembered beyond the immediate familial realm.

Perhaps the most notable intersection between social practices and the *nei-wai* distinction as a normative distinction between genders is the infamous practice of footbinding, in which the female body is concealed and marked through human means as a sign of *wen* 文, that is, a sign of culture and civility in the illiterate realm of *nei*. Through binding their own feet and the feet of their daughters, women—the purely functionary beings limited to the realm of *nei*—come to mimic their male counterparts in making and transmitting this unique "culture of ours" through wraps and needles, instead of words and brushes. In other words, in footbinding, women subvert the Confucian way of being civilized, by trimming their raw flesh instead of cultivating their whole person. Yet this subversion also reflects the structural limitation that is imposed on women as gendered beings, who have no legitimate access to the realm of *wai,* the realm of literary learning, governance, and personal accomplishment. And it is this desire to be remembered through perpetuating a male heir in the familial realm and through virtuous self-cultivation and accomplishment in the extrafamilial realm that underpins the problem of gender disparity in Chinese society. Women, the illiterate, nameless beings concealed in the realm of *nei*, are not and cannot be fully personed. In short, the problem of gender disparity in Chinese society is also a problem of the ritual boundary of the *nei* and the *wai* as a gender-based division of labor and sphere of activities. The dynamic interplay between the *nei* and the *wai*, on the one hand, robs women of any legitimate access to the *wai* realm of literary learning, and on the other hand, conceals women's achievement, especially in the areas of *wen* and *zheng*.

Women's incomplete personhood is further accentuated by the Confucian ethical project of self-cultivation that begins with the study and appropriation of the classics, the words of past sages, and the Confucian ideal of *junzi* who are not only filial and ritually deferential, but more importantly, are able to lead the people by their virtuous examples. By contrast, due to the *nei-wai* distinction, women, the limited beings, are forever incomplete. The Confucian project of self-cultivation and the ideal of *junzi*, although they are not gender specific in their moral content, are nevertheless beyond the reach of women as gendered beings of *nei*. Hence, what needs to be rectified in Confucianism is the gender-based division of labor of *nei-wai*, instead of the whole Confucian framework of the achieved personhood of *ren,* its emphasis on filial piety, or even the importance of familial continuity embodied in the practice of passing on the family name and in the practice of ancestor worship, both part of the grand notion of filial piety. In other words, in our hybrid Confucian feminism, the *nei-wai* distinction as a gender distinction will need some modifications in order to create a feminist space within.

But first of all, let us outline the basic assumptions of our hybrid feminist theory that is Confucian and feminist at the same time. First of all, our Confucian feminism presupposes a relational self situated in a web of relations that are not just external, "add-ons" to some "core" self supposed to exist prior to the external relations. Instead, the self is conceived to be coextensive with the web of relations, which are constitutive of one's substantial self. And one's moral worth in turn is measured against one's practical achievement in sustaining harmonious social relations beginning with the parent-child relation, since it is in the parent-child relation that one first finds oneself in the world. The virtue of filial piety, which emphasizes the reciprocal care between parent and child, is our starting point of being human. The parent is to be affectionate, and the child filial; that is to say, the child must be ritually proper and responsive to the parent's wishes. Without locating oneself in social relations, one is without a substantial existence, and hence one is not fully personed in the world. This starting point is Confucian through and through, since it is entirely consistent with the Confucian achieved personhood of *ren*, in which a person becomes a "person" only through embodying specific social virtues that can only be actualized in specific social relations and roles, starting with familial relations and roles.

One possible objection to this is that there is a danger in presupposing an unequal worth among human beings. The danger, of course, lies in the possible human rights abuse inflicted on those who fall below the socially defined minimal qualification for being a person. That is to say, if rights and entitlements depend on the actual contribution of a person measured in accordance with the success of her social relations, there will be no safety net for those who fail to achieve. The discourse on the natural rights of man is indeed a familiar one in Western political theory in modern times. Hobbes's natural equality of man (and woman) marks the beginning of modern contractual theory in which all men are said to be equal and free without qualification. Such an absolute equality in Western political theory, as exemplified in Locke's theory, is by and large rooted in the theory of divine creation, which provides a metaphysical ground for the claim of absolute equality. However, if one is to reject the sort of metaphysical ground upon which a person is a person without qualification, the importance of social relations must consequently be substantiated not just as "part" of the self but as the very "essence" of the self. In other words, a person is a person only if it is a person-in-relations. Severance of all social relations, in a sense, makes oneself unpersoned. The parent-child relation in which one first finds oneself in the world must be substantiated prior to other relations that expand one's self in the world. However, the virtue of filial piety is not limited to the natural relation between birthparents and their children. It certainly can be extended to accommodate modern nontraditional families in which primary caregivers are grandparents, foster parents, relatives, or even social workers in an orphanage. The point of emphasizing the importance of filial piety is to transform the conventional lineal relationship between the caring and the cared-for into a reciprocal one, so that there is no "naturalized" duty or obligation required of one toward the other without reciprocity. Filial piety is the gateway to humanity at the minimal level. One's genuine care for others is the starting point of being human, without which one is not entitled to anything in return. There is, in a word, no entitlement without qualification in Confucian ethics.

Some scholars argue that some sort of basic respect owed to others is needed in ethics in order to deal with an issue such as slavery or the abuse of human rights.[5] Most noticeably, the Kantian universal "respect for persons" is taken to be an indispensable ethical principle despite all the criticism of the abstract nature of the person presupposed in Kantian ethics. But if the end is to assert some sort of "universal" principle upon which all people are treated with respect and care, the virtue of filial piety can do a better job than the abstract respect for persons of Kantian ethics. A genuine care for others, not just respect for an abstract person, can be achieved and "universalized" by extending the virtue of filial affection found in the natural relation between parent and child to strangers. This extension is achievable since every person is also a person in the parent-child relation; that is to say, everyone is someone's father, mother, son, or daughter, not just an abstract person without social relations. The genuine affection that one has for one's family can be extended to strangers, who are also persons-in-relations. Furthermore, filial care can also be extended to every sentient being that is also situated in the natural relation of parent-offspring. The virtue of filial piety not only asserts the fundamental relatedness of one's personhood in the world, but more importantly is able to give the Kantian abstract "respect for persons" a concrete content and to extend it from the human world to the world of all sentient beings.

Secondly, in the outline of a Confucian feminism, we propose the centrality of the virtue of *ren* as the culmination of one's achieved personhood. The virtue of filial piety is the starting point of being human, but a person is also a person in an ever-enlarging web of relations. While family is the focused center, community, society, state, and the world at large are the extended field of the relational self. Or, if you will, family, community, state, and the world at large are a series of concentric circles. The self is enlarged as the circle of one's concerns and relations is enlarged. The circle of concerns for one's family is not perceived to be separate from or in conflict with one's concern for the state or the world at large. As argued earlier, the private virtue of filial piety is not a separate virtue from political good; instead it is the building block, the foundation upon which the actualization of extended public good depends. In other words, Confucian ethics assumes the priority of the family, and familial virtue as the necessary condition for the actualization of public virtue. An unfilial son/daughter is also an untrustworthy subject, and one way to ensure the harmony and longevity of the state is to groom trustworthy subjects by grooming filial sons/daughters. Once the foundation is firm, the embodiment of public good would be firm as well. Or, to put it in contemporary political rhetoric, strong family values mitigate social discord.

The virtue of *ren*, as pointed out in chapter 2, begins with the virtue of filial piety, which is also the beginning of being human. It is not surprising that not just etymologically, or paronomasitically, but also philosophically, the virtue of *ren* and the concept of person are one and the same in Confucian ethics. Beyond being filial and deferential at home, a person of *ren* is also a person of *yi*, of *li*, of *zhi*, of *shu*, of *xin*, etc. This is so because to be *ren* is also to be a person who embodies specific social excellence appropriate to specific social relations. And since there is no metaphysical ground upon which a person is a person without qualification, the scope of one's social relations is also the scope of one's substantial self. The self must, as it were, extend outward to actualize itself, and at the minimal level, the self must constantly sustain the existing, familial relations, through which the self first comes into existence. In the course of one's lifetime, as the web of relations is extended from the family to the world at large, so is the range of different social virtues that are required in order to continue to sustain those relations. The virtue of *ren,* though comprehensive in its scope, is not an "original" principle underlying all other particular virtues existing prior to all others as the necessary condition for their actualization. Instead, the virtue of *ren* as the culmination of one's personhood can only be actualized in each particular relation governed by a particular social excellence appropriate to that relation.

By affirming the virtue of *ren* as the highest achievement of a relational personhood, our Confucian feminism also affirms a practical ethic without the need for a metaphysical grounding. It affirms the priority of human relations; the community in which one is located must be the starting point, the focused center, and the world at large, the world of the Other, is the extended field where care for others is not just an abstract respect for persons with impersonal laws of reason, but a genuine care with a concrete ritual content. However, the virtue of *ren* does not give rise to a strictly communitarian ethic in which one's circle of concerns is limited to one's community or one's family. Instead, the ethic of *ren* acknowledges the priority of meeting the needs of one's community as the starting point and at the same time stresses the need to extend that genuine care for one's own to the world of others. Hence, taking the virtue of *ren* as the ethical ideal, our Confucian feminism is able to, on the one hand, address the feminist need for a concrete morality taking human relations as the priority, and, on the other hand, is able to meet the ethicist demand for a "universal" ethical principle to ensure some sort of basic "human rights," or a sense of "justice" and "fairness" owed to a person as a person without qualification.

Lastly, in our Confucian feminism, we affirm the complementarity and reciprocity of *yin-yang* and *nei-wai* as the basic structure of human relations. We suppose that in a world of concrete human relations, complementarity and reciprocity characterize the very nature of each relation. The power structure of each particular relation is not that of domination and submission in which the superior has an absolute power over the inferior. In the Confucian world, although it is true that social relations are hierarchical in nature, they are also reciprocal and complementary through and through. For instance, although in the father-son relation, the father and son are socially unequal, the legitimacy of the father's authority over the son depends on the reciprocal care that the father and the son have for each other. If the father is not ritually affectionate toward the son, the son then ceases to be obligated by his filial duty toward the father. In "historical" reality, the legend of sage-king Shun who defied his vicious father in marriage yet was still considered virtuous illustrates the point here. The father is entitled to the son's filial submission only insofar as the father is righteous in his own conduct. Our Confucian feminism assumes no fundamental supremacy embodied in the position of the father regardless of the actual virtuous achievement of the father. That is to say, by affirming the hierarchical nature of human relation, we do not thereby affirm the value of patriarchy as articulated in Western political theory that grants an absolute power to the position of the father, since the power of the father as a social superior in Confucian ethics is tempered by reciprocity. There is no such thing as right without obligation, let alone absolute authority, in Confucian ethics. The point here is that each social relation, although hierarchal in nature, is also reciprocal and complementary.

Our Confucian feminism asserts the basic hierarchical, yet complementary and reciprocal scheme of Confucian human relations in which inequality based on ability or moral authority is the starting point among particulars rather than an absolute equality without qualification. Parents and children are not socially equal and they should not be equal, nor are teachers and students, or the elderly and the young. The assumption in Confucian ethics is that the socially inferior must observe a basic sense of deference toward the socially superior, so that there is a sense of harmony and continuity in the complex web of human relations in which the knowledge of the past is passed on from the elderly to the young, from the parent to the child, and from the teacher to the student. The knowledge of the past signifies more than the literary, intellectual tradition of the past that can be understood independently of one's appreciation of the past. Here the knowledge of the past also signifies the ritual tradition, and the sense of continuity of one's familial and cultural identity, which can only be learned through embodying particular kinship and social roles. And hence observing a basic deference toward the socially superior is essential to the continuity of the ritual and intellectual tradition of the past. Such a social inequality changes over the course of one's lifetime. One is neither definitely socially inferior nor superior, and each relation is premised on complementarity and reciprocity instead of domination and submission.

In order to meet the challenges of feminism, the hierarchical relation between husband and wife, and the gender-based division of labor in terms of the *nei* and the *wai* will need rectification. Within the Confucian ethical system, there is no necessity that a wife must be subordinated to her husband. In the traditional account, the husband-wife relation is modeled after the ruler-minister relation and therefore the husband is socially superior and wife socially inferior. However, the ruler-husband and minister-wife analogy is fallacious, since unlike the ruler-minister relation, the husband-wife relation is personal and intimate in nature. And unlike the contractual nature of the relation between the ruler and the minister, the bond between a husband and a wife (or in the modern sense of partnership) is ideally assumed to last for a lifetime and the life after. The gender-based hierarchy in the husband-wife relation will lose its justification if women are allowed full access to cultural resources like their male counterparts. In the modern age, an alternative analogy for the relation between husband and wife would be the relation between friends, which is one of the Confucian five relations. Although it is true that the basic scheme for all human relations in the Confucian world is hierarchical in nature including friendship, the assumed hierarchy in friendship is not gender based.

The hierarchy in friendship is mostly based on ability and moral authority. The association between friends is strictly voluntary, and the duration of that association depends on an assumed common goal. Such a free association in which people are bound together for a self-defined common goal best approximates the relation between the husband and the wife in the modern age. This rectification of the relation between husband and wife and the gender-based division of labor is made within the Confucian framework without resorting to any metaphysical basis for absolute equality. In other words, the problem of gender disparity derived from the gender-based division of labor in terms of the *nei* and the *wai* distinction and the hierarchical relation of husband and wife can be addressed by using resources available within the Confucian tradition. With this rectification, the theoretical justification for women's liberation is no longer limited to the liberal argument of individual rights accompanied by an implicit theist assumption of an absolute equality for all. Our Confucian feminism affirms the Confucian tradition while taking account of feminist concerns for gender parity. The end result of creating the hybrid identity of Confucian feminism is a qualified inequality among the unequal based on ability and moral authority instead of gender per se. Once the gender-based hierarchy and division of labor is taken away from the relation between husband and wife, what is left is a more flexible rearrangement of the division of labor within one's household in which a woman can be in charge of all or part of the *wai* and a man all or part of the *nei,* or vice versa, depending on the common goal set in that particular relationship by its participants.

Once the gender-based division of labor is eradicated, women will no longer be confined to the limited realm of *nei,* and hence would also be able to achieve the highest cultural ideal of *junzi,* who are not only ritually proper at home but also are fully cultured, leading the masses by their virtuous example. But eradicating the gender-based boundary of the *nei* and the *wai* would directly challenge the normative gender identity and consequently the sense of civility in the Chinese world. The difficulty is not so much whether such a change should be made; rather, the question here is whether such a change can be justified by the Confucian tradition itself, or whether any change in gender relations can only be made possible by importing Western ethical theories. To put it another way, the question is whether Confucianism is perceived as a sexist ideology through and through, and hence, as far as the issue of women's oppression is concerned, no rectification is possible from within Confucianism.

Confucianism as a living tradition thrives on incorporating others into its expanding self; its adaptability has been proven again and again in history. For instance, the first wave of expansion of Confucianism occurred in its incorporation of the theory of *yinyang wuxing* during the late Qin and early Han in order to survive politically first in the Qin under its anti-*Ru* policies, and subsequently to compete with the popular *Yinyangjia* as well as *Daojia* in the Han. The second wave of expansion, as commonly known, occurred during the Song period and the result is the rise of *Daoxue* and *Lixue*—that is "Neo-Confucianism"—which in reality is more of a mixed plate of Confucianism, Daoism, and Buddhism. Now the new challenge that lies ahead for Confucianism is feminism. The making of Confucian feminism, as Tu Wei-ming put it, would be the third wave of expansion of Confucianism, whose survival again is on the line.[6] The goal of making Confucian feminism, of course, is more than simply keeping Confucianism alive in the twenty-first century. It is an affirmation of the dynamic nature of Confucianism, so that one can be a Confucian and a feminist without apology, just as one can be an Aristotelian and a feminist, a Kantian and a feminist, or an existentialist and a feminist at the same time, despite some sexist statements made in that specific intellectual tradition.

REFLECTIONS AND CONCLUSIONS

In the end, this project eventually is personal. Like de Beauvoir, who wrote *The Second Sex* in order to answer the personal question of what it means to be a woman, I am trying to answer to myself what it means to be a Chinese Confucian woman. Through the eye of Western feminism, I see my own reflection as an Other. The tension between being a feminist and being a Chinese is a tension between the need to form a universal sisterhood where all women are assumed to share some sort of common roots of oppression and the need to substantiate and affirm my own cultural identity that in turn dissolves the assumed commonality among women across cultural boundaries. As a feminist and as a Chinese, I am trying to resolve such a tension. At the same time, I feel compelled to prioritize my own cultural identity, since I am lost in a theoretical space where women exist as ahistorical, acultural beings. In that abstract theoretical space, Western cultural assumptions, however, are privileged in transnational feminist discourse. That privileging of Western ethical theories in turn makes it impossible for me to be a feminist and at the same time a Chinese whose substantial identity is rooted in the larger, cultural framework of Confucianism—the emblem of Chinese high culture.

This project is intended to seek reconciliation between feminism and Confucianism by proposing a hybrid ethical theory in which Confucianism is not just a convenient scapegoat for the oppression of Chinese women. Instead, Confucianism is seen as a dynamic working of different voices and indeterminate meanings in orthodox teachings that afford the Chinese people sufficient conceptual tools to engage in internal critiques of the social abuse of women without resorting to a total rejection of their Confucian root. In other words, one need not be a Marxist, a liberal, an existentialist, or a radical separatist to be a feminist of some sort, since it would no longer be an oxymoron to be a feminist and a Confucian at the same time. By sorting out the cultural elements of being a woman within the cultural boundaries of China, I also seek to add to the epistemological portrait of the roots of women's oppression whose model of liberation is no longer limited to the Kantian autonomous subject, the Cartesian agendered cogito, liberal individual rights, or Marxist material equality. Now it is also possible to take Confucian relational, virtue-based personhood as a viable goal for women's liberation. As the epistemological portrait of the roots of women's oppression is enriched by the study of Confucianism, so is the range of the possibility for women's liberation in feminist ethics and in the theoretical imagination.

NOTES

CHAPTER 1. INTRODUCTION

1. The term *Western feminist* here primarily is used to refer to an ideological orientation that frames Chinese women's liberation in accordance with Western intellectual tradition. In this way, a feminist and/or sinologist who is de facto Chinese or have Chinese ancestry could fall into the category of "Western Feminist" and a feminist and/or sinologist who is de facto Westerner could fall outside of that category insofar as their ideological orientation is concerned. So that the empirical problem that so and so is a Westerner yet advocates such and such position or so and so is a Chinese yet advocates such and such position can be resolved.

2. To say this is not to deny the importance of Daoism and Buddhism in the lives of Chinese people. After all, Confucianism, Daoism, and Buddhism are understood as three essential teachings in Chinese narratives of their intellectual traditions. But the unique position and privileges that Confucianism enjoyed in Chinese history is unparalleled within the other two prominent teachings. Also, while there is considerable scholarship devoted to the compatibility between Daoism and feminism or the Daoist penchant for "feminine" virtues, scholarship that explores a possible feminist space within the Confucian tradition is almost nonexistent. This project aims at opening up that feminist space in order to lay a foundation for the construction of Confucian feminism.

3. For the postcolonial discourse in feminist scholarship, see, for instance, *Signs* (1995), special issue on "Postcolonial, Emergent, and Indigenous Feminisms"; Also Grewal and Kaplan (1994); John (1996).

4. Raphals (1998).

5. Watson (1986).

6. The husband-wife relationship here is used analogically, not biologically, so that it can also be used to accommodate alternative sexual relationships.

CHAPTER 2. CONFUCIANISM, CHINESENESS, AND *REN* VIRTUOUS PERSONHOOD

1. Julia Kristeva (1977), 66–99. Also see Olga Lang (1946), 42–43; Helen F. Snow (1967), 38; Katie Curtin (1975), 10; Marjorie Topley 1975; Margery Wolf 1975 and 1994; Elisabeth Croll (1978), 12–14; Phyllis Andors (1983), 126–27; Emily Honig and Gail Hershatter (1988), 274. For the anti-Confucian sentiment during the May Fourth Movement, see Hua R. Lan and Vanessa L. Fong 1999.

2. Wolf (1994), 253.

3. Chenyang Li (2000), 1.

4. Frederic Wakeman remarked in the round table discussion on De Bary's *The Trouble with Confucianism* that: "The trouble with Confucianism ... was that it had no name in premodern China." Wakeman (1994), 19. For the Jesuit's invention of "Confucianism," see Lionel M. Jensen's *Manufacturing Confucianism*, 1997.

5. The term *ru* is also found in the *Zhouli*, a ritual text of Zhou. In the traditional account, the *Zhouli* is said to have been compiled by the Duke of Zhou; yet scholars generally agree that the *Zhouli* was probably compiled between the fourth and second century BCE. See William Boltz's "*Chou li*", in *Early Chinese Texts: A Bibliographical Guide* (1993), 24–32. The term *ru* is also found in the *Zouzhuan* commentary of *Chunqiu*; see Duke Ai, the twenty-first year. For the translation, cf. James Legge, *The Chun Tsew with the Tso Chuen* (1960) V, 853.

6. For the passages in the *Zhouli* and the commentaries, see Hu Shi (1953), 2–3.

7. See especially "*Yiwenzhi*" of the *Book of Latter Han*, "*Ruxue*" of the *Old Book of Tang*, and "*Rulinzhuan*" of the *History of Qing*.

8. William Boltz's "*Shou wen chieh tzu*," in *Early Chinese Texts* (1993), 429–42.

9. Quoted in Hu Shi's "*Shou Ru*" (1953), 6. Also see Lionel Jensen (1997), 295.

10. Jensen (1997), 294–95, 300.

11. Ibid., 156.

12. Ibid., 170.

13. The rivalry between *Rujia* and *Mojia* is clearly recorded in the *Zhuangzi* in the "*Qiwulun*" chapter: "*Dao* is obscured by partial achievements; speech is obscured by eloquent verbiage. Therefore there are disputes between *Ru* and *Mo* over what is right and wrong [儒墨是非]. They invariably affirm what their opponents deny and deny what their opponents affirm." Also in the "*Tianyun*" chapter of *Zhuangzi*, it is said once the minds of the people become deviant, the world is in a state of unrest, and, "Hence, all under heaven are in a great panic, and both *Ru* and *Mo* arise [天下大駭儒墨皆起]." In the "*Xianxue*" chapter of *Hanfeizi*, the world's most illuminating learning is *Ru* and *Mo* (世之顯學儒墨也). In the *Mencius*, *Mo*, *Ru*, *Yang* are characterized as three main schools of thought (7B/26). Cf. James Legge, *The Works of Mencius*, (1960) II, 491. For the translation of *Zhuangzi*, see Victor H. Mair, *Wandering on the Way: Early Taoist Tales and Parables of Chuang Tzu*, (1998), 15, 141.

14. For the translation, cf. Yi-Pao Mei, *The Ethical and Political Works of Motse* (1929), 202.

15. See especially *"Tanggong"* pt. I & II of *Liji*. Cf. James Legge, *Li Chi: Book of Rites* (1967) I, 120–201.

16. Yi-Pao Mei (1929), 202–203.

17. Ibid., 203n1.

18. Ibid.

19. Jensen (1997), 194–95.

20. For the term *rufu*, see *Mozi*, *"Gongmeng"* chapter; *Zhuangzi*, *"Shoujian"* and *"Tianzifang"* chapters; and *Liji*, *"Ruxing"* chapter.

21. Jensen (1997), 197.

22. See especially *Lunheng*, chapter 52 *"Shiyin."* Also see Jensen (1997), 192–93.

23. Peter Boodberg, "The Semasiology of Some Primary Confucian Concepts" (1953), 329.

24. Cf. Mair (1998), 203–204, 335.

25. Hu Shi (1953), 2–3. For an in-depth discussion of Hu Shi's *"Shou Ru,"* see Jensen (1997), esp. ch.3.

26. See *Xunzi*, esp. ch. 2, *"Xiushen,"* chapter 6, *"Feishierzi,"* and chapter 19, *"Lilun."*

27. Cf. Homer H. Dubs, *The works of Hsuntze* (1966), 110–11.

28. Cf. Legge (1967) II, 409–10.

29. Cf. Legge, ibid., 405, 409. The same passage can also be found in the *Kongzi jiayu* (Confucius Family Discourses), chapter 5, "Explaining the Conduct of *Ru.*"

30. Cf. Dubs (1966), 111–12.

31. *Shiji*, ch. 6; quoted in A. C. Graham's *Disputers of the Tao: Philosophical Argument in Ancient China* (1989), 32.

32. *Shiji*, ch. 6; cf. Graham, *Disputers*, 32–33.

33. Graham, ibid., 33.

34. Cf. E. A. Kracke Jr., "Region, Family and Individual in the Chinese Examination System," in *Chinese Thought and Institutions* (1957), 253.

35. Cf. Homer H. Dubs, *The History of the Former Han Dynasty by Pan Ku* (1944) II, 348.

36. Kracke (1957), 253.

37. Cf. Niu Zhipin (1995), 131–44, 138–39.

38. *"Ruxue shan"* (Part I of *Ru* Learning), *Liezhuan* (Biography) 139, in the *Old Book of Tang*.

39. For the Song *Ru*'s delineation of the transmission of the orthodox *Ru* learning, see Thomas A. Wilson, *Genealogy of the Way: the Construction and Uses of the Confucian Tradition in Late Imperial China* (1995), esp. Appendix A and B.

40. *The History of Song*; also see Peter K. Bol, "Seeking Common Ground: Han Literati under Jurchen Rule" (1987), 468.

41. On the connection between Song *Ru* and the Buddhist tradition of genealogy, see Thomas A. Wilson (1995), 114. For the connection between Song's *Daoxue* and Daoism, see Wing-tsit Chan, *A Source Book in Chinese Philosophy* (1963), 460.

42. Wing-tsit Chan (1963), 462, 496; and his *Chu Hsi and Neo-Confucianism* (1986), 595.

43. Wing-tsit Chan (1986), 599–600; also see Thomas Wilson (1995), 39–40.

44. For instance, see Jin *Ru*, Yuan Haowen and Wang Ruoxu's, attacks on Song's *Daoxue*; as quoted in Peter K. Bol (1987), 532, n258.

45. Kracke (1957), 254.

46. Bol (1987), 470.

47. Benjamin A. Elman, "Political, Social, and Cultural Reproduction via Civil Service Examinations in Late Imperial China" (1991), 13.

48. Ibid., 17.

49. Ibid., 22.

50. Bol (1987), 528.

51. John W. Dardess, *Confucianism and Autocracy: Professional Elites in the Founding of The Ming Dynasty* (1983), 14–16; also see Bol (1987), 527.

52. Bol (1987), 535.

53. Kracke (1957), 263.

54. Ibid. However, John Dardess gave a slightly different number of degrees awarded annually. According to Dardess, in 1315, the Yuan quota for the highest degree (*Qinshi*) was set at twenty-five for *Hanren*, twenty-five for *Nanren*, or an annual all-Chinese average of about seventeen degrees altogether. Cf. Dardess (1983), 17.

55. For instance, under Qubilai's rule, no Han could become a prime minister, the highest civil post in the state; all prime ministers were ethnic Mongolians; see Dardess, 104. Also as Thomas Wilson pointed out, during the first half of the Yuan, Han were recruited by the state as functionary clerks (*li* 吏) not as officials (*guan* 官); see Wilson (1995), 50.

56. Bol (1987), 483–93.

57. Ibid., 469.

58. Ibid., 488–93.

59. Quoted in Peter Bol, with some modification in the translation, cf. Bol (1987), 536.

60. As quoted in Jensen (1997), 170. Also quoted in Dardess (1983), 22.

61. Quoted in Dardess, with some modification in the translation; cf. Dardess (1983), 23.

62. Song Lian, "*Qirujie*" (1970). For a discussion of the essay, see Dardess (1983), 158–62; also Jensen (1997), 171.

63. Song Lian, "*Qirujie*" (1970).

64. Wilson (1995), 51–52.

65. Dardess (1983), 17.

66. Kracke (1957), 263.

67. Cf. Benjamin A. Elman, *Classicism, Politics, and Kinship: The Ch'ang-chou School of New Text Confucianism in Late Imperial China* (1990), 16.

68. Elman (1991), 14.

69. Kracke (1957), 263–64.

70. Elman (1990), 275.

71. Wilson (1995), 53.

72. Ibid., 36, 52.

73. Elman (1990), "Introduction," xxi–xxxiii.

74. Quoted in Jensen (1997), 43.

75. Ibid., 49.

76. Ibid., 53.

77. For other possible meanings of *Ru*, see Jensen, ibid.

78. For the myth of Han identity, see Hall and Ames, *The Democracy of the Dead: Dewey, Confucius, and the Hope for Democracy in China* (1999), esp. ch. 1. For the meaning of Confucianism as a cultural narrative, see Ames, "New Confucianism: A Native Response to Western Philosophy" (1999), 23–52.

79. For instance, Wing-tsit Chan, "Chinese and Western Interpretations of *Jen* (Humanity)" (1975), 107.

80. Lin Yu-sheng, "The Evolution of the Pre-Confucian Meaning of *Jen* and the Confucian Concept of Moral Autonomy" (1974–75), 172–73, n3.

81. Wing-tsit Chan (1975), 107 and Lin Yu-sheng, ibid.

82. Wing-tsit Chan, ibid.

83. Fang Ying-hsien, "[On the origins of *ren*: the transformation of the concept from the time of the *Book of Songs* and the *Book of Documents* to Confucius]" (1976), 22.

84. Cf. de Beauvoir (1989), xxi–xxii.

85. Jonathan Barnes, *The Complete Works of Aristotle* (1984); cf. *Generation of Animals*, 737a 28–30.

86. Genevieve Lloyd, *The Man of Reason: "Male" and "Female" in Western Philosophy* (1984), x. For other feminist critiques of Western philosophy, see Sandra Harding and Merrill B. Hintikka (1983); Jean Grimshaw (1986); Morwenna Griffiths and Margaret Whitford (1988); Louise M. Antony and Charlotte Witt (1993); Bat-ami Bar On (1994); and Janet A. Kourany (1998). For the distinctive "feminine" gender traits in psychology, see especially Nancy Chodorow (1974); Carol Gilligan (1982); and Nel Noddings (1984).

87. Peter Boodberg, "The Semasiology of Some Primary Confucian Concepts" (1953), 328.

88. See *Mencius*, 7B/16, *Zhongyong* 20 and 25; for translation, cf. James Legge (1960)I, 405, 149; and (1960) II, 485.

89. Hall and Ames, *Thinking Through Confucius* (1987), 114; also see Tu Wu-ming (1985), 84.

90. See for example, Wing-tsit Chan, "Evolution of the Confucian Concept *Jen*" (1955), 295–319; also see, Lin Yu-sheng (1974); and Fan Ying-hsien (1976).

91. For the translation, cf. James Legge (1960) III, 354.

92. Cf. Legge (1960) IV, 127.

93. Legge III, 292.

94. Cf. Ames and Rosemont (1998), 226; all the translations of the *Analects* or *Lunyu*, unless noted otherwise, are based on Ames and Rosemont's with some minor modifications of my own.

95. For the date of compilation of the texts, see Anne Cheng, "*Ch'un ch'iu, Kung yang, Ku liang* and *Tso chuan*," and Chang I-jen, William G. Boltz, and Michael Loewe, "*Kuo yu*," in *Early Chinese Text* (1993), 67–76, 263–68.

96. *Zuozhuan*, the "Fourteenth Year of the Duke of Xi"; cf. Legge (1960) V, 161–62.

97. *Guoyu*, the "Discourse of Zhou"; cf. Fang Yin-hsien (1976), 24.

98. For the connection between *ren* and the concept of a complete person in the Spring and Autumn period, see Fang (1976).

99. *Guoyu*, the "Discourse of Qi"; cf. Fang Yin-hsien (1976), 24.

100. Cf. Ames and Rosemont (1998), 159–60.

101. Cf. Legge (1960) II, 333.

102. *Xunzi*, chapter 27, "*Dalue*."

103. For *ren* as a general virtue, see Wing-tsit Chan (1975), 107–109; and Tu Wei-ming (1985), 81–92.

104. Legge (1960) II, 414.

105. See for instance, Ambrose Y. C. King (1985); Hall and Ames (1987), 110–25. Also Lin Yu-sheng (1974), 193.

106. Fei Xiaotong 1992; esp. chapter 5, "The Morality of Personal Relationships," 71–79.

107. Legge (1960) II, 282.

108. Hu Shi (1919), 116; also see King (1985), 57.

109. Herbert Fingarette (1983); as quoted in Ames and Rosemont (1998), 48.

110. The five relations are father-son, ruler-minister, husband-wife, siblings, and friends. Cf. *Mencius* 3A/4; Legge II, 251–52.

111. King (1985), 58.

112. Ames (1994).

113. Legge (1960) II, 456, 314.

114. Ibid., 295.

115. Legge (1960) I, 357.

116. Ibid., 406.

117. Ibid.

118. Hall and Ames (1987), 118.

CHAPTER 3. *YIN-YANG*, GENDER ATTRIBUTES, AND COMPLEMENTARITY

1. The sense of universal womanhood beyond the limited, traditional kinship roles associated with the female sex in the modern use of the term *nuxing* is clearly

shown in the translation of the Western concept of feminism as *nuxing zhuyi*, and all feminist and women's writings fall into the literary category of *nuxing wenxue*.

2. For more details on the invention of the term *nuxing*, and the communists' use of the term *funu* in political discourse, see Barlow (1994a and 1994b). For the term *nuxing* as a fictional representation of a universal "womanhood" in the literary discourse during the May Fourth Movement, see Ching-ki Stephen (1988).

3. Cf. Legge (1960) IV, 1.

4. Other examples from the *Book of Songs* can be found in poems 9, 23, 42, and 58. (For the conversion between the poem number and the page number in Legge's translation, see Legge (1960) IV, "Concordance Table," v–xiv.) It is true that the word *nu* in certain poems refers to married women as well, such as poem 82, but mostly it refers to unmarried girls or young brides. By the same token, the word *nu* in the infamous passage (17.25) of the *Analects* where Confucius disparaged *nuzi* along with petty men as lacking ritual propriety can arguably be interpreted as referring to young girls who are not yet properly ritualized and hence gendered. However, this is not an apology for Confucius's "sexist" remark. Rather the point here is to draw attention to the absence of the concept of gender independent of kinship relations in the Confucian tradition.

5. *Liji*, "Miscellaneous Records," pt. I and commentary; cf. Legge (1967) I, 137.

6. The term *xiong-ci* also appears in the *Daodejing*, where the distinction between the human and the natural world seen less explicit. The elusive writing style of the *Daodejing* makes a definitive interpretation of the term *xiong-ci* difficult. It is not clear whether *xiong* and *ci* mentioned in chapter 28 and the word *ci* in chapter 10 signify the gender relation between man and woman in the human world, or the so-called "masculine and feminine" qualities associated with the male and female sex.

7. *Mozi*, ch. 6; cf. Mei (1929), 26–27.

8. *Xunzi*, ch. 5; cf. Dubs (1966), 71–72. However in Eric L. Hutton's translation, the term *nannu* was rendered as "male and female"; see Hutton (2003), 114.

9. The view of gender as determined by inborn biological, sexual differences could be traced as far back as Aristotle. The Aristotelian biological essentialism in gender discourse was challenged in de Beauvoir's *The Second Sex* where she separated sex from gender, the former being the biological fact, the latter the process of acculturation. After de Beauvoir, the conceptual separation between sex and gender has become a common assumption in modern feminist discourse. However some contemporary feminists such as Judith Butler and Denise Riley have questioned the validity of the duality between sex and gender, nature and culture, etc. Judith Butler (1990 and 1993); and Denise Riley (1988). Also see Elizabeth V. Spelman (1988).

10. Richard W. Guisso (1981), 48.

11. Margery Wolf (1985), 112; as quoted in Barlow (1989), 318.

12. Barlow (1994a), 255.

13. Ibid., 256.

14. Needham (1956) II, 33; as quoted in Ames (1981), 1. A similar assessment of Daoism as the feminine can also be found in Ellen Marie Chen: "*Tao* is said again and again in the *Tao Te Ching* to be a female principle ... ; it is empty, dark, and yielding, all characteristics of the female" (1969), 399.

15. Needham (1956) II, 105; as noted in Ames (1981), 21. The speculation of a matriarchal society in the pre-Zhou China can also be found in Ellen Marie Chen's work (1969), 401–405. For the connection between Daoism and the existence of a matriarchal, primitive society in ancient China, see especially Sandra A. Wawrytko (2000), 163–98.

16. Cf. Genevieve Lloyd (1984). The term *Cartesian* here does not refer so much to Descartes himself; in fact Descartes had very little to say about the nature of woman. His mind-body metaphysical duality, on the contrary, was used by eighteenth-century Enlightenment writers to advocate gender equality. Rather, the term *Cartesian* here is used to refer to the historical and cultural use of Cartesianism in gender discourse. Here I am following Susan Bordo's distinction between Descartes and Cartesianism: "[I]t is the dominant cultural and historical renderings of Cartesianism, not Descartes 'himself,' that are the object of our criticisms" (Bordo [1999], 2). For more details on the historical use and the misuse of Cartesianism, see Stephen Gaukroger (1995), cf. esp. "Introduction."

17. For the classificatory aspect of *yin-yang* correlations as the basic binary scheme in Chinese cosmology, see Graham (1986 and 1989).

18. Black (1989), 185; and Raphals 1998, esp. 139–40.

19. For more details on the linguistic structure and the semantic meaning of the term *yin-yang*, see Xu Fuguan (1961), cf. no. 19, pt. I, 4. Also see Bernhard Karlgren (1957), cf. no. 651, 173 and no. 720, 188–98. Rubin (1982), 140–41. Graham (1986), 70–71.

20. It is true that the term *yin-yang* occurs in the *Yijing* as well; but it only appears in the later attached commentaries and appendices, which were probably compiled around the late Qin or the early Han period. The crucial difference between the *Zhouyi* and later attached commentaries of the *Yijing* will be discussed later in detail. In the *Shujing*, the term *yin-yang* only occurs once in the "*Zhouquan*" chapter of the "ancient text." Scholars generally agree that the ancient text is a later forgery composed around the early fourth century CE. Hence, the earliest appearance of the term *yin-yang* in Chinese literature must be accorded to the *Shijing*, whose status as a Zhou text is generally accepted. For more details, see Edward L Shaughnessy (1993b), 376.

21. *Shijing* poem 35; cf. Legge (1960) IV, 55.

22. Ibid., poem 174; ibid., 276.

23. Ibid., poem 250; ibid., 483.

24. Cf. Legge (1960) IV, 488; and Xu Fuguan (1961) I, 4–5.

25. For the references of the six *qi* in *Guanzi* and *Guoyu*, see Raphals (1998), 148–49.

26. *Zhuangzi* ch. 1; cf. Victor H. Mair (1998), 5.

27. Ibid., ch. 22; ibid., 212.

28. Ibid., ch. 6; ibid., 58.

29. *Zuozhuan*, Duke Zhao, the "first year;" cf. Legge (1960) V, 573–74, 580–81.

30. Raphals (1998), 147; Xu Fuguan (1961) I, 5–6; and Graham (1986), 71.

31. *Mozi*, ch. 27; cf. Yi-Pao Mei (1929), 144.

32. Cf. note 7.

33. Raphals (1998), 158–60. I am greatly in debt to Raphals for the following analysis on the complementarity of the *yin-yang nan-nu* correlation found in the *Mozi*.

34. *Shiji*, ch. 130; cf. Rubin (1982), 141; Raphals (1998), 143n13.

35. *Hanshu* ch. 30; cf. Rubin, ibid., 140–41; also see Raphals, ibid.

36. Tang Chunyi (1976); as quoted in Rubin (1982), 140.

37. *Daodejing*, ch. 42; Ames and Hall (2003), 142–43. All translations of DDJ are based on Ames and Hall's (2003) with some modifications of my own. Also cf. D. C. Lau (1963), 49.

38. Ames and Hall (2003), 120; D. C. Lau (1963), 33.

39. *Zhuangzi*, ch. 25; cf. Mair (1998), 264.

40. *Xunzi*, ch. 19; cf. Homer Dubs (1928), 235.

41. *Lushi chunqiu* in the later imperial catalogues was classified under the section of the "Mixed." It is traditionally attributed to Lu Buwei who died in 235 BCE, but his in-house scholars around 239 BCE probably composed it. For more details on the origins and the authenticity of the text, see Michael Carson and Michael Loewe (1993), 324.

42. *Lushi chunqiu* 5.2; cf. Raphals (1998), 151.

43. For relevant passages in the *Baihutong*, see Raphals (1998), 164–65 n99–103.

44. *Yijing*, "*Shougua*" commentary 3.10; cf. Wilhelm and Baynes (1961), 294.

45. Ibid., "*Dazhuan*" commentary IA, 1.1; cf. Wilhelm and Baynes (1961), 301.

46. *Chunqiu fanlu*, ch. 43; cf. Raphals (1998), 163.

47. *Zhuangzi*, ch. 33.

48. See for instance Shaughnessy (1996), 1–13. According to Fung Yu-lan, the word *yi* of *Yijing* originally means "easy," and hence the *Yijing* should be understood as "Divination Made Easy." See Fung Yu-lan (1952) I, 380; also see Graham (1989), 359.

49. However, in recent scholarship, the supposed derivation of the sixty-four hexagrams from the eight core trigrams has been questioned, since all numerical symbols regularly appear in sets of six instead of three in the study on Western Zhou bronzes and the late Shang oracle bones. The eight core trigrams, as Edward Shaughnessy speculated, might in fact appear later than the sixty-four hexagrams. In any case, *qian-kun* is not the primary binary. Shaughnessy (1993a), 216–28.

50. *Zuozhuan*, Duke Zhao, the "seventh year"; cf. Legge (1960), 614–15, 619. Also see Shaughnessy (1996), 7–8.

51. *Yijing*, "*Dazhuan*" commentary II, 6.1; cf. Wihelm/Baynes (1961), 369.

52. See, for instance, Shaughnessy (1993a), 221. As he wrote, "[T]here can be no question that the commentaries were not produced by Confucius," and "[I]n general it would seem that they attained their present form in the mid-third to the early second century B.C., with the probable exception of the *Hsu kua* which would seem to date from the Later Han period."

53. Graham (1986), 13.

54. Graham (1989), 359.

55. Cf. Graham (1986), 76. The interpretation of the term *wuxing* found in the *Xunzi* as referring to five forms of moral conduct instead of five processes is enforced by the finding of the "*Wuxing*" chapter attributed to Zisizi, Confucius's grandson. In the new found chapter, the term *wuxing*, with a slight variation, refers to *ren, li, yi, zhi*, and *sheng*. A list of the five virtues unconnected with the term *wuxing* can also be found in the *Mencius* 7B/24. However, neither in Zisizi's "*Wuxing*" chapter nor in the *Mencius*, is the five-virtue correlated with the five-process. At this time due to the lack of any textual evidence, it is still not clear whether the *wuxing* as five forms of moral conduct found in *Xunzi* functions as a derivative concept of the five-process or an independent concept all together.

It is possible that Zou Yan's *wude* theory had already incorporated the five kinds of moral conduct into the *wuxing*. In the "*Hongfan*" 洪範 chapter of the *Book of Documents* where the term *wuxing* first appears, one also finds other correlative terms such as the five happiness (*wufu* 五福), five works (*wushi* 五事), five standards of chronology (*wusi* 五祀), three virtues (*sande* 三德), six unfavorable extremes (*luji* 六極), etc.

The complex correlation between *wuxing* and the five forms of moral conduct can also be found in the later Han text—*Baihutong*—where the five virtues were incorporated into the *wuxing* theory. As shown in the following table:*

(Five Processes)	Wood	Fire	Earth	Metal	Water
(Four Seasons)	Spring	Summer		Autumn	Winter
(Four Directions)	East	South	(Center)	West	North
(Five Colors)	Green	Red	Yellow	White	Black
(Five Viscera)	Liver	Heart	Spleen	Lungs	Kidney
(Five Conducts)	Ren	Li	Xin	Yi	Zhi

*table adopted from Graham (1989), 382. Cf. Baihutong, ch. 30, "Instinct and Emotion."

A similar correlation between the five-conduct and *wuxing* can also be found in the *Yueling* calendar of *Liji*, which, in part, was taken from the third-century BCE text *Lushi chunqiu*; for more see, Rubin (1982), 136, 143.

56. For the term *wuxing*, see *Xunzi* ch. 6. And for the term *yin-yang* see ch. 17 and ch. 19.

57. Xunzi in chapter 6 following his negative assessment of the *wuxing* theory also said that Zisi (the grandson of Confucius) and Mencius help spread the unworthy *wuxing* theory. (c.f. *Xunzi* 6). This accusation, however, cannot be substantiated, since in the present version of the *Mencius* there is no mention of the *wuxing* theory at all. But it is possible that after the death of Mencius, his followers integrated the *wuxing* and *yinyang* concept into the Mencius tradition. As for Zisi, the authenticity of the latest discovery of the writings on the *wuxing* theory attributed to him has yet to be assessed. But the initial dating of the "*Wuxing*" chapter is around 300 BCE.

58. For instance, see Ames and Rosemont (1998), 114–15; Lau (1979), 88; and Graham (1986), 9. The usual rendering of the word *yi* found in the passage 7.17 as a reference to the *Yijing* often appeals to the authority of the biography of Confucius found in Sima Qian's (c.145–90 BCE) *Shiji*, in which Confucius was said to have a deep interest in the *Yijing* in the later years of his life. "Late in life, Confucius enjoyed the *Yi*, putting in order the *Tuan, Xi, Xiang, Shougua* and *Wenyan* [i.e., the commentaries], thrice wearing out the leather binders in reading the *Yi*" (*Shiji* 47; cf. Ames and

Rosemont [1998], 241n108, and Raphals [1998], 145n19). The accuracy of Sima Qian's account of Confucius is difficult to assess. But one thing should be kept in mind is that the *Shiji* was compiled around the late second and early first century BCE after the consolidation and the institutionalization of *Yijing* as one of the five classics in 136 BCE. And therefore the association between the *Yijing* and Confucian thoughts or Confucius himself after the Han became natural and necessary. In the outer chapter—"Heavenly Movements" of Zhuangzi—Confucius was also said to be proficient in the six classics including the *Yijing*. This chapter, as recent scholars point out, was probably compiled around the late second century BCE; cf. Roth (1993), 56–57.

59. *Xunzi*, ch. 1; cf. Dubs (1928), p. 36–37. The *Yijing* plays no significant role in the text, *Xunzi*. However, according to Han scholar Liu Xiang who compiled the text, *Xunzi*, in its present form, Xunzi was proficient in the *Yijing*. Also, John Knoblock noted that in the *Shiji* it was recorded that Meng Xi, a Han scholar of the Xunzi tradition, was an expert in the *Yijing*. In chapter 5 of *Xunzi*, the *Yijing* is mentioned as an authority, but is not correlated with the concept of *yinyang* or *wuxing*; and in chapter 27, there are three paragraphs devoted to explicating the *Yijing*. Overall, there is no explicit textual evidence indicating that Xunzi was particularly concerned with the *Yijing* or the *qiankun, yinyang* concept in his writings, since other classics, such as the *Songs*, and the *Rituals*, are evoked as the authority far more frequently than the *Yi*. C.f. Knoblock (1988)I, 42–48.

60. For instance, see Rubin (1982); and Xu Fuguan (1961).

61. Traditionally, the grand synthesis of the *yinyang* and the *wuxing* concepts is attributed to Dong Zhongshu; yet several scholars have contested this attribution. See Sarah A. Queen (1996). According to Queen, the grand synthesis began at least as early as the third century BCE. Queen also questioned Dong Zhongshu's authorship on the *wuxing* chapters which might be in fact compiled by anonymous writers during the Latter Han (c.f. 3 and 101).

62. For a brief account of the *Yinyangjia*, see Wing-tsit Chan (1963), 244–50. Also see Vitaly A. Rubin, for his critique of Chan's account of the *Yinyangjia* (1982), 131–32. The biography of Zou Yan as recorded in the *Shiji*, says: "[Zou Yan] he therefore examined deeply into the increase and decrease of *yin* and *yang* and wrote essays totaling more than one hundred thousand words about strange permutations and about the rise and fall of great sages" (*Shiji* 74); quoted in Rubin (1982), 142.

63. Sima Qian wrote, "In this time [the time of the Warring States] only Zou Yan had a clear view of the movements of *wude*, and he disclosed the difference between appearance and disappearance [of *de* or power] in such a manner as to become famous among the rulers." (*Shiji* 26); and, "Zou Yan won fame among the rulers for his theories of *yin* and *yang* . . ." (*Shiji* 74); cf. Rubin (1982), 142.

64. Graham (1986), 12–13.

65. For more details on Zou Yan's *wude* theory and his influence on the first dynasty Qin, see Sima Qian's *Shiji*, ch. 6, ch. 26, ch. 28, ch. 34, ch. 44, ch. 46, ch. 74, and ch. 76; cf. Rubin (1982), 141–50; and Graham (1986), 11–13, n15.

66. *Chunqiu fanlu*, ch. 43.

67. Ibid., ch. 43, 44, 46, 51, and 53.

68. *Shiji*, ch. 6; cf.Graham (1989), 371–72.

69. For Dong Zhongshu's role in establishing the Confucian Classics including the *Yijing* as the state orthodox in the early Han under Emperor Wu, see Queen (1996), esp. "Introduction," 2, 24–25, and "Conclusion," 227–28. Also see Sivin (1995), 36–37; Graham (1989), 378.

The intensity of the struggle between the *Fajia* and *Rujia* during the early Han is apparent in the civil service recruitment system in the early Han. According to the *Han Shu*, in 141 BCE, all Legalists were excluded from government posts. This was followed by a drastic reduction in the number of imperial scholars and a change in their fields of required expertise that was limited to the *Five Classics*. Cf. Hans Bielenstein (1980), ch. 6, "Civil Service Recruitment," esp. 138.

70. For the *Yijing*, cf. notes 44 and 51. For the *Chunqiu fanlu*, cf. ch. 43.

71. *Yijing*, "*Dazhuan*" commentary IA, 1.1, 4–7; cf. Wilhelm/Baynes (1961), 301–308.

72. Black (1986), 174–78.

73. *Chunqiu fanlu*, ch. 46.

74. Ibid., ch. 70.

75. Ibid., ch. 53.

76. Ibid.

77. Furth (1999), 301–302.

78. Ibid., 46, 52.

79. Raphals (1998), 169–93, ch. 7, "Yin-Yang in Medical texts."

80. Ibid., 182, 184.

81. Black (1986), 185.

82. Furth (1998), 3.

83. Furth (1998), 1. As she wrote, "It is well known that Chinese cosmology based on the interaction of the forces of yin and yang made sexual difference, a relative and flexible bipolarity in natural philosophy. On the other hand, Confucianism constructed gender around strict hierarchical kinship roles" (1).

84. Topley (1975), 78. A similar view can also be found in Lily Xiao Hong Lee (1994), 13; and Olga Lang (1968), 43. For more recent scholarship on the correlation between the *yin-yang* cosmology and gender hierarchy, see Bert Hinsch (2002).

CHAPTER 4. NEI-WAI, GENDER DISTINCTIONS, AND RITUAL PROPRIETY

A version of this chapter under the title "*Neiwai*, Civility, and Gender Distinctions" was first published in *Asian Philosophy* 14:1 (March 2004): 41–58. Reprint with permission.

1. Both in philosophy and in Chinese gender studies, studies on the term *nei-wai* have been rather sketchy. For a more in-depth study on *nei-wai* see Raphals 1998, esp. ch. 8 and 9. For a brief discussion on the shifting nature of the *nei-wai* boundary, see Ames (1994), 204–205.; Ko (1994), 12–14, 143–47; Mann (1997), 15, 223–24; Ebrey (1993), 23–27; Hu Ying (1997), 72–99. Hu's essay focuses on the representation of *nei* as familiar homeland and *wai* as barbaric outerland in fictional writings.

2. Lang (1968), 10–11, 333.

3. As quoted in Hay (1994), 8.

4. See for example, Raphals (1998) esp. ch.8 and 9; Ko (1994); Mann (1997); Ebrey (1993).

5. Raphals (1998), 213.

6. For instance, see *Liji*, "*Neize*" chapter where the proper gender sphere for man and woman is defined along the line of the *nei* and *wai*; cf. Legge (1967) I, 449–79. As for the *Yijing*, see, for example, hexagram 37—*Jiaren*; trans. cf. Wilhelm/Baynes (1977), 214–24.

7. Cf. Legge (1960) III, IV & V. However the term *nei-wai* does occur in the *Zuozhuan*. For the compiling date of the *Zuozhuan*, see Loewe (1993), 67–76.

8. *Daxue*, ch. 10; trans. cf. Legge (1960) I, 375–76.

9. *Zhongyong*, ch. 25. All translation of *Zhongyong* is based on Ames and Hall's with some modifications of my own; cf. Ames and Hall (2001), 106. Also cf. Legge (1960) I, 418–19.

10. *Mencius* 7B24; Legge (1960) II, 489–90.

11. *Mencius* 1B/5; Legge II, 164.

12. *Mencius* 6B/6; Legge II, 434.

13. *Shujing*, "The Books of Zhou," "*Hongfan*" chapter; cf. Legge (1960) III, 337–38.

14. Ibid., "*Jiuhao*" chapter; cf. Legge (1960) III, 407. For other passages containing the term *nei-wai*, see Legge III, 654, 664.

15. Yu Ying-shi (1967), 4.

16. Cf. Hay (1994), 12.

17. Cf. Yu Ying-shi (1967), 40.

18. *Hou Hanshu*, 116 *chuan*. A similar description of other barbarian tribes can also be found in the *Hou Hanshu* from 115 to 120 *chuan*.

19. Chu Tung-tsu (1965). For the concept of *li*, see ch. 7, esp. 226–41.

20. *Zuozhuan*, Duke Zhao, the fifth year; cf. Legge (1960) V, 601, 604.

21. *Zuozhuan*, Duke Zhao, the twenty-fifth year; Legge V, 704, 708.

22. See note. 20.

23. *Zuozhuan*, Duke Yin, the eleventh year; Legge V, 31, 33.

24. *Liji*, "Questions of Duke Ai;" cf. Legge (1967)II, 266.

25. *Xunzi*, ch. 2; trans. cf. Dubs (1928), 45.

26. *Xunzi*, ch. 8; cf. Dubs, 118. A similar passage is also found in chapter 11 where Xunzi said, "A state without *li* will not be in good order. That *li* is able to straighten the state is because *li* to the state is like a scale to heavy and light, rope and ink to the crooked and straight and a measurement to square and circle." My own translation.

27. *Liji*, "Record of Music;" cf. Legge (1967)II, 98.

28. Ibid.; Legge (1967)II, 100.

29. *Xunzi*, ch. 5; cf. Dubs (1928), 71.

30. *Huainanzi*, II, Ia; as quoted in Chu Tung-tsu (1965), 233n25.

31. *Huainanzi*, 6, 1b; cf. Chu, Ibid., 233n26.

32. *Hanshu* 58,3b; cf. Chu, Ibid., 233n31.

33. *Xunzi*, ch. 19; Dubs (1928), 213.

34. *Xunzi*, ch. 5; Ibid., 72.

35. Hay (1994), 12–19.

36. Raphals (1998), 207.

37. *Mozi*, ch. 9; cf. Yi-Pao Mei (1929), 40.

38. *Mozi*, ch. 35; Mei, 185–86. For more passages in the *Mozi* dealing with the concept of *nannuzhibie*, see Raphals (1998), 207–208. Regarding the passage in chapter 19 of *Mozi* in which the downfall of King Zhou of Shang was linked to a series of natural anomalies including women becoming men, Raphals speculated the woman here refers to Moxi. However, Moxi was in the Xia dynasty not Shang. Hence, the woman who was denounced for crossing the boundary of gender propriety, in my estimation, probably referred to Danji of Shang instead. See Raphals (1998), 208.

39. *Guanzi*, Book XI, ch. 31, "The Prince and His Ministers II"; trans. cf. Rickett (1985) I, 412–13.

40. *Guanzi*, Book XXI, ch. 65, "Explanation to the Section on Nine Ways to Failure"; cf. Rickett I, 110–11.

41. *Guanzi*, Book XXI, ch. 66, "Explanation to the *Ban Fa*"; cf. Rickett I, 145.

42. *Guanzi*, Book X, ch. 30, "The Prince and His Ministers I"; cf. Rickett I, 403.

43. *Shujing*, the "Book of Xia," chapter "*Kaoyaomo*;" cf. Legge (1960) III, 74. For more details on the five-zone theory, see Yu Ying-shih (1986), 379n6.

44. Yu Ying-shih (1986), 379–80.

45. *Chunqiu fanlu*, ch. 6, "The Way of the Ruler."

46. Yu (1986), 381–82.

47. Yu (1967), 66–67.

48. Ibid., 67.

49. On the Han treatment of barbarians, see Yu (1967), ch. 4, 91.

50. Ames (1994), 204–208.

51. Ko (1994), 144–45.

52. *Baihutong*, ch. 17, "Plowing and Gathering Mulberry-leaves;" trans. cf. Tjan Tjoe Som (1952). For a partial translation, see Paul R. Goldin (2003), 170–76.

53. Mann (1997), 151.

54. Hisayuki Miyakawa (1960), 31.

55. Yu (1967), 87.

56. Ibid.

57. Francesca Bray (1995), 132.

58. *Guliang zhuan* 4/7b (fourteenth year of Duke Huan, eighth month); cf. Mann (1997), 151–52.

59. *Liji*, "*Neize*" chapter; cf. Legge (1967) I, 471–72.

60. The Confucian "six arts" consists of archery, arithmetic, ritual, music, charioteering, and calligraphy. See Tu Wu-ming (1985), 76.

61. *Liji*, "*Neize*"; cf. Legge (1967) I, 472

62. Ibid.; Legge I, 478.

63. Ibid.; Legge I, 478–79.

64. Ibid.; Legge I, 470.

65. Ibid.; Legge I, 77.

66. *Guanzi*, Book V, ch. 13, "Eight Observations"; cf. Rickett I, 226.

67. Hay (1994), 13.

68. *Guanzi*, Book I, ch. 3, "On the Cultivation of Political Power"; cf. Rickett I, 95.

69. Ebrey (1993), 24.

70. Cf. ibid., 24n7.

71. *Xunzi*, ch. 10, "A Wealthy State."

72. Ibid.

73. Ko (1994), 12.

74. Cf. Ebrey (1993), 23–24n2; also see Hu Ying (1997), 79; and Ping Yao (2003a), 414–18.

75. See Ko (1994); Mann (1997); and Widmer (1989).

76. Ko (1994), 12.

77. *Mencius* 4A/5; cf. Legge (1960) II, 295.

78. *Daxue* "The text"; cf. Legge III, 357.

79. For the metaphor of "concentric circles," see Tu Wei-ming (1985), 171–81; for its Stoic root, see James Tiles (2000), 314–15.

80. *Lienuzhuan* "The Daughter of Shen of Zhaonan" (4.1). For a complete list of chapter titles in the *Lienuzhuan*, cf. Raphals (1998), appendix one, 263–67. For a partial translation of the text, see Pauline C. Lee (2003), 149–61.

81. *Xunzi*, ch. 27, "*Dalue*"; cf. Hutton (2003), 117.

82. *Zhongyong*, ch. 12; Legge (1960) I, 393.

83. *Mencius* 6B/6; Legge II, 434. Also see Bryan Van Norden (2003), 108.

84. Mann (1997), 223. For more details on the "civil society" debate, see *Modern China* 19:2 (April 1993), special issue, esp. William T. Rowe, "The Problem of 'Civil Society' in Late Imperial China": 139–57; and Frederic Wakeman, "The Civil Society and Public Sphere Debate: Western Reflections on Chinese Political Culture," 108–38.

85. Rowe (1993), 139.

86. According to William Rowe, "civil society," in its early use, referred to the condition of being governed; that is, "civil" or "political society" is contrasted with the ungoverned "state of nature." The notion of "civil society" as an autonomous entity contrary to the state is a later development. Rowe (1993), 141–42.

87. Rowe (1993), 148, 147. Also see M. Bonnin and Y. Chevrier (1991), 579–82; quoted in Rowe, 147.

88. Elman (1990), 27.

89. Cf. *Lunyu* 15.22, 7.31.

90. *Shujing*, the "Books of Zhou," "*Hongfan*" chapter; Legge (1960) III, 331.

91. Barlow (1989), 325.

92. For instance, Francis L. K. Hsu (1968), 83, 592–93. Kay Ann Johnson (1983), 25 as quoted in Rubie S. Watson (1991), 363.

93. Ortner (1981), 396–97.

94. Ibid.

95. Ibid., 397.

96. Watson (1991), 348.

97. *Liji*, "*Jiaotesheng*" chapter; cf. Legge (1967) I, 441.

98. *Kongzi jiayu*, ch. 26, "*Penminjie*."

99. *Lienuzhuan*, Book I "*Muyi*," see esp. "'Her Serenity' Ji of Lu" (1.9), "The Mother of Zifa of Chu" (1.10), "The Mother of Meng Ke of Zou" (1.11), "The Mother-teacher of Lu" (1.12), and "The Mother of Tian Ji of Qi" (1.14); Book III "*Ren Zhi*," see esp. "The Mother of Zang Sun of Lu" (3.9), "The Old Woman from Qu Wu in Wei" (3.14), and "The Mother of General Gua of Zhao" (3.15); Book VI "*Biantong*," see esp. "The Mother of Jiangyi of Chu" (6.2). For more details, see Raphals 1998, Appendix Two: The Intellectual Stories, 271–76, 218n15. For a partial translation of *Yanshi jiaxun*, see Ping Yao (2003b), 245–49.

100. *Lienuzhuan* (1.11) "The Mother of Meng Ke of Zou."

101. The institutionalization of the regency began from 87 BCE in the Han onward to the last dynasty of Qing in the early twentieth century. Cf. Hans Bielenstein (1980), 151.

102. Chu Tung-tsu (1965), 25, 28–29.

103. For instance, under the Tang and Song law, parents could be punished for killing their child, but the punishment was one degree less than that imposed for killing with intent if the child was unfilial. But under the Yuan, Ming, and Qing law, parents might go unpunished for killing an unfilial child. Furthermore, under the Qing law, parents could ask the court to banish their unfilial son to remote provinces until they requested a return for their son. Cf. Chu Tung-tsu (1965), 23–27, 121.

104. As quoted in Yang Lien-sheng (1992), 17.

105. As quoted in Raphals (1998), 219, n17.

106. Marina H. Sung (1981), 69n30.

107. *Liji*, "*Jiaotesheng*"; cf. Legge (1967) I, 441. In chapter 3, "Posthumous Names," of the *Baihutong*, it also says that even the spouse of a feudal lord should not receive a posthumous name, because she has no rank; cf. Tjan I, 373.

108. *Baihutong*, ch. 40, "Marriage"; cf. Tjan I, 261.

109. Ibid.; Tjan I, 249–50.

110. *Liji*, "*Huanyi*"; Legge (1967) II, 429.

111. Ibid.; Legge II, 429–30.

CHAPTER 5. DIDACTIC TEXTS FOR WOMEN AND THE WOMANLY SPHERE OF *NEI*

1. Cf. Raphals (1998), 6 n15.

2. Cf. Mann (1997), 205.

3. Cf. Raphals (1998), 19 n31. Also Pauline C. Lee (2003).

4. Raphals (1998), 28.

5. Ibid., see esp. ch. 4, "The Textual Matrix of the *Lienu zhuan*," 87–112.

6. Ibid., 117.

7. Ibid., see ch. 5, "Talents Transformed in Ming Editions," 113–38; also see Appendix 5, 285–89.

8. For more details on the number of virtuous women recorded in all twenty-four dynasties of China, cf. Chen Dongyuan (1937), 430–39. Also cf. *Suishu*, for the Sui dynasty, Book 80, ch. 45, "*Lienuzhuan*." For Tang, cf. *Jiu Tangshu*, Book 193, ch. 143, "*Lienuzhuan*," and *Xin Tangshu*, Book 205, ch. 130, "*Lienuzhuan*." And for Song, *Songshi*, Book 460, ch. 219, "*Lienuzhuan*."

9. See Chen Dongyuan (1937), 430–39. Also cf. *Mingshi*, Book 301–303, ch. 189–91, "*Lienuzhuan*;" and *Qingshi*, Book 507–10, ch. 293–96, "*Liezhuan*." However, the number of women's biographies recorded in major dynastic histories is slightly different in Chiao Chien's estimation: Sui 15, Tang 31, Song 52, Yuan 166, and Ming 257; cf. Chiao Chien (1971).

10. See *Qingshi* (History of Qing), Book 507, ch. 293, "*Lienuzhuan*."

11. Cf. Raphals (1998), 12n4. Also see Mark Edward Lewis (1990), 73n89, n90.

12. For more details, see Andrew H. Plak (1987).

13. Carlitz (1991), 118–19.

14. Ibid., cf. 128–31.

15. Ibid.

16. Raphals (1998), 118.

17. Cao Xueqin and Gao E (1978), 53; cited in Clara Wing-chung Ho (1995), 198n27. Also, for a brief survey of traditional instruction books for women, see Tienchi Martin-Liao (1985), 165–89.

18. *Hou Hanshu*, Book 114, ch. 74, "*Lienuzhuan*," the story—"Wife of Cao Sishu" (i.e., Bao Zhao). Interestingly, an achieved, talented woman, such as Bao Zhao, with an impressive pedigree, in the dynastic biography is still first and foremost remembered as a bearer of the gender kinship role.

19. Nancy Lee Swann (1968); cf. ch. 5, "Her Share in the *Han Shu*," esp. 65. Also see ch. 6, 8, 9.

20. Ibid., cf. ch. 4, 5. For a complete translation of *Nujie*, see Swann (1968) and Robin R. Wang (2003), 177–88.

21. Yu-shih Chen (1996), 245.

22. Ibid., 233.

23. Swann (1968), 84–85.

24. Lily Xiao Hong Lee (1994), 22–23.

25. Raphals (1998), 245n51.

26. Lan Dingyuan, *Nuxue*, "Introduction." The *Nulunyu* in Lan's assessment is only for elementary learning and is unrefined and inelegant. Zhang Xuecheng, in his popular work "*Fuxue*" also criticized the *Nulunyu* for being unrefined and pretentious as well. Both are cited in Tienchi Martin-Liao (1985), 174.

27. Martin-Liao, ibid. Also for a complete translation of *Nulunyu*, see Robin R. Wang (2003), 327–40, reprint of Heying Jenny Zhan and Robert Bradshaw (1996).

28. Ibid. For a slightly different account of the lives of the two Sung sisters, see Zhan and Bradshow (1996); Wang (2003), 327.

29. Empress Ma, though a former peasant, was self-educated, widely read, and regularly conducted study groups on the *Classics* for court ladies. She was also remembered for her ability to admonish and restrain the founding Ming Emperor, Taizu, who was well known for his violence and cruelty in several occasions. Moreover, Empress Ma had natural feet! This might come as a shock especially during the Ming when the practice of footbinding was relatively common; yet given her former peasant status, it is understandable why she did not have her feet bound. Emperor Taizu defended Empress Ma for not having bound feet after he rose to power; and after her death, Taizu was said to mourn her deeply and did not replace her as empress. For more details, cf. Wm. Theodore de Bary (1994), 44.

30. Cf. Hu Wenkai (1957), 170–624; also see, Clara Wing-chung Ho (1995), 203n46.

31. Cf., Clara Wing-Chung Ho (1995), 206–207.

32. Mann (1992), 42n4.

33. Ibid., 44.

34. Clara Wing-Chung Ho in her study on Qing scholars' views on women's education stated that most Qing scholars such as Chen Hongmou (1696–1771), Zhou Guangye (1730–1798), and Li Zhaolou (1769–1841) all shared the view that women should be taught to read and write, although the main purpose was to enable them to properly perform wifely roles and duties. Cf. Ho (1995), 193.

35. See David Nivison (1966), 263.

36. For trans., see Mann (1992), 49–51. Mann translated "*ciming*" 辭命 "deferential obedience." Yet throughout my research on the term *ciming*, I have not found any reference that suggests such a translation. The first occurrence of the term *ciming* is in the *Mencius*, where it is used to signify one's ability to master speech (*Mencius* 2A/2, cf. Legge II, 192, and *Mencius* 2A/9, cf. Legge II, 207). Another variation of the term *ciming* is "*ciling*" 辭令, which is in the *Zouzhuan*, Duke Xiang the thirty-first year (cf. Legge V, 561, 565), *Liji*, "The Meaning of Capping," *Mozi*, "The Inquiry of Duke Lu," and *Shiji*, "The Biography of Chu Yuan."

37. Mann (1992), 53–54.

38. Cf. Clara Wing-Chung Ho (1995), 199.

39. Cf. Mann (1992), 53–54.

40. Ibid., cf. 56.

41. Cf. Nivison (1966), 263.

42. For more details, see Mary Briody Mahowald (1994).

CHAPTER 6. CHINESE SEXISM AND CONFUCIANISM

1. Raphals (2002), 285.

2. Ibid.

3. Mahowald (1994), 25, 31.

4. Ibid., 103.

5. Ibid., 193.

6. Ibid., 196.

7. Ibid., 199.

8. For more, see Rosenlee's book review of Bryan van Norden's *Confucius and the Analects: New Essays, The Philosophical Quarterly* 53:213 (October 2003): 609–13.

9. For instance, the assumed prevalence of female infanticide in China is questioned in Holmgren (1981), 158–63. Holmgren's essay concentrates on late-nineteenth and early-twentieth-century China. For a more recent study of infanticide, see Croll (2000), ch. 3. Croll maintained that even today in China, the birth of a girl is still a source of disappointment to the family and often results in the abuse, neglect, and abandonment of both the mother and the daughter.

10. *Hanfeizi,* "*Liufan*" chapter; quoted in Cai Xianlong (1979), 87.

11. *Yanshi jiaxun* [*Family instructions for the Yan Clan*], ch. 5, "*Zhijia*" [Managing one's family]; cf. Chen Dongyuan (1937), 66–67. Also see Ping Yao (2003b).

12. *Mencius* 4A/26; Legge (1960)II, 313.

13. *Kongzi jiayu,* Book 6, ch. 26, "*Benmingjie*"; also see *Lienuzhuan,* "Honorable Woman of Bao of Song" (2.7).

14. *Baihutong,* "*Jiachu*" (Marriage) chapter; cf. Tjan Tjoe Som (1952)I, 251, 257.

15. Cf. Cai Xianlong (1979), 98–99.

16. Ibid., 99.

17. Ayscough (1937), 54; O'Hara (1945), 3.

18. Cf. Legge (1960)III, 208.

19. Ibid., 618.

20. Legge (1960)IV, 458–59.

21. *Xiaojing,* ch. 1, "*Kaizong mingyi.*" For translation, see Patricia B. Ebrey (2003a), 374–75.

22. *Mencius* 5A/22; Legge (1960)II, 345–46.

23. *Xunzi,* ch. 29, "*Zidao*" [The Way of Son].

24. Cf. *Xiaojing,* ch. 15, "*Jianzheng.*" Cf. Ebrey (2003), 378–79.

25. *Mencius* 4A/28; Legge (1960)II, 315.

26. Legge (1960)III, 392. *Xiaojing,* ch. 11, "*Wuxing*" (Five punishments); Ebrey (2003), 378.

27. *Mencius* 4A/28; Legge (1960)II, 314.

28. *Liji,* "*Jitong*" chapter; cf. Legge (1967)II, 237–38.

29. *Xiaojing,* ch. 10, "*Jixiaoxing.*" Cf. Ebrey (2003), 380.

30. *Liji*, "*Hunyi*" chapter; cf. Legge (1967)II, 428.

31. Cf. Watson (1991a), 240.

32. Cf. Ebrey (1992), 635.

33. Watson (1991a), 243.

34. *Baihutong*, "Marriage" chapter; cf. Tjan (1952)I, 250. Also see *Liji*, "*Zengzi wen*" chapter; Legge (1967)I, 322.

35. *Kongzi jiayu*, ch. 26, "*Benmingjie*."

36. See Ban Zhao's biography in the *Hou Hanshu*; cf. Swann (1968), ch. 4, "The Life of Pan Chao." For the kinship title, "*Dajia*", see Swann (1968), 52n7. For another variation "Dagu", see *Nuxiaojing*; for trans. see Patricia B. Ebrey (2003b), 380–90, 374n2.

37. Watson (1986), 619.

38. Ibid.

39. *Baihutong*, "Marriage" chapter; cf. Tjan (1952)I, 223–24.

40. Louie and Edwards (1994), 135–48.

41. Cf. Li Yu-ning (1992), 106. For trans. of "The Ballad of Mulan", see Robin R. Wang (2003), 250–54.

42. Cf. Jackson (1997), 1. As for Korean women's participation in footbinding, see Levy (1966), 253–54.

43. *Liji*, "*Jiaotesheng*" chapter; cf. Legge (1967)I, 439. *Yijing*, commentary of the thirty-second hexagram "*Heng*" (i.e., constancy); cf. Wilhelm/Baynes (1961), 135. However in the *Shijing*, song 45 "*Pozhou*" in the "*Yongfeng*" section is traditionally interpreted as a widow's protest against being urged by her mother to remarry. This is different from the explicit command of *Liji* in regard to widow fidelity as part of the wifely virtue, since in the *Shijing* it is rather a display of the widow's own determination to remain widowed despite being urged to do otherwise; cf. Legge (1960)II, 73–74.

44. *Liji*, "*Tangong*" chapter; cf. Legge (1967)I, 151–52, 152n1.

45. Cf. Dong Jiazun (1979), 139–40. Also see Niu Zhipin (1995), 131.

46. Cf. *Mencius* 1B/5; Legge (1960)II, 163–64; *Mencius* 3B/3; Legge, 268.

47. Cf. Liu Jihua (1995), 103. Also see Dong Jiazun (1979), 140.

48. Elvin (1984), 11–12.

49. Dong Jiazun (1979), 146.

50. Liu Jihua (1995), 107; also Dong Jiazun (1979), 151.

51. Ibid.

52. *Yanshi jiaxun*, chapter 5, "Managing One's Family"; cf. Chen Dongyuan (1937), 66–67.

53. Dong Jiazun (1979), 152.

54. Ibid., 153.

55. *Jiu Tangshu*, Book 193, ch. 143, "*Lienu*," story of "The Concubine of the King of Chu;" cf. Niu Zhipin (1995), 136.

56. Dong Jiazun (1979), 154–58. Also see Nie Chongqi (1979), 130–31. The number of Tang princesses who remarried is given by Nie as twenty-seven.

57. Chen Dongyuan (1937), 132.

58. Dong Jiazun (1979), 161.

59. *Jinsilu* 6.13 "The Way to Regulate the Family," compiled by Zhu Xi and Lu Zuqian; cf. Wing-tsit Chan (1967), 177. For a partial translation, see Robin R. Wong (2003), 316–26.

60. Cf. Chen Lungjie (1992), 346.

61. Chen Dongyuan (1937), 139.

62. *Jinsilu* 6.17; cf. Wing-tsit Chan (1967), 179.

63. *Jinsilu* 6.13; cf. Ibid., 177.

64. Cf. Chen Dongyuan (1937), 138.

65. Ibid., 138–39.

66. Cf. Liu Jihua (1995), 114; and Chen Dongyuan (1937), 173. Also, see the *History of Yuan*, Book 200, ch. 87, "*Lienu*" section I, the biography of "Woman Tuotuoni." Tuotuoni was a Mongol native who resisted her two stepsons in their efforts to consummate with her after the death of their father, as was part of the Mongol custom. Court historians, who were probably ethnically Han, celebrated her extraordinary act of courage in defying the Mongol custom. The Yuan imperial court itself later outlawed this native custom of Mongolia. Tuotuoni, a Mongol native, in the biography, denounced such a native custom as an act of beasts. This of course reflected the Han's influence on the Mongols.

67. Elvin (1984), 134.

68. Chien Chiao (1971), 207. Chien Chiao estimated the number of virtuous women's biographies in the Yuan dynastic history to be 166. Chen Dongyuan gave a higher number, around 187. Cf. Chen Dongyuan (1937), 180.

69. Elvin (1984), 114.

70. Ibid., 124.

71. Mann (1987), 40n8.

72. Mann (1987), 41; also see Chen Dongyuan (1937), 179; and Liu Jihua (1995), 116.

73. Chen Dongyuan (1937), 179; Elvin (1984), 133; Mann (1987), 41; and Liu Jihua (1995), 118.

74. Liu Jihua (1995), 117.

75. For the story of Gu Yanwu, see Peterson (1968), 144–45; Mann (1997), 25n28.

76. For the early Qing's bans and its later reversal in 1851 on widow suicide, see Elvin (1984), 126–29; Mann (1997), 25–26.

77. Ropp (1981), 128, 130. Also see Chen Dongyuan (1937), 246–5; Liu Jihua (1995), 117–18.

78. Mann (1987), 41–42; Liu Jihua (1995), 122–23.

79. For the Qing law on forced remarriage of chaste widows, see Sommer, (1996), Appendix I, 119–20.

80. Levy (1966), and Jackson (1997). For a more balanced study of footbinding, see Ko (2001).

81. Mohanty (1991):cf. "Introduction," esp. 29.

82. Chen Dongyuan (1937), 125; Levy (1966), 17. For other accounts of the origin of footbinding, see Jia Shen (1979), 183–85.

83. See Fu Yuechen (1979), 165–80. However, according to Jia Shen, the practice of footbinding might have already taken place during the Tang. He drew this conclusion from the existence of arch-shaped lamps found in Tibet that were commonly called the shoes of Tang princesses who were married off to Tibet to form an alliance between the Tang court and the invading barbarian tribe; cf. Jia Shen (1979), 186.

84. See Jia Shen (1979), 187.

85. For Zhu Xi's alleged involvement in promoting the practice of footbinding, see Levy (1966), 44. For the rejection of that tale, see Ebrey (1990), 217n39.

86. See Chen Dongyuan (1937), 161–72. For the brilliance of Li Qingzhao's poems, see Fatima Wu (2003), 435-6.

87. For trans., cf. Patricia Ebrey (1990), 217; and Levy (1966), 65. Also see Jia Shen (1979), 189.

88. However, in different regions, customs also varied; some might start as early as age two or three and some as late as age twelve or thirteen. The ideal age is usually at six or seven, since besides the greater flexibility the foot-bond affords at this age, it is also an age when the process of self-conscious gender marking begins. Cf. Jackson, (1997), 27; Blake (1994), 678.

89. Blake (1994), 676.

90. For trans. cf. Headland (1895), 559.

91. Quoted in Jia Shen (1979), 187.

92. Ibid.

93. Blake (1994), 676.

94. Ibid.

95. *Liji*, "*Neize*" chapter; cf. Legge (1967)I, 478.

96. Ibid., 479.

97. *Zhuangzi*, ch. 17; for trans. cf. Mair (1998), 159.

98. Jackson (1997), 28, 33.

99. Cf. Levy (1966): ch. 2, "Origin and Presence," esp. 53.

100. Ko (1997), 12–15.

101. Ibid., 10.

102. Ibid., 16.

103. For the history of the queue, see Godley (1994), esp. 54–57.

104. Ko (1997), 22.

105. Levy (1966), 79.

106. Ko (1997), 21–22.

107. For the anti-footbinding movement in the late nineteenth century and early twentieth century organized by official-literati as well as gentry dissents, see Pao Chia-lin (1979), 266–95. For early footbinding critics in the seventeenth and eighteenth century prior to the influence of Western missionaries, see Ropp (1981),

120–289. Also see Jia Shen (1979), 189–92. For Western writings on footbinding, 1300–1890, see Ebrey (1999).

CHAPTER 7. TOWARD A CONFUCIAN FEMINISM—
FEMINIST ETHICS IN-THE-MAKING

1. For critiques of the category of "woman," see Riley (1988).

2. See Kaplan (1994); Mohanty (1991).

3. Kaplan (1994), 138.

4. Ibid., 144.

5. See for instance, James Tiles (2000). Despite his critique of the abstract nature of Kantian ethics, Tiles took Kant's respect for person as one of his three proposed measures of morality. For more, see Rosenlee (2003b). Besides Kant's penchant for abstract personhood, Kantian ethics also imports a great deal of moral theology as well by making God the regulative ideal for morality. For more critique of Kant on the connection between Kantian ethics and theology, see Rosenlee (2003a).

6. I am here acknowledging my indebtedness to Tu Wei-ming for the term of the third wave Confucianism.

BIBLIOGRAPHY

Ames, Roger T., and David L. Hall, trans. (2003) *A Philosophical Translation of Dao De Jing: Making this Life Significant*. New York: Ballantine Books.

———. (2001) *Focusing the Familiar: A Translation and Philosophical Interpretation of the Zhongyong*. Honolulu: University of Hawaii Press.

Ames, Roger T. (1999) "New Confucianism: A Native Response to Western Philosophy." *China Studies* (*Zhongguo yanjiu*) 5:23–52.

Ames, Roger T., and Henry Rosemont Jr., trans. (1998) *The Analects of Confucius: A Philosophical Translation*. New York: Ballantine Books.

Ames, Roger T. (1994) "The Focus-Field Self in Classical Confucianism." In *Self as Person in Asian Theory and Practice*, ed. Roger T. Ames, Wimal Disanayake, and Thomas P. Kasulis. Albany: State University of New York Press.

———. (1981) "Taoism and the Androgynous Ideal." In *Women in China*, ed. Richard W. Guisso and Stanley Johannesen. New York: Philo Press.

Andors, Phyllis. (1983) *The Unfinished Liberation of Chinese Women 1949–1980*. Bloomington: Indiana University Press.

Antony, Louise M., and Charlotte Witt, eds. (1993) *A Mind of One's Own: Feminist Essays on Reason and Objectivity*. Boulder: Westview.

Ayscough, Florence. (1937) *Chinese Women: Yesterday and Today*. Boston: Houghton Mifflin.

Bar On, Bat-ami, ed. (1994) *Modern Engendering: Critical Feminist Readings in Modern Western Philosophy*. Albany: State University of New York Press.

Barlow, Tani E. (1994a) "Theorizing Woman: *Funu, Guojia, Jiating* (Chinese Women, Chinese State, Chinese Family)." In *Body, Subject and Power in China*, ed. Angela Zito and Tani E. Barlow. Chicago: University of Chicago Press.

———. (1994b) "Politics and Protocols of Woman." In *Engendering China: Women Culture, and the State*, ed. Christina K. Gilmartin, Gail Hershatter, Lisa Rofel, and Tyrene White. Cambridge: Harvard University Press.

———. (1989) "Asian Perspective: Beyond Dichotomies." *Gender and History* 1:3: 318–30.

Barnes, Jonathan. (1984) *The Complete Works of Aristotle.* Princeton: Princeton University Press.

Bielenstein, Hans. (1980) *The Bureaucracy of Han Times.* Cambridge: Cambridge University Press.

Black, Alison. (1989) "Gender and Cosmology in Chinese Correlative Thinking." In *Gender and Religion: On the Complexity of Symbols,* ed. Caroline W. Bynum, Stevan Harrell, and Paula Richman. Boston: Beacon Press.

Blake, Fred. (1994) "Foot-binding in Neo-Confucian China and the Appropriation of Female Labor." *Signs* (Spring):676–712.

Bol, Peter K. (1987) "Seeking Common Ground: Han Literati under Jurchen Rule." *Harvard Journal of Asiatic Studies* 47:2 (Dec.):461–538.

Boltz, William (1993a) "*Chou li.*" In *Early Chinese Texts: A Bibliographical Guide,* ed. Michael Loewe. The Society for the Study of Early China and the Institute of East Asian Studies. Berkeley: University of California Press.

———. (1993b) "*Shou wen chieh tzu.*" In *Early Chinese Texts: A Bibliographical Guide,* ed. Michael Loewe. The Society for the Study of Early China and the Institute of East Asian Studies. Berkeley: University of California Press.

Bonnin, M., and Y. Chevrier. (1991) "Autonomy during the Post-Mao Era." *China Q.* 123:569–93.

Boodberg, Peter. (1953) "The Semasiology of Some Primary Confucian Concepts." *Philosophy East and West* 2:4:317–32.

Bordo, Susan, ed. (1999) *Feminist Interpretations of Rene Descartes.* University Park: Pennsylvania State University Press.

Bray, Francesca. (1995) "Textile Production and Gender Roles in China, 1000–1700." *Chinese Science* 12:115–37.

Butler, Judith. (1993) *Bodies that Matter: On the Discursive Limits of "Sex."* New York: Routledge.

———. (1990) *Gender Trouble: Feminism and the Subversion of Identity.* London: Routledge.

Cai, Xianlong. (1979) "[The Origin of the System of Chinese Polygamy]." In *Zhongguo funushi lunji* [Readings in the Chinese Women's History]. First edition. Ed. Pao Chia-lin. Taipei: Cowboy.

Cao, Xueqin, and Gao E. (1978) *Dream of the Red Chamber.* Trans. Yang Hsienyi and Gladys Yang. Beijing: Foreign Languages Press.

Carlitz, Katherine. (1991) "The Social Uses of Female Virtue in Late Ming Editions of *Lienu Zhuan.*" *Late Imperial China* 12:2 (December):117–52.

Carson, Michael, and Michael Loewe. (1993) "*Lu shih ch'un ch'iu.*" In *Early Chinese Texts: A Bibliographic Guide,* ed. Michael Loewe. The Society for the Study of Early China and the Institute of East Asian Studies. Berkeley: University of California Press.

Chan, Ching-ki Stephen. (1988) "The Language of Despair: Ideological Representations of the 'New Woman' (*xing nuxing*) by May Fourth Writers." *Modern Chinese Literature* 4:1–2:19–39.

Chan, Wing-tsit, ed. (1986) *Chu Hsi and Neo-Confucianism.* Honolulu: University of Hawaii Press.

Chan, Wing-tsit. (1975) "Chinese and Western Interpretations of *Jen* (Humanity)." *Journal of Chinese Philosophy* 2:107–29.

——, trans. (1967) *Reflections on Things at Hand*. New York: Columbia University Press.

——, trans. (1963) *A Source Book in Chinese Philosophy*. Princeton: Princeton University Press.

——. (1955) "Evolution of the Confucian Concept *Jen*." *Philosophy East and West* 4:295–319.

Chang, I-jen, William G. Boltz, and Michael Loewe. (1993) "*Kuo yu*." In *Early Chinese Texts: A Bibliographical Guide*, ed. Michael Loewe. The Society for the Study of Early China and the Institute of East Asian Studies. Berkeley: University of California Press.

Chen, Dongyuan. (1937) *Zhongguo funu shenghuo shi* [History of the Lives of Chinese Women]. Shanghai: Shangwu yinshuguan.

Chen, Lungjie, comp. (1992) *Jinsilu xiangzhu jiping* [A Detailed Collection of the Commentaries of *Jinsilu*]. Taipei: Taiwan xueshen shuzhu.

Chen, Ellen Marie. (1969) "Nothingness and the Mother Principle in Early Chinese Taoism." *International Philosophical Quarterly* 9:391–405.

Chen, Yu-shih. (1996) "The Historical Template of Pan Chao's *Nu Chieh*." *T'oung-Pao* 82:230–57.

Cheng, Anne. (1993) "*Ch'un ch'iu, Kung yang, Ku liang* and *Tso chuan*." In *Early Chinese Texts: A Bibliographical Guide*, ed. Michael Loewe. The Society for the Study of Early China and the Institute of East Asian Studies. Berkeley: University of California Press.

Chiao, Chien. (1971) "Female Chastity in Chinese Culture." *Bulletin of the Institute of Ethnology, Academia Sinica* 31:205–12.

Chodorow, Nancy. (1974) *The Reproduction of Mothering: Psychoanalysis and the Sociology of Gender*. Berkeley: University of California Press.

Chu, Tung-tsu. (1965) *Law and Society in Traditional China*. Paris: Mouton.

Croll, Elisabeth. (2000) *Endangered Daughters: Discrimination and Development in Asia*. London: Routledge.

——. (1978) *Feminism and Socialism in China*. London: Routledge and Kegan Paul.

Curtin, Katie. (1975) *Women in China*. New York and Toronto: Pathfinder Press.

Dardess, John W. (1983) *Confucianism and Autocracy: Professional Elites in the Founding of The Ming Dynasty*. Berkeley: University of California Press.

De Bary, Wm. Theodore. (1994) "Roundtable Discussion: Wm. Theodore De Bary. *The Trouble with Confucianism*." *China Review International* 1:1 (Spring):9–47.

De Beauvoir, Simone. (1989) *The Second Sex*. Trans. H. M. Parshley. New York: Vintage Books.

Dong, Jiazun. (1979) "[Investigation into the Custom of Widow Remarriage from the Han to Song]." In *Zhongguo funushi lunj* [Readings in the Chinese Women's History]. First edition. Ed. Pan Chia-lin. Taipei: Cowboy.

Dubs, Homer H., trans. (1966) *The Works of Hsuntze*. Reprint. Taipei: Ch'eng-wen.

——, trans. (1944) II. *The History of the Former Han Dynasty by Pan Ku*. 3 volumes. The American Council of Learned Societies.

Ebrey, Patricia B. (2003a) "The Book of Filial Piety." In *Images of Women in Chinese Thought and Culture*, ed. Robin R. Wang. Indianapolis: Hackett.

——. (2003b) "The Book of Filial Piety for Women." In *Images of Women in Chinese Thought and Culture*, ed. Robin R. Wang. Indianapolis: Hackett.

——. (1999) "Gender and Sinology: Shifting Western Interpretations of Footbinding, 1300–1890." *Late Imperial China* 20:2 (Dec.): 1–34.

——. (1993) *The Inner Quarters: Marriage and the Lives of Chinese Women in the Sung Period*. Berkeley: University of California Press.

——. (1992) "Women, Money, and Class: Ssu-ma Kuang and Sung Neo-Confucian Views on Women." In *Papers on Society and Culture of Early Modern China*. Comp. Academia Sinica, Institute of History and Philology. Taipei: Academia Sinica.

——. (1990) "Women, Marriage, and the Family in Chinese History." In *Heritage of China: Contemporary Perspectives on Chinese Civilization*, ed. Paul S. Ropp. Berkeley: University of California Press.

Elman, Benjamin A. (1991) "Political, Social, and Cultural Reproduction via Civil Service Examinations in Late Imperial China." *Journal of Asian Studies* 50:1 (February):7–28.

——. (1990) *Classicism, Politics, and Kinship: The Ch'ang-chou School of New Text Confucianism in Late Imperial China*. Berkeley: University of California Press.

Elvin, Mark. (1984) "Female Virtue and the State in China." *Past and Present* 104:111–52.

Fang, Ying-hsien. (1976) "[On the Origin of *Ren*: the Transformation of the Concept of *Ren* from the Time of the *Book of Songs* and the *Book of Documents* to Confucius]." *Ta-lu Tsa-chih* 52:3 (March):22–34.

Fingarette, Herbert. (1983) "The Music of Humanity in the Conversations of Confucius." *Journal of Chinese Philosophy* 10:331–56.

Fei, Xiaotong. (1992) *From the Soil: The Foundations of Chinese Society*. Trans. Gary G. Hamilton and Wang Zheng. Berkeley: University of California Press.

Fu, Yuechen. (1979) "[The life of Tang Women.]" In *Zhongguo funushi lunji* [Readings in the Chinese Women's History]. First edition. Ed. Pan Chia-lin. Taipei: Cowboy.

Fung, Yu-lan. (1952) *A History of Chinese Philosophy*. Trans. Derk Bodde. Princeton: Princeton University Press.

Furth, Charlotte. (1999) *A Flourishing Yin: Gender in China's Medical History, 960–1665*. Berkeley: University of California Press.

——. (1998) "Androgynous Males and Deficient Females: Biology and Gender Boundaries in Sixteenth- and Seventeenth-Century China." *Late Imperial China* 9:2 (Dec.):1–31.

Gaukroger, Stephen. (1995) *Descartes: An Intellectual Biography*. Oxford: Clarendon Press.

Gilligan, Carol. (1982) *In a Different Voice: Psychological Theory and Women's Development*. Cambridge: Harvard University Press.

Godley, Michael R. (1994) "The End of the Queue: Hair as Symbol in Chinese History." *East Asian History* 8:53–72.

Goldin, Paul R. (2003) "Comprehensive Discussions in the White Tiger Hall." In *Images of Women in Chinese Thought and Culture*, ed. Robin R. Wang. Indianapolis: Hackett.

Graham, A. C. (1989) *Disputers of the Tao: Philosophical Argument in Ancient China*. Chicago: Open Court.

———. (1986) *Yin-Yang and the Nature of Correlative Thinking*. Occasional Paper and Monograph Series No.6. Kent Ridge, Singapore: Institute of East Asian Philosophies.

Griffiths, Morwenna, and Margaret Whitford, eds. (1988) *Feminist Perspectives in Philosophy*. Bloomington: Indiana University Press.

Grimshaw, Jean. (1986) *Feminist Philosophers: Women's Perspective on Philosophical Traditions*. Brighton, England: Wheatsheaf Books.

Guisso, Richard W. (1981) "Thunder Over the Lake: The Five Classics and the Perception of Woman in Early China." In *Women in China*, ed. Richard W. Guisso and Stanley Johannesen. New York: Philo Press.

Hall, David L., and Roger T. Ames. (1999) *The Democracy of the Dead: Dewey, Confucius, and the Hope for Democracy in China*. Chicago: Open Court.

———. (1987) *Thinking Through Confucius*. Albany: State University of New York Press.

Harding, Sandra, and Merrill B. Hintikka, eds. (1983) *Discovering Reality: Feminist Perspectives on Epistemology, Metaphysics, Methodology, and Philosophy of Science*. Dordrecht: D. Reidel.

Hay, John. (1994) *Boundaries in China*. London: Reaktion Books.

Headland, Isaac Taylor. (1895) "The *Nu Erh Ching*; or *Classic for Girls*." *The Chinese Recorder* 26:12 (December):554–60.

Hinsch, Bret. (2002) *Women in Early Imperial China*. Oxford: Rowman and Littlefield.

Ho, Clara Wing-chung. (1995) "The Cultivation of Female Talent: Views on Women's Education in China during the Early and High Qing Periods." *Journal of the Economic and Social History of the Orient (JESHO)* 38:2:191–223.

Holmgren, J. (1981) "Myth, Fantasy, or Scholarship: Images of the Status of Women in Traditional China." *The Australian Journal of Chinese Affairs* 6:147–70.

Honig, Emily, and Gail Hershatter. (1988) *Personal Voices: Chinese Women in the 1980's*. Stanford: Stanford University Press.

Hu, Shi. (1953) "*Shou Ru*" [On the Concept of *Ru*]. In *Hu Shi Wencun* [Preserved Works of Hu Shi]. Volume 4: Reprint. Taipei: Yuandong.

———. (1919) *Zhongguo zhexueshi dakang* [*An Outline of the History of Chinese Philosophy*]. Shanghai: Commercial Press.

Hu, Wenkai. (1957) *Lidai funu zhuzuo kao* [A Survey of Women's Writings throughout the Ages]. Shanghai: Gujichubanshe.

Hu, Ying. (1997) "Re-configuring *Nei/wai*: Writing the Woman Traveler in the Late Qing." *Late Imperial China* 19:1 (June):72–99.

Hutton, Eric L., trans. (2003) *Xunzi*. In *Images of Women in Chinese Thought and Culture*, ed. Robin R. Wang. Indianapolis: Hackett.

Hsu, Francis L. K. (1968) "Chinese Kinship and Chinese Behavior." In *China in Crisis*. 2 volumes. Ed. Ping-ti Ho and Tang Tsou. Chicago: University of Chicago Press.

Jackson, Beverley. (1997) *Splendid Slippers: a Thousand Years of an Erotic Tradition*. Berkeley: Ten Speed Press.

Jensen, Lionel M. (1997) *Manufacturing Confucianism: Chinese Traditions and Universal Civilization*. Durham and London: Duke University Press.

Jia, Shen. (1979) "[An Investigation into Chinese Women's Footbinding]." In *Zhongguo funushi lunji* [Readings in the Chinese Women's History]. First edition. Ed. Pan Chia-lin. Taipei: Cowboy.

John, Mary. (1996) *Discrepant Dislocations: Feminism, Theory, and Postcolonial Histories*. Berkeley: University of California Press.

Johnson, Kay Ann. (1983) *Women, the Family, and Peasant Revolution in China*. Chicago: University of Chicago Press.

Kaplan, Caren. (1994) "The Politics of Location as Transnational Feminist Critical Practice." In *Scattered Hegemonies: Postmodernity and Transnational Feminist Practices*, ed. Inderpal, Grewal and Caren Kaplan. Minneapolis: University of Minnesota Press.

Karlgren, Bernhard. (1957) *Grammata Serica Recensa*. Stockholm.

King, Ambrose Y. C. (1985) "The Individual and Group in Confucianism: A Relational Perspective." In *Individualism and Holism: Studies in Confucian and Taoist Values*, ed. Donald Munro. Ann Arbor: University of Michigan Press.

Knoblock, John, trans. (1988) *Xunzi: A Translation and Study of the Complete Works*. 3 volumes. Stanford: Stanford University Press.

Ko, Dorothy. (2001) *Every Step a Lotus: Shoes for Bound Feet*. Berkeley: University of California Press.

——. (1997) "The Body as Attire: the Shifting Meanings of Footbinding in Seventeenth-Century China." *Journal of Women's History* 8:4 (Winter):8–27.

——. (1994) *Teachers of the Inner Chambers: Women and Culture in Seventeenth Century China*. Stanford: Stanford University Press.

Kourany, Janet A., ed. (1994) *Philosophy in Feminist Voice: Critique and Reconstructions*. Princeton: Princeton University Press.

Kracke, E. A. Jr. (1957) "Region, Family, and Individual in the Chinese Examination System." In *Chinese Thought and Institutions*, ed. John K. Fairbank. Chicago: University of Chicago Press.

Kristeva, Julia. (1977) *About Chinese Women*. Trans. Anita Barrows. New York: Urizen Books.

Lan, Hua R., and Vanessa L. Fong, eds. (1999) *Women in Republican China: A Sourcebook*. Armonk: M. E. Sharpe.

Lang, Olga. (1946) *Chinese Family and Society*. New Haven: Yale University Press.

Lau, D. C., trans. (1979) *The Analects*. London: Penguin Books.

——, trans. (1963) *Lao Tzu—Tao Te Ching*. London: Penguin Books.

Lee, Lily Xiao Hong. (1994) *The Virtue of Yin: Studies on Chinese Women*. Broadway: Wild Peony.

Lee, Pauline C, trans. (2003) *Biographies of Women*. In *Images of Women in Chinese Thought and Culture*, ed. Robin R. Wang. Indianapolis: Hackett.

Legge, James, trans. (1967) *Li Chi: Book of Rites*. 2 volumes. Reprint. New York: University Books.

——, trans. (1960) I. *Confucian Analects, The Great Learning, The Doctrine of the Mean*. In *The Chinese Classics*. 5 volumes. Reprint. Hong Kong: Hong Kong University Press.

——, trans. (1960) II. *The Works of Mencius*. In *The Chinese Classics*. 5 volumes. Reprint. Hong Kong: Hong Kong University Press.

——, trans. (1960) III. *The Shoo King* or *The Book of Historical Documents*. In *The Chinese Classics*. 5 volumes. Reprint. Hong Kong: Hong Kong University Press.

——, trans. (1960) IV. *The She King* or *The Book of Poetry*. In *The Chinese Classics*. 5 volumes. Reprint. Hong Kong: Hong Kong University Press.

——, trans. (1960) V. *The Chun Tsew with the Tso Chuen*. In *The Chinese Classics*. 5 volumes. Reprint. Hong Kong: Hong Kong University Press.

Lewis, Mark Edward. (1990) *Sanctioned Violence in Early China*. Albany: State University of New York Press.

Levy, Howard S. (1966) *Chinese Footbinding: The History of a Curious Erotic Custom*. New York: Walton Rawls.

Li, Chenyang, ed. (2000) *The Sage and the Second Sex: Confucianism, Ethics, and Gender*. Chicago: Open Court.

Li, Yu-ning. (1992) "Historical Roots of Changes in Women's Status in Modern China." In *Chinese Women through Chinese Eyes*, ed. Li Yu-ning. New York: M. E. Sharpe.

Lin, Yu-sheng. (1974) "The Evolution of the Pre-Confucian Meaning of *Jen* and the Confucian Concept of Moral Autonomy." *Monumenta Serica* 31 (1974–75):172–204.

Liu, Jihua. (1995) "The Historical Evolution of Chinese Concept of Chastity." In *Zhongguo funushi lunji* [Readings in the Chinese Women's History]. Fourth volume. Ed. Pao Chia-lin. Taipei: Cowboy.

Lloyd, Genevieve. (1984) *The Man of Reason: "Male" & "Female" in Western Philosophy*. Minneapolis: University of Minnesota Press.

Loewe, Michael. (1993) "*Chun chiu, Kung yang, Ku liang and Tso chuan*." In *Early Chinese Texts: A Bibliographical Guide*, ed. Michael Loewe. The Society for the Study of Early China and the Institute of East Asian Studies. Berkeley: University of California Press.

Louie, Kam, and Louise Edwards. (1994) "Chinese Masculinity: Theorizing *Wen* and *Wu*." *East Asian History* 8:135–48.

Mahowald, Mary Briody, ed. (1994) *Philosophy of Woman: An Anthology of Classic to Current Concepts*. Third edition. Indianapolis: Hackett.

Mair, Victor H., trans. (1998) *Wandering on the Way: Early Taoist Tales and Parables of Chuang Tzu*. Reprint. Honolulu: University of Hawaii Press.

Mann, Susan. (1997) *Precious Records: Women in China's Long Eighteenth Century.* Stanford: Stanford University Press.

———. (1992) "'*Fuxue*' (Women's Learning) by Zhang Xuecheng (1728–1801): China's First History of Women's Culture." *Late Imperial China* 13:1 (June):40–62.

———. (1987) "Widows in the Kinship, Class, and Community Structures of Qing Dynasty China." *Journal of Asian Studies* 46:1 (February):37–56.

Martin-Liao, Tienchi. (1985) "Traditional Handbooks of Women's Education." In *Woman and Literature in China*, ed. Anna Gerstlacher, Ruth Keen, Wolfgang Kubin, Margit Miosga, and Jenny Schon. Bochum: Brockmeyer.

Mei, Yi-Pao, trans. (1929) *The Ethical and Political Works of Motse*. London: Arthur Probsthain.

Miyakawa, Hisayuki. (1960) "The Confucianization of South China." In *The Confucian Persuasion*, ed. Arthur F. Wright. Stanford: Stanford University Press.

Mohanty, Chandra T., Ann Russo, and Lourdes Torres, eds. (1991) *Third World Women and the Politics of Feminism*. Indianapolis: Indiana University Press.

Needham, Joseph. (1956) *Science and Civilisation in China*. 5 volumes. Cambridge: Cambridge University Press.

Nie, Chongqi. (1979) "[On the Evolution of the Question of Women's Remarriage in History.]" In *Zhongguo funushi lunji* [Readings in the Chinese Women's History]. First edition. Ed. Pan Chia-lin. Taipei: Cowboy.

Nivison, David S. (1966) *The Life and Thought of Chang Hsueh-cheng (1738–1801)*. Stanford: Stanford University Press.

Niu, Zhipin. (1995) "[From Divorce and Remarriage to View the Concept of Women's Chastity in the Tang Dynasty.]" In *Zhongguo funushi lunji* [Readings in the Chinese Women's History]. Fourth volume. Ed. Pao Chia-Lin. Taipei: Cowboy.

Noddings, Nel. (1984) *Caring: A Feminine Approach to Ethics and Moral Education*. Berkeley: University of California Press.

O'Hara, Albert Richard. (1945) *The Position of Women in Early China*. Washington: The Catholic University of America Press.

Ortner, Sherry B. (1981) "Gender and Sexuality in Hierarchical Societies: the Case of Polynesia and Some Comparative Implications." In *Sexual Meanings: the Cultural Construction of Gender and Sexuality*, ed. Sherry B. Ortner and Harriet Whitehead. Cambridge: Cambridge University Press.

Pao, Chia-lin. (1979) "[Women's Thought during the *Xinhai* Revolution.]" In *Zhongguo funushi lunji* [Readings in the Chinese Women's History]. First edition. Ed. Pao Chia-lin. Taipei: Cowboy.

Peterson, Willard J. (1968) "The Life of Ku Yen-wu (1613–1682)." *Harvard Journal of Asiatic Studies* part I, 28:114–56.

Plaks, Andrew H. (1987) *The Four Masterworks of the Ming Novel*. Princeton: Princeton University Press.

Queen, Sarah A. (1996) *From Chronicle to Cannon: the Hermeneutics of the 'Spring and Autumn' According to Tung Chung-shu*. Cambridge: Cambridge University Press.

Raphals, Lisa (2002) "A Woman Who Understood the Rites." In *Confucius and the Analects: New Essays*, ed. Bryan van Norden. Oxford: Oxford University Press.

———. (1998) *Sharing the Light: Representations of Women and Virtue in Early China*. Albany: State University of New York Press.

Riley, Denise. (1988) *"Am I that Name?" Feminism and the Category of "Woman."* Minneapolis: University of Minnesota Press.

Rickett, W. Allyn, trans. (1985) *Guanzi: Political, Economic, and Philosophical Essays from Early China*. 2 volumes. Princeton: Princeton University Press.

Ropp, Paul S. (1981) *Dissent in Early Modern China: Ju-lin wai-shih and Ch'ing Social Criticism*. Ann Arbor: University of Michigan Press.

Rosenlee, Li-Hsiang Lisa. (2003a) "Book review: Bryan van Norden's *Confucius and the Analects: New Essays*." *The Philosophical Quarterly* 53:213 (October):609–13.

———. (2003b) "Book review: James E. Tiles' *Moral Measures: An Introduction to Ethics West and East*." *Philosophy East and West* 53:3 (July):425–30.

———. (2000) "Book review: Lisa Raphals's *Sharing the Light*." *Philosophy East and West* 50:1 (Jan.):149–53.

Roth, H. D. (1993) "*Chuang tzu*." In *Early Chinese Texts: A Bibliographical Guide*, ed. Michael Loewe. The Society for the Study of Early China and the Institute of East Asian Studies. Berkeley: University of California Press.

Rowe, William T. (1993) "The Problem of 'Civil Society' in Late Imperial China." *Modern China* 19:2 (April):139–57.

Rubin, Vitaly A. (1982) "The Concepts of *Wu-hsing* and *Yin-yang*." *Journal of Chinese Philosophy* 9:131–57.

Shaughnessy, Edward L., trans. (1996) *I Ching: The Classic of Changes*. New York: Ballantine Books.

Shaughnessy, Edward L. (1993a) "*I Ching (Chou I)*." In *Early Chinese Texts: A Bibliographical Guide*, ed. Michael Loewe. The Society for the Study of Early China and the Institute of East Asian Studies. Berkeley: University of California Press.

———. (1993b) "*Shang Shu (Shu Ching)*." In *Early Chinese Texts: A Bibliographic Guide*, ed. Michael Loewe. The Society for the Study of Early China and the Institute of East Asian Studies. Berkeley: University of California Press.

Sivin, Nathan. (1995) "State, Cosmos, and Body in the Last Three Centuries B.C." *Harvard Journal of Asiatic Studies* 55:1:5–37.

Snow, Helen F. (1967) *Women in Modern China*. Paris: Mouton.

Sommer, Matthew H. (1996) "The Use of Chastity: Sex, Law, and the Property of Widows in Qing China." *Late Imperial China* 17:2 (December):77–130.

Song, Lian. (1310–1381) "*Qirujie*." In *Song wenxian gong quanji* [The Collected Works of the Cultural Eminent during the Song]. Reprint. Taipei: Zhonghua shuju, 1970.

Spelman, Elizabeth V. (1988) *Inessential Woman: Problems of Exclusion in Feminist Thought*. Boston: Beacon Press.

Sung, Marina H. (1981) "The Chinese Lieh-nu Tradition." In *Women in China: Current Directions in Historical Scholarship*, ed. Richard W. Guisso and Stanley Johannesen. New York: Philo Press.

Swann, Nancy Lee. (1968) *Pan Chao: Foremost Woman Scholar of China*. Reprint. New York: Russell and Russell.

Tang, Chunyi. (1976) *Zhongguo zhexue yuanlun, Yuan Dao* [An Original Exposition of Chinese Philosophy. Exposition of *Dao*]. Taipei: Xinya shuyuan yanjiusuo.

Tiles, James E. (2000) *Moral Measures: An Introduction to Ethics West and East*. London: Routledge.

Tjoe, Som Tjan, trans. (1952) *Po Hu Tung: The Comprehensive Discussions in the White Tiger Hall*. 2 volumes. Leiden: E. J. Brill.

Topley, Marjorie. (1975) "Marriage Resistance in Rural Kwangtung." In *Women in Chinese Society*, ed. Margery Wolf, and Roxane Witke. Stanford: Stanford University Press.

Tu, Wu-ming. (1985) *Confucian Thought: Selfhood as Creative Transformation*. Albany: State University of New York Press.

Van Norden, Bryan, trans. (2003) *Mencins*. In *Images of Women in Chinese Thought and Culture*, ed. Robin R. Wang. Indianapolis: Hackett.

———, ed. (2002) *Confucius and The Analects: New Essays*. Oxford: Oxford University Press.

Wakeman, Frederic. (1994) "Roundtable Discussion: Wm. Theodore de Bary. *The Trouble with Confucianism*." *China Review International* 1:1 (Spring):9–47.

———. (1993) "The Civil Society and Public Sphere Debate: Western Reflections on Chinese Political Culture." *Modern China* 19:2 (April):108–38.

Wang, Robin R, ed. (2003) *Images of Women in Chinese Thought and Culture: Writings from the Pre-Qin Period through the Song Dynasty*. Indianapolis: Hackett.

Wang, Xiang, ed. (1789–1852) *Nusishu* [Four Books for Women]. Daoguang edition, 1838.

Watson, Rubie S. (1991a) "Wives, Concubines, and Maids: Servitude and Kinship in the Hong Kong Region, 1900–1940." In *Marriage and Inequality in Chinese Society*, ed. Rubie S. Watson and Patricia B. Ebrey. Berkeley: University of California Press.

———. (1991b) "Afterword: Marriage and Gender Inequality." In *Marriage and Inequality in Chinese Society*, ed. Rubie S. Watson and Patricia B. Ebrey. Berkeley: University of California Press.

———. (1986) "The Name and the Nameless: Gender and Person in Chinese Society." *American Ethnologist* 13:619–31.

Wawrytko, Sandra A. (2000) "Prudery and Prurience: Historical Roots of the Confucian Conundrum Concerning Women, Sexuality, and Power." In *The Sage and the Second Sex: Confucianism, Ethics, and Gender*, ed. Chenyang Li. Chicago: Open Court.

Widmer, Ellen. (1989) "The Epistolary Worlds of Female Talent in Seventeenth-Century China." *Late Imperial China* 10:2:1–43.

Wilhelm, Richard, and Cary F. Baynes, trans. (1961) *The I Ching or Book of Changes*. Bollingen Series XIX. One-volume edition. Reprint. New York: Pantheon Books.

Wilson, Thomas A. (1995) *Genealogy of the Way: the Construction and Uses of the Confucian Tradition in Late Imperial China*. Stanford: Stanford University Press.

Wolf, Margery. (1994) "Beyond the Patrilineal Self: Constructing Gender in China." In *Self as Person in Asian Theory and Practice*, ed. Roger T. Ames, Wimal Disanayake, and Thomas P. Kasulis. Albany: State University of New York Press.

——. (1985) *Revolution Postponed: Women in Contemporary China*. Stanford: Stanford University Press.

——. (1975) "Women and Suicide in China." In *Women in Chinese Society*, ed. Margery Wolf, and Roxane Witke. Stanford: Stanford University Press.

Wu, Fatima, trans. (2003) "The Ci of Shuyu." In *Images of Women in Chinese Thought and Culture*, ed. Robin R. Wang. Indianapolis: Hackett.

Xu, Fuguan. (1961) "[On the Evolution of the Concept of *Yin-yang* and *Wuxing*, and the Question Concerning the Explanation of the Formative Era of Other Related Texts]." *Minju Pinglun* (*The Democratic Review*) 12:19–21: three parts; pt. I:4–9, pt. II:4–9, pt. III:5–14.

Yang, Lien-sheng. (1992) "Female Rulers in Ancient China." In *Chinese Women through Chinese Eyes*, ed. Li Yu-ning. Armonk, NY: M. E. Sharpe.

Yao, Ping. (2003a) "Precepts for Family life." In *Images of Women in Chinese Thought and Culture*, ed. Robin R. Wang. Indianapolis: Hackett.

——. (2003b) "Family Instructions to the Yan Clan." In *Images of Women in Chinese Thought and Culture*, ed. Robin R. Wang. Indianapolis: Hackett.

Yu, Ying-shih. (1986) "Han Foreign Relations." In *The Cambridge History of China*, ed. Denis Twitchett and Michael Loewe. Volume I. Cambridge: Cambridge University Press.

——. (1967) *Trade and Expansion in Han China: A Study in the Structure of Sino-Barbarian Economic Relations*. Berkeley: University of California Press.

Zhan, Heying Jenny, and Robert Bradshaw. (1996) "The Book of Analects for Women." *Journal of Historical Sociology* 9:261–68.

Zhang, Xuecheng (1728–1801) "*Fu xue*" [Women's learning]. In *Zhangshi yishu* [Bequeathed Writings of Master Zhang], ed. Liu Chenggang. Jiayetang edition.

INDEX

Ames, Roger, and Henry Rosemont, 59
Aristotle (Aristotle's Virtue Ethics), 16, 19, 36, 116, 120–21, 149, 159
Augustine, 116
Ayscough, Florence, 123

Baihutong (*White Tiger Hall*), 55, 80, 93, 123, 126, 128
Ban, Gu, 103, 116
Ban, Zhao, 8, 76, 100, 103–09, 111, 115–16, 127, 131
Barlow, Tani, 45, 48, 88
Beauvoir, de, Simone, 3, 35–6, 150, 159
"Biographies of *Ru*" (*Rulinliezhuan*), 17, 18, 27
Blake, Fred, 140–41
Black, Alison, 64, 67
Bol, Peter K., 30
Boodberg, Peter, 22, 37

Cai, Yong, 78
Carlitz, Katherine, 101
Chen, Hongmou, 47–8
Chen, Yu-shih, 105
Cheng, Hao, 27
Cheng, Yi, 27, 119, 133–34
Che, Ruoshui, 140
Child-bride/servant, 9–10, 15, 153
Christianity, 17
Chunqiu (*Spring and Autumn*), 71
Chunqiu fanlu (*Luxuriant Dew of the Spring and Autumn*), 50, 56, 60, 62–6, 78

Chu, Tung-tsu, 73, 91–2
Civil Service Examination, 4, 8, 11, 16, 26–30, 32
Cixi Empress of Qing, 91
Concubinage, 9, 10, 15, 122–23, 146, 153
Confucius, 4, 17–8, 20–6, 31–2, 34, 36, 56, 58, 62, 74, 119–21, 124–25, 128, 138, 141
Confucian Feminism, 150, 152, 154–59

Daodejing (*Classics of Dao and De*), 54–5
Daojia (Daoism), 18, 28, 33, 49, 149, 152, 159
Daxue (*Great Learning*), 18, 27, 59, 71, 85
Descartes or Cartesian Duality, 49, 67, 149, 160
Dong, Zhongshu, 26, 50, 56, 60, 62, 65–6, 119

Ebrey, Patricia, 83, 139
Elman, Benjamin, 29, 87
Elvin, Mark, 135
Existentialism, 16, 146, 150–51, 159–60

Fajia (Legalism), 18, 62–3
Fan, Zhongyen, 132
Fang, Ying-hsien, 36
Fei, Xiaotong, 39
Female Infanticide, 9, 10, 15, 122–23, 153
Fingarette, Herbert, 40

First Emperor of Qin, 25, 26, 61, 131
First Empress Dowager, Lu, of Han, 105
Five Classics, 18, 27–8, 37, 47, 61–2, 70–1, 129, 130
"Five-zone" (*Wufu*), 78
Footbinding, 9–11, 15, 122, 129–30, 138–39, 140–46, 153
Foucault, 69
Four Books (*Sishu*), 8, 18, 27–8, 32, 35, 59, 70–2, 103, 123, 129–30
Four Books for Women (*Nusishu*), 8, 81, 95, 108
Fude (Women's Excellence), 81, 104
Fugong (Women's Work), 81, 82, 104–5, 142
Furong (Women's Comportment), 82, 104
Furth, Charlotte, 66–7
"*Fuxue*" (Women's Learning), 109–11, 114
Fuyan (Women's Speech), 82, 104–5, 110, 112, 114–15

Graham, A. C., 25, 58, 61
Gu, Yanwu, 136
Guan, Daosheng, 111
Guanzi (Book of Guanzi), 51, 70, 76, 82, 97, 130
Gui, Youguang, 136
Guifan (Model Women), 99–100, 109
Guisso, Richard, 47
Guoyu (Discourse of the States), 38, 51, 97–8

Hall, David, and Roger Ames, 34, 42
Hanfezi (Book of Hanfezi), 25, 61, 97, 122
Hanshu (The Official History of the Former Han), 54, 70, 75, 79, 96, 103, 105, 116
Hay, John, 76, 83
Hobbes, 154
Hongloumeng (Dream of the Red Chamber), 103, 108
Hou Hanshu (The Official History of the Latter Han), 73, 103
Hua, Mulan, 129
Huangdi neijing (Inner Classic of the Yellow Emperor), 66

Huainanzi (Book of Huainanzi), 70, 97
Hu, Shi, 21, 23–4

Jackson, Beverley, 139
Jensen, Lionel, 19, 34
Jesuits, 17–8, 33–4
Jiaonu yigui (Inherited Guide for Educating Women), 47
Jing Jiang, 120
Jinsilu (Reflections on Things at Hand), 133

Kant (Kantian), 3, 16, 67, 116, 120–21, 150, 155, 159–60
Kaplan, Caren, 151–52
King, Ambrose, 40
Ko, Dorothy, 79, 84–5, 144
Kongzi jiayu (Family Discourses of Kongzi), 89–90, 123
Kracke, E. A., 26
Kristeva, Julia, 16

Lan, Dingyuan, 107
Lang, Olga, 69
Lee, Lily Xiao Hong, 106
Legge, James, 51
Levy, Howard, 139
Li, Chenyang, 16
Liang, Hungyu, 129
Liang, Lanyi, 113
Liang, Xi, 80
Liberalism, 16, 146, 160
Lienu (Virtuous Women), 7, 95–6, 132
Lienuzhuan (Biographies of Virtuous Women), 7, 86, 89–90, 96–101, 123, 131
Liji (Book of Rites),10, 18, 21, 23–4, 27, 46, 71, 82, 84, 89, 92–3, 104, 108, 112, 115, 119, 122, 125–28
Lin, Puqing, 129
Lin, Yu-sheng, 35
Li, Qingzhao, 111, 139
Liu, Xiang, 7, 95–101, 131
Lloyd, Genevieve, 36, 49
Lunheng (Critical Evaluation of Doctrines), 22
Lunyu (The Analects), 10, 18, 20–1, 23, 27, 36, 38–40, 42, 59, 71, 74, 85, 87, 107, 124–25, 142
Lushi chunqiu (Springs and Autumns of Master Lu), 54–5, 97

Mann, Susan, 80, 86, 112
Mao, Qiling, 136
Marxism, 160
May Fourth Movement, 1, 21, 45, 121
Meadows, Thomas Taylor, 91
Mei, Yi-Pao, 21
Mencius, 25, 36, 39, 71–2, 90, 123, 125, 130
Mencius (*Book of Mencius*), 27, 37, 39, 41, 59, 71, 85–6, 97, 125, 130
Ming Taizu, 32
Mohanty, Chandra T., 139, 151
Mojia (The School of Mozi), 18, 20–1, 23, 55
Mozi, 20–1
Mozi (*Book of Mozi*), 20–1, 23, 46, 51, 53, 70, 76
Mu, Guiying, 129

Needham, Joseph, 49
Neo-Confucianism (*Daoxue* or *Lixue*), 16, 27–8, 33, 130, 149, 159
Neixun (*The Regulation for the Inner Quarter*), 8
Neixun (*Instruction for the Inner Quarters*), 108
Nietzsche, 116, 120–21, 150
Nuerjing (*Classic for Girls*), 140
Nufan jielu (*Concise Records of Model Women*), 8
Nufan jielu (*Concise Selection of Model Women*), 109–10, 114
Nujie (*The Admonition for Women*), 8, 100, 103–9, 115–16, 131
Nulunyu (*The Analects for Women*), 8, 107–8

Ortner, Sherry B., 88–9

Princess Pingyang of Tang, 129
Plato, 17, 37

Qian-kun, 21, 48, 56–8, 60, 63–4
Qin, Liangyu of Ming, 129
Qin, Zheng, 38

Raphals, Lisa, 7, 53, 66, 70, 76, 97, 99, 102, 106, 119–20

Ricci (Father Ricci), 33
Rich, Adrienne, 151
Rowe, William, 86

Sancong (Threefold Following or Dependence), 70
Sanguozhi (*Memoirs of the Three Kingdoms*), 80
"Seven Reasons for Expelling One's Wife" (*Qichu*), 123
Shen, Yunying, 129
Shiji (*Records of History*), 54, 79, 101
Shijing (*Book of Songs*), 25–6, 37, 45, 71–2, 96, 104, 108–9, 111–12, 114–15, 123–24
"*Shou Ru*" (A Discourse on *Ru*), 22–3
Shouwen (*Explanation of Patterns*), 19, 46, 143
Shouwen jiezi gulin (*Explanation of Patterns, Elaboration of Graphs*), 19
Shujing (*Book of Documents*), 25, 36–7, 60, 71–2, 78, 87, 96, 108, 123–25
Side (Four Womanly Virtues), 81, 102, 104–5, 110–13
Sima, Guang, 84–5, 126
Sima, Qian, 54
Song, Lian, 31–2
Song, Ruohua, 107
Song, Ruozhao, 107
Song, Tingfen, 107
Sung, Marina, 92

Tang, Junyi, 54
"Three Grounds that A Wife Cannot Be Expelled" (*Sanbuchu*), 126
Topley, Marjorie, 68
Tu, Wei-ming, 16, 149, 159

Utilitarianism, 146

Watson, Rubie S., 10, 89, 127, 128
Wang, Xiang, 8, 103, 109
Wang, Wei, 31–2
Widow Chastity or Widowhood, 9–11, 15, 122, 129–31, 134–39, 146
Wolf, Margery, 16, 47, 149, 151
Wude (Five-power), 60–2
Wulun (Five Relations), 40, 46

W*uxing* (Five Processes), 48, 56, 58–61, 159
Wu, Zetian, 26, 91, 132

Xiaojing (*Book of Filial Piety*), 10, 124–25
Xiaoxue (*Elementary Learning*), 108
Xu, Fuguan, 51
Xunzi, 31–2, 46, 61, 74–5, 83, 125
Xunzi (*Book of Xunzi*), 23, 54–5, 59, 70, 86, 97
Xu, Shen, 19

Yanshi jiaxun (*Family Instructions for the Yan Clan*), 90, 123, 131
Yantie lun (*Discourse on Salt and Iron*), 70, 73
Yan, Zhitui, 123, 131
Yang, Guifei, 123
Yijing (*Book of Changes*), 21, 36, 55–6, 58–60, 62–4, 66, 71, 108, 130
Yinyangjia (The School of Yinyang), 18, 54, 60–1, 159
Yuan, Mei, 110–13, 115

"*Yuan Ru*," (The Origin of *Ru*), 21, 23, 31
Yun, Zhu, 114–15
Yu, Ying-shih, 73–4, 81

Zhang, Binglin, 21–2
Zhang, Cai, 28
Zhanguoce (*Strategies of the Warring States*), 97
Zhang, Xuecheng, 107, 109–15
Zhou, Dunyi, 28
Zhongyong (*Focusing the Familiar*), 18, 27, 37, 41–2, 59, 71, 86
Zhouli (*The Rites of Zhou*), 18–9
Zhuangzi (*Book of Zhuangzi*), 21–2, 51–2, 54–6, 61, 143
Zhuangzi, 143
Zhu, Xi, 27–8, 32, 108, 133, 139
Zi Chong, 80
Zisizi, 130
Zou, Yan, 58, 60–2
Zuozhuan (*Zuo Annal*), 38, 51–2, 57, 73–4, 81, 97–8

www.ingramcontent.com/pod-product-compliance
Lightning Source LLC
Chambersburg PA
CBHW020732240426
43665CB00052B/455